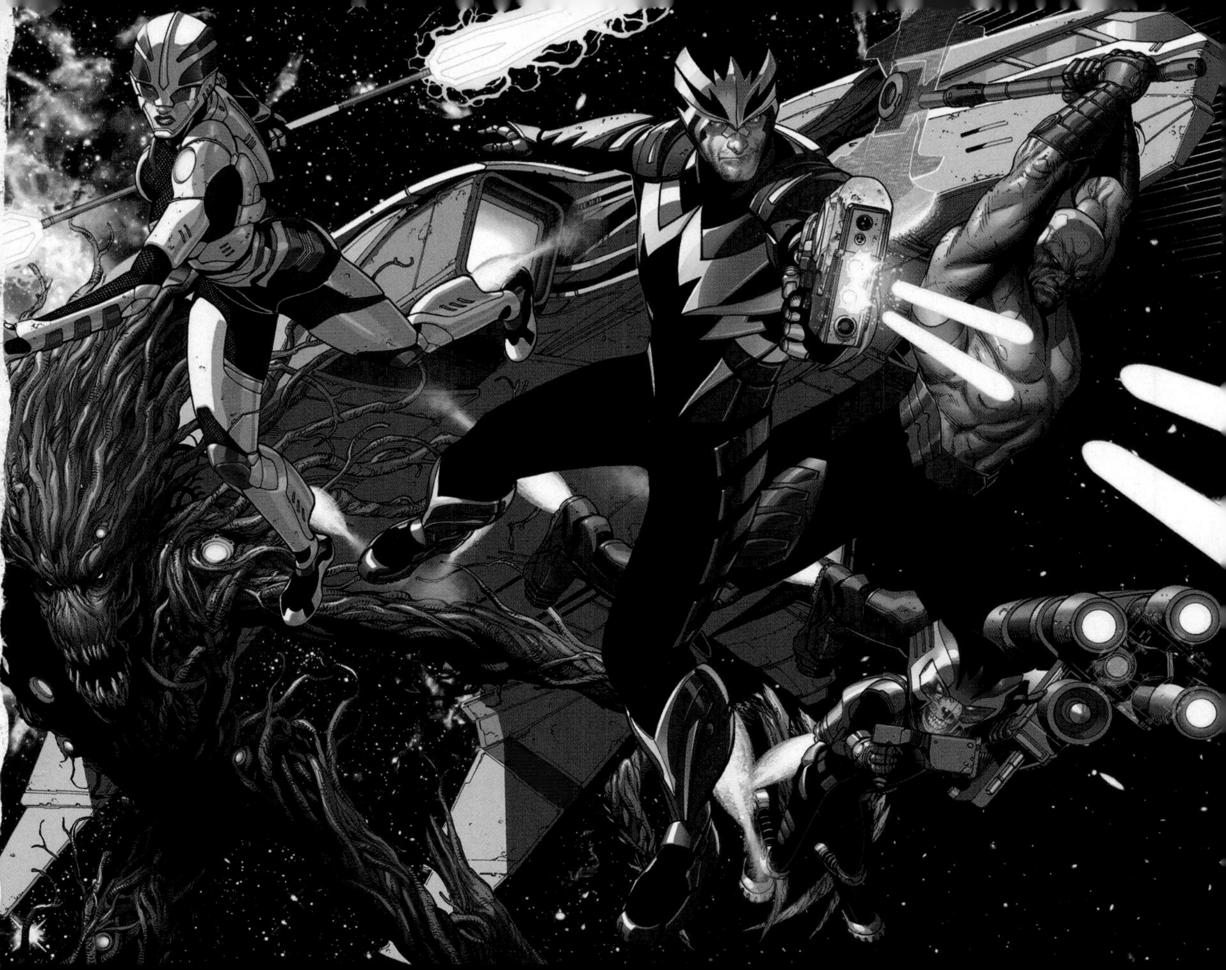

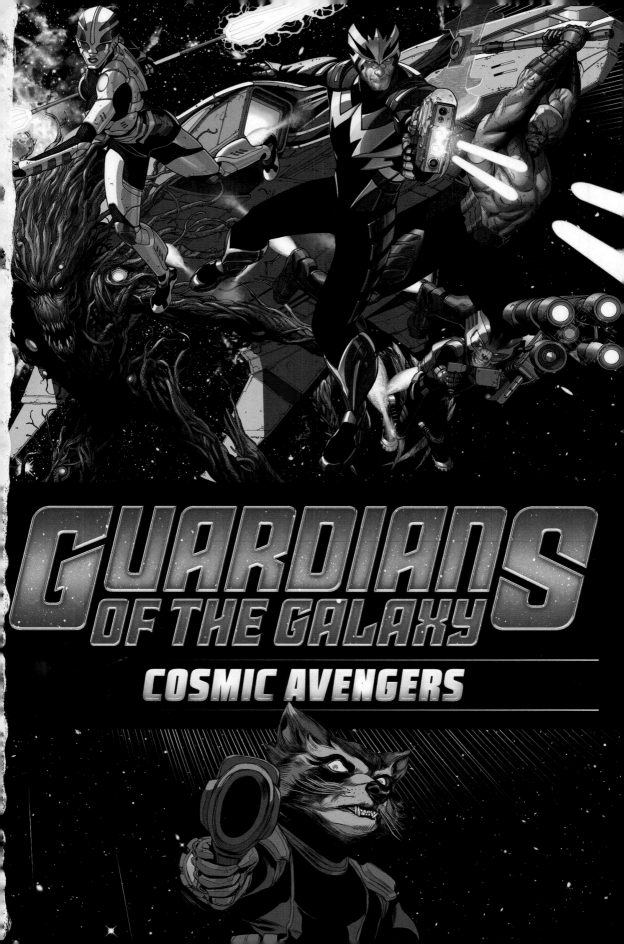

GUARDIANS OF THE GALAXY

COSMIC AVENGERS

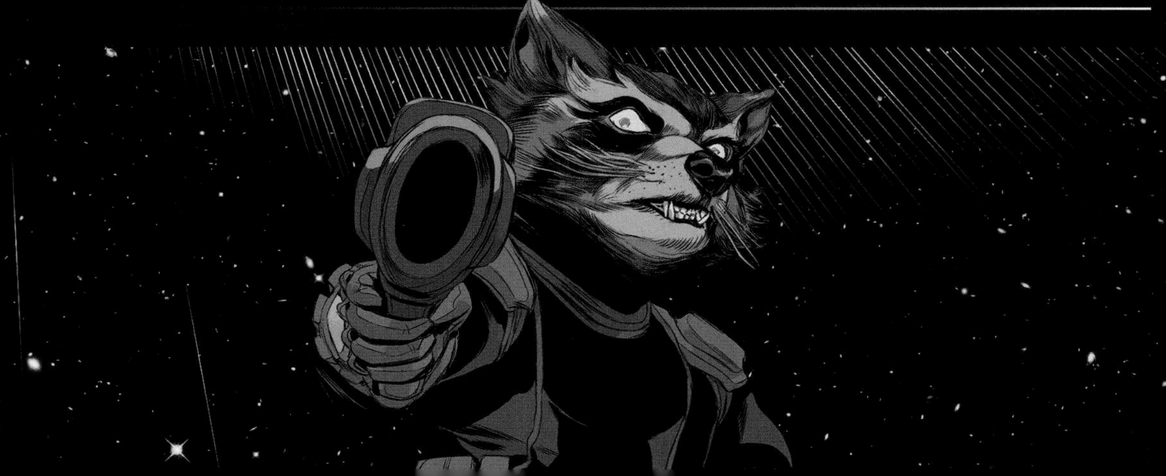

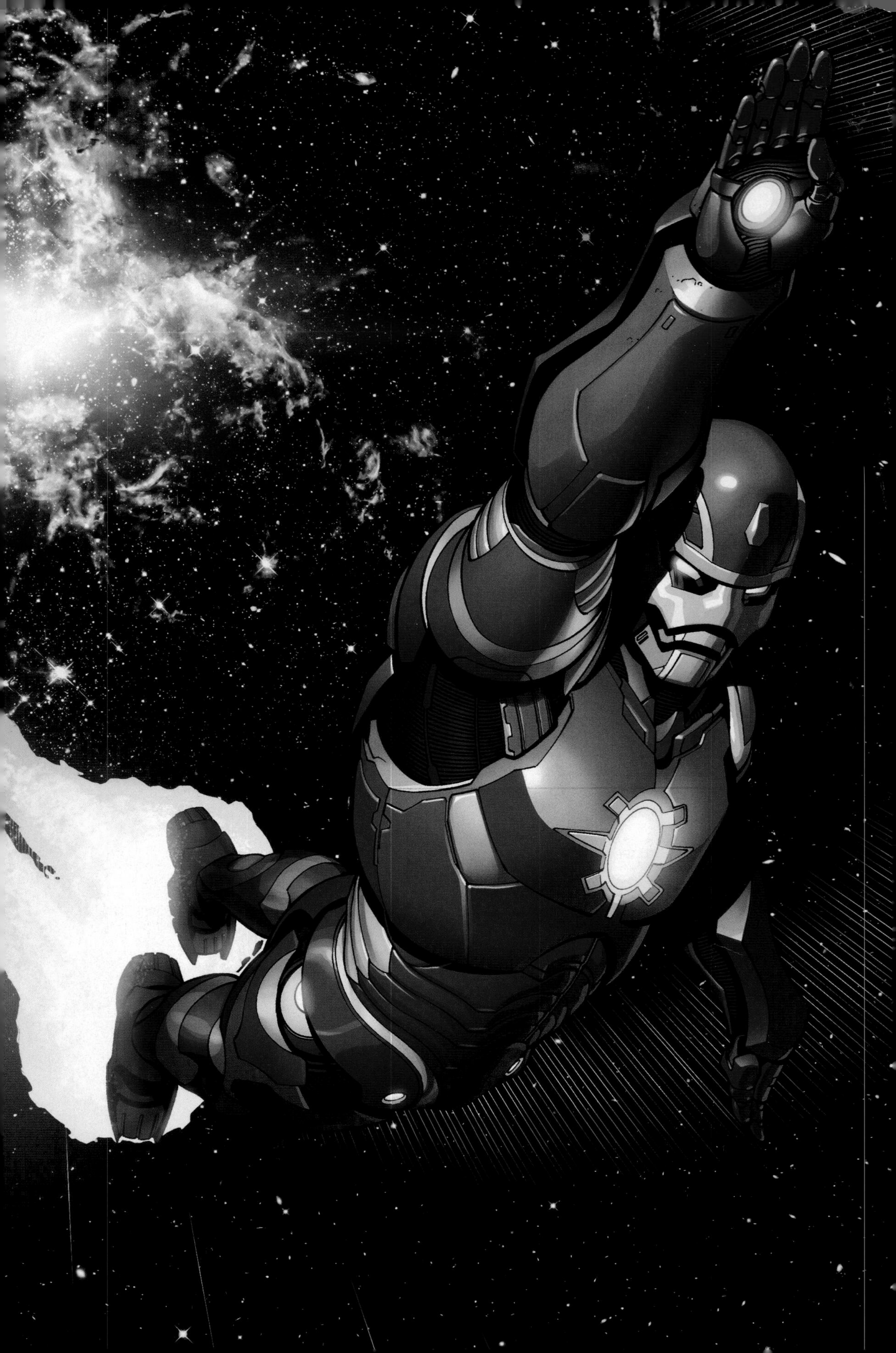

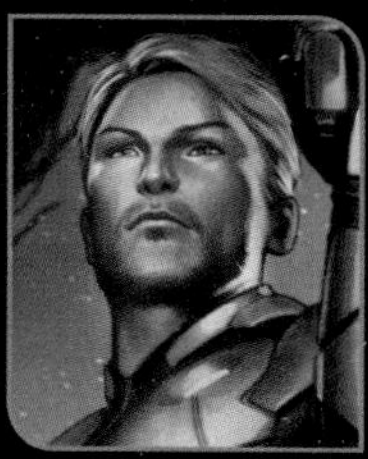

STAR-LORD

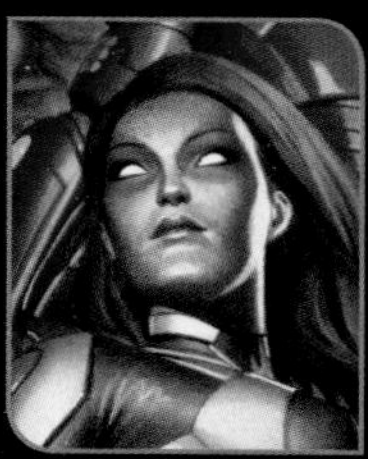

GAMORA

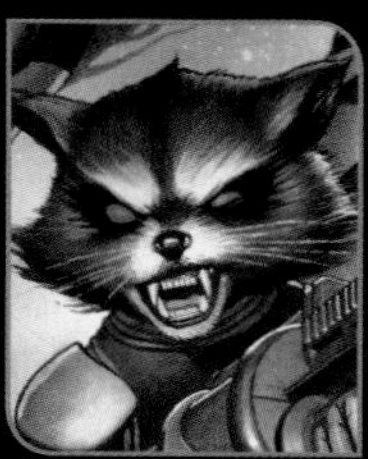

ROCKET RACCOON

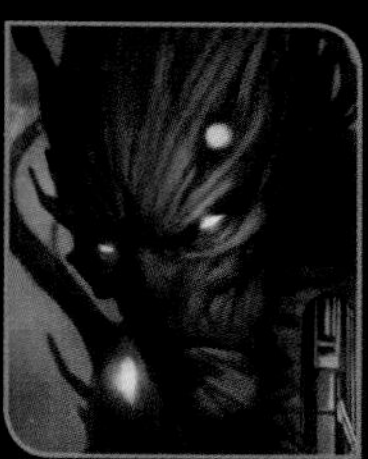

GROOT

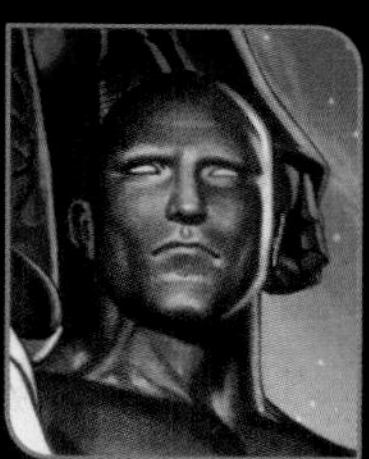

DRAX

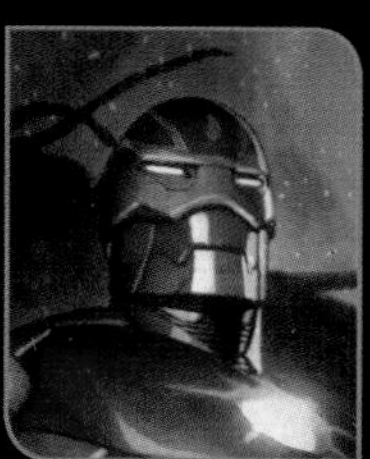

IRON MAN

GUARDIANS OF THE GALAXY

COSMIC AVENGERS

WRITER: **BRIAN MICHAEL BENDIS**
PENCILERS: **STEVE McNIVEN** (#0.1, 1-3) & **SARA PICHELLI** (#2-3)
INKERS: **JOHN DELL** WITH **MARK MORALES** (#2), **STEVE McNIVEN** (#2-3) & **SARA PICHELLI** (#2-3)
COLORIST: **JUSTIN PONSOR** COVER ART: **STEVE McNIVEN, JOHN DELL & JUSTIN PONSOR**
LETTERER: **VC'S CORY PETIT** ASSISTANT EDITOR: **ELLIE PYLE** EDITOR: **STEPHEN WACKER**

TOMORROW'S AVENGERS

WRITER: **BRIAN MICHAEL BENDIS**
ART: **MICHAEL AVON OEMING** & **RAIN BEREDO** (DRAX), **MING DOYLE** & **JAVIER RODRIGUEZ** (ROCKET RACCOON) AND **MICHAEL DEL MUNDO** (GAMORA & GROOT)
LAYOUTS (DRAX, ROCKET RACCOOON, GAMORA): **YVES BIGEREL**
LETTERER: **VC'S JOE CARAMAGNA** COVER ART: **MING DOYLE** EDITOR: **SANA AMANAT**
SENIOR EDITOR: **STEPHEN WACKER**

COLLECTION EDITOR: **JENNIFER GRÜNWALD** ASSISTANT EDITORS: **ALEX STARBUCK & NELSON RIBEIRO**
EDITOR, SPECIAL PROJECTS: **MARK D. BEAZLEY** SENIOR EDITOR, SPECIAL PROJECTS: **JEFF YOUNGQUIST**
SVP OF PRINT & DIGITAL PUBLISHING SALES: **DAVID GABRIEL** BOOK DESIGNER: **RODOLFO MURAGUCHI**

EDITOR IN CHIEF: **AXEL ALONSO** CHIEF CREATIVE OFFICER: **JOE QUESADA**
PUBLISHER: **DAN BUCKLEY** EXECUTIVE PRODUCER: **ALAN FINE**

GUARDIANS OF THE GALAXY VOL. 1: COSMIC AVENGERS. Contains material originally published in magazine form as GUARDIANS OF THE GALAXY #1-3 and #0.1, and GUARDIANS OF THE GALAXY: TOMORROW'S AVENGERS #1. First printing 2013. ISBN# 978-0-7851-6828-7. Published by MARVEL WORLDWIDE, INC., a subsidiary of MARVEL ENTERTAINMENT, LLC. OFFICE OF PUBLICATION: 135 West 50th Street, New York, NY 10020. **Printed in the U.S.A**. ALAN FINE, EVP - Office of the President, Marvel Worldwide, Inc. and EVP & CMO Marvel Characters B.V.; DAN BUCKLEY, Publisher & President - Print, Animation & Digital Divisions; JOE QUESADA, Chief Creative Officer; TOM BREVOORT, SVP of Publishing; DAVID BOGART, SVP of Operations & Procurement, Publishing; C.B. CEBULSKI, SVP of Creator & Content Development; DAVID GABRIEL, SVP of Print & Digital Publishing Sales; JIM O'KEEFE, VP of Operations & Logistics; DAN CARR, Executive Director of Publishing Technology; SUSAN CRESPI, Editorial Operations Manager; ALEX MORALES, Publishing Operations Manager; STAN LEE, Chairman Emeritus. For information regarding advertising in Marvel Comics or on Marvel.com, please contact Niza Disla, Director of Marvel Partnerships, at ndisla@marvel.com. For Marvel subscription inquiries, please call 800-217-9158. **Manufactured between 6/28/2013 and 8/12/2013 by R.R. DONNELLEY, INC., SALEM, VA, USA.**

10 9 8 7 6 5 4 3 2 1

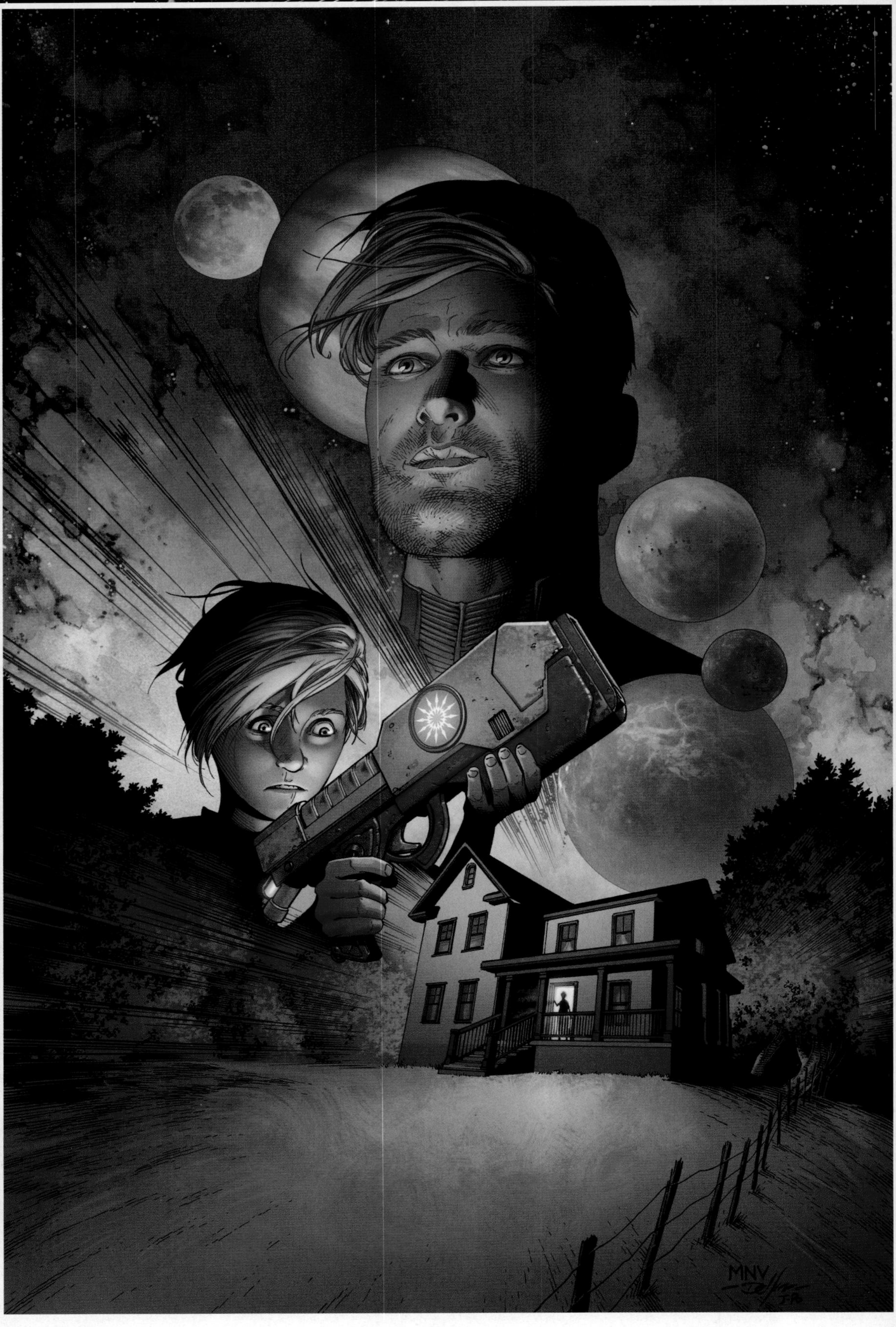

0.1

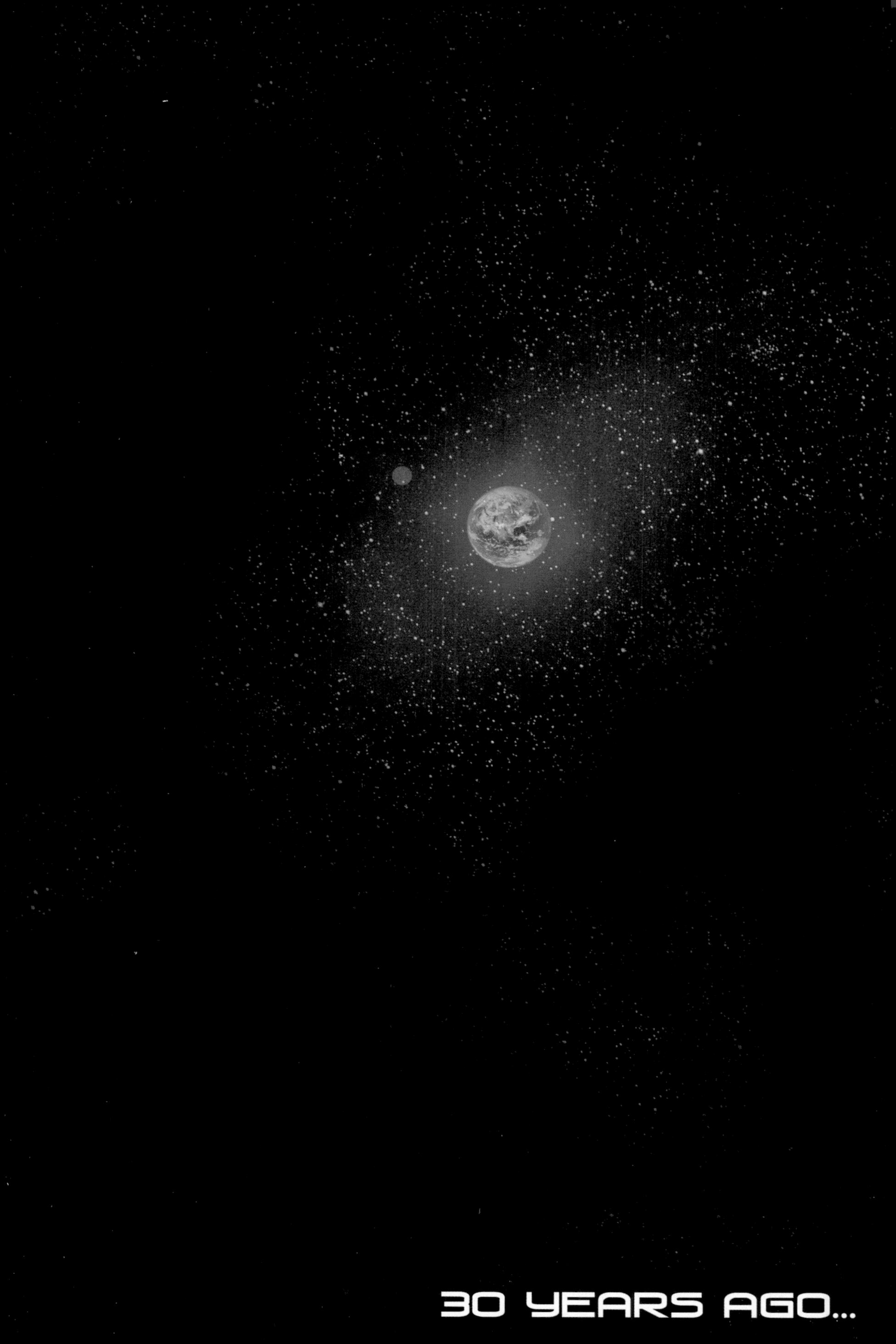
30 YEARS AGO...

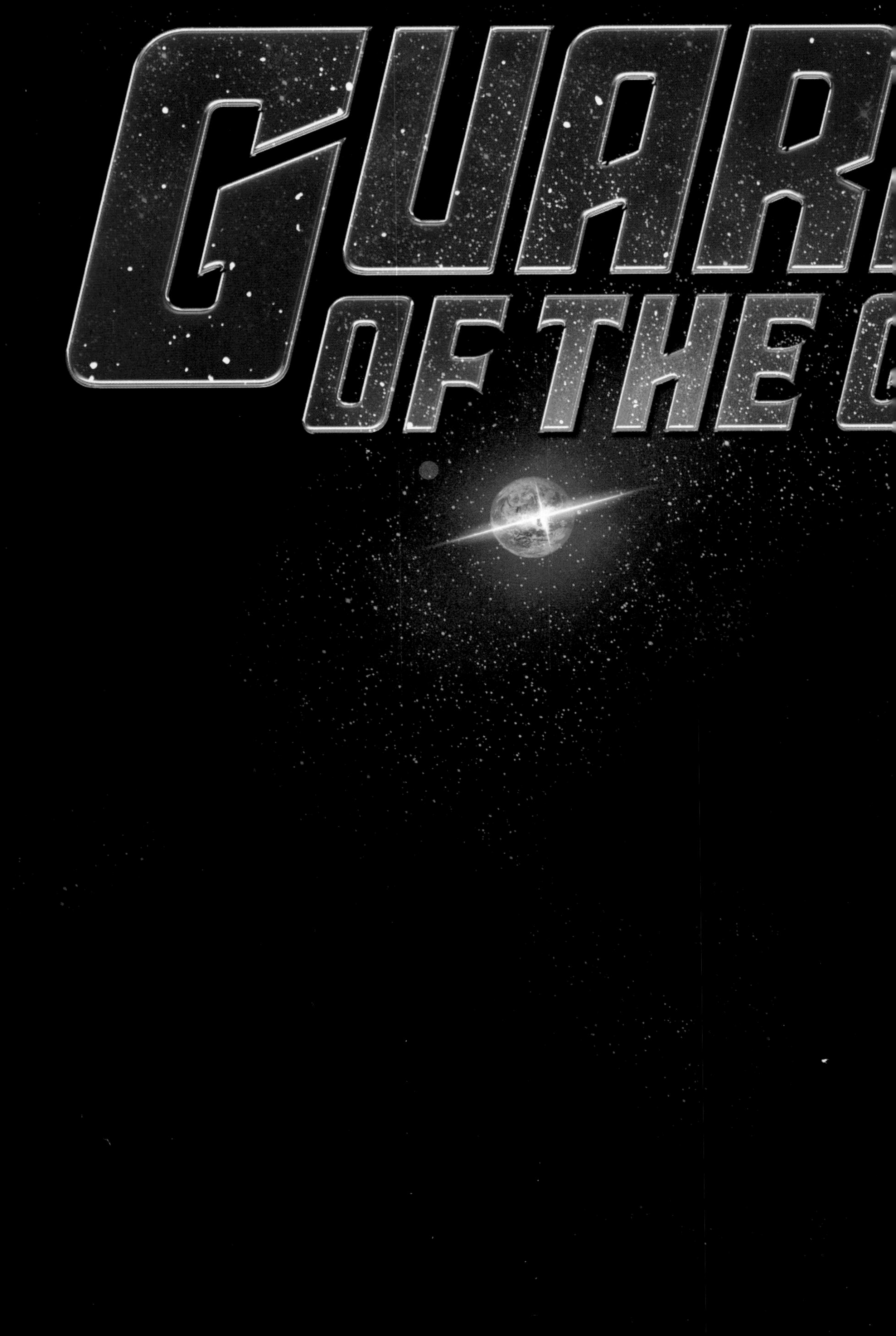
OF THE

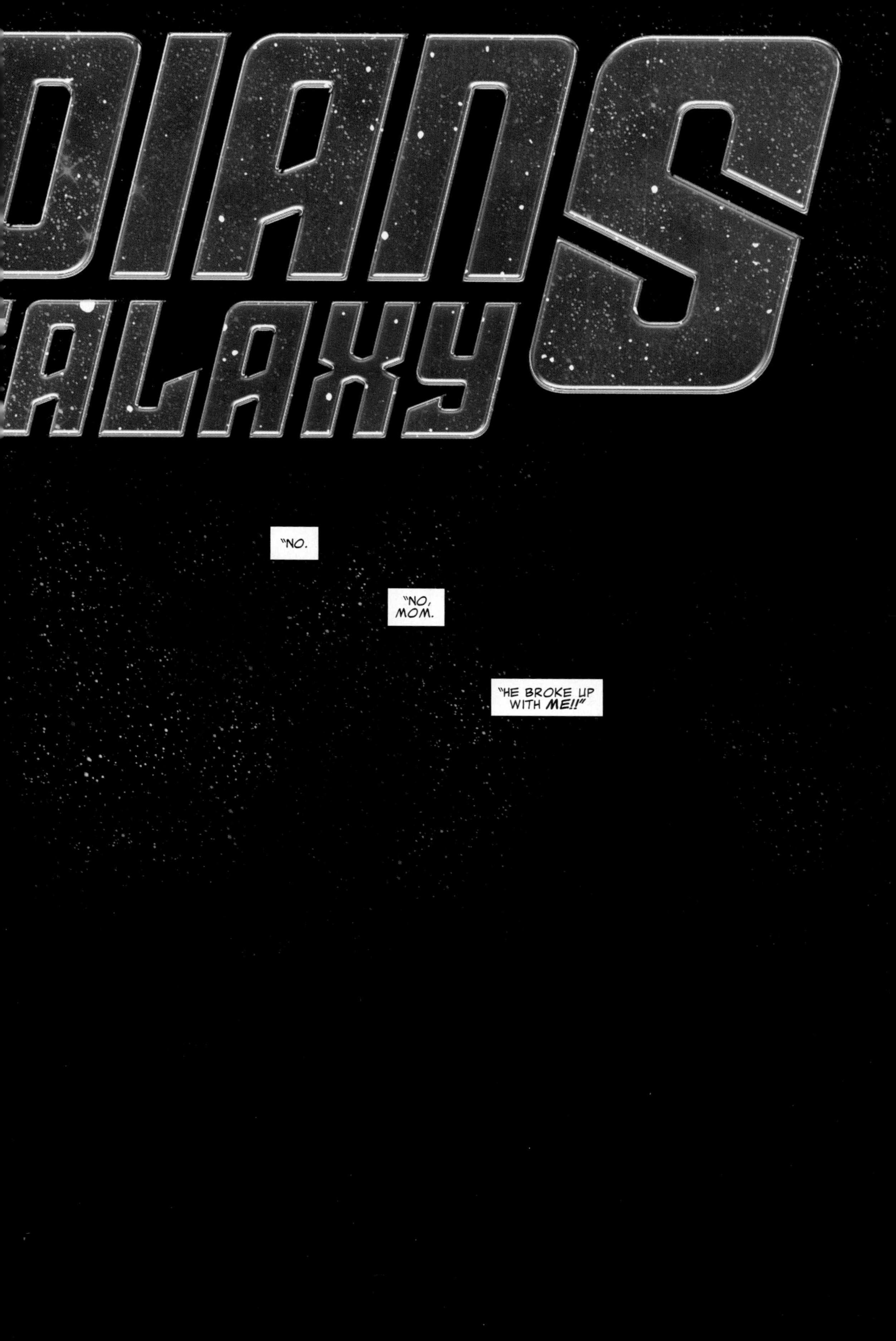
"NO.
"NO, MOM.
"HE BROKE UP WITH ME!!"

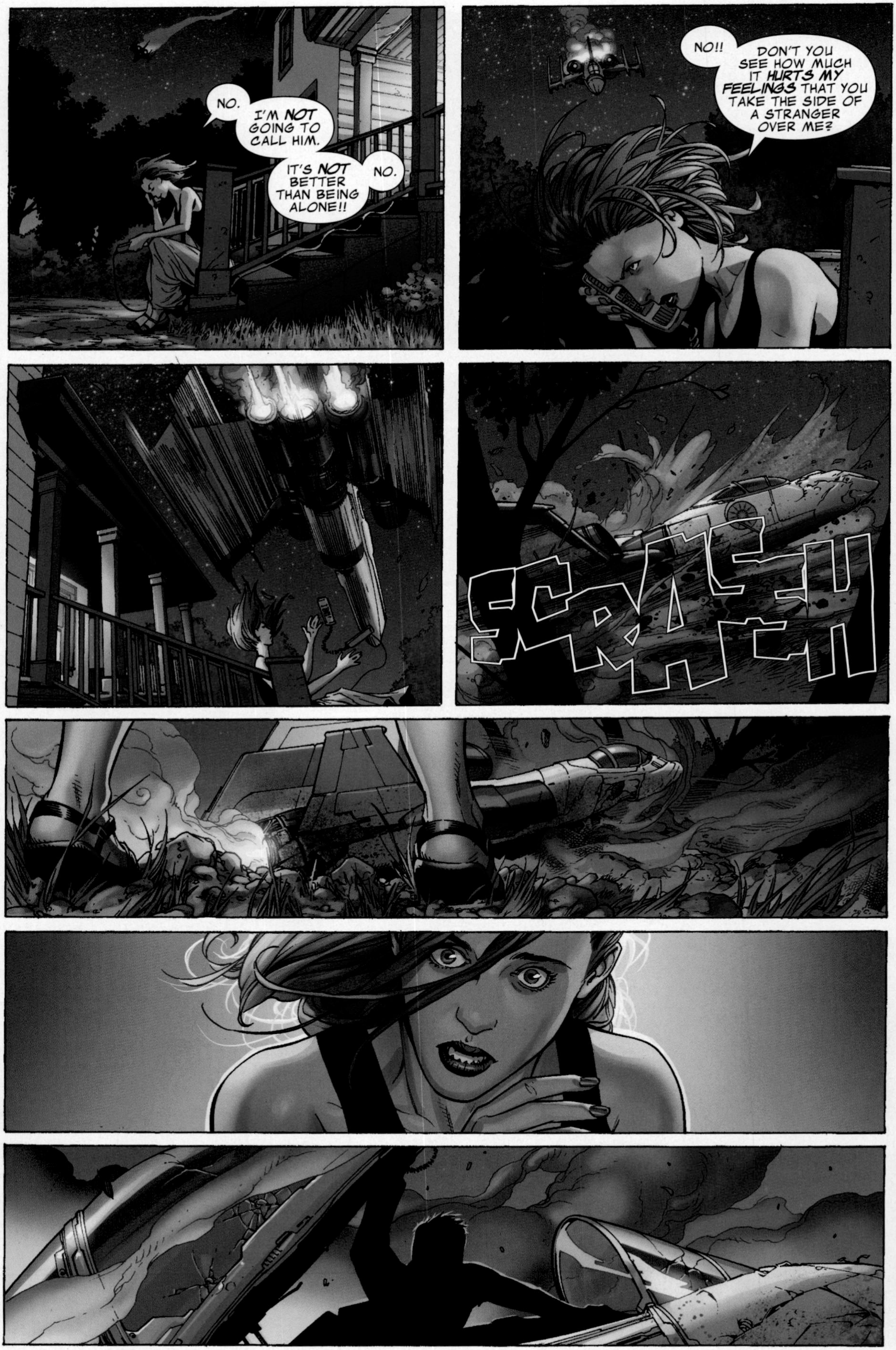
NO.
I'M **NOT** GOING TO CALL HIM.
IT'S **NOT** BETTER THAN BEING ALONE!!
NO.
NO!!
DON'T YOU SEE HOW MUCH IT **HURTS MY FEELINGS** THAT YOU TAKE THE SIDE OF A STRANGER OVER ME?
SCRATCH

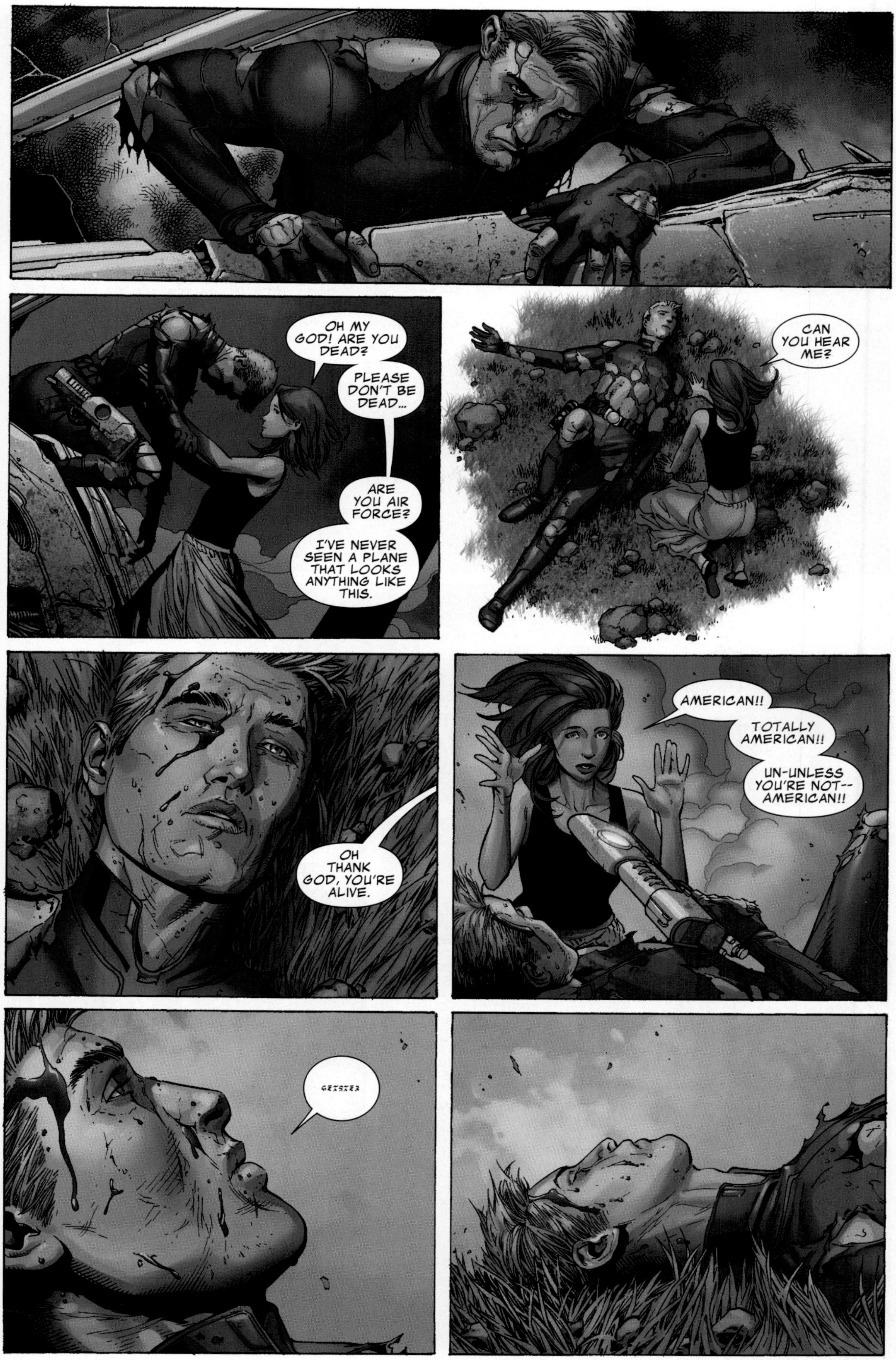
OH MY GOD! ARE YOU DEAD?
PLEASE DON'T BE DEAD...
ARE YOU AIR FORCE?
I'VE NEVER SEEN A PLANE THAT LOOKS ANYTHING LIKE THIS.
CAN YOU HEAR ME?
OH THANK GOD, YOU'RE ALIVE.
AMERICAN!!
TOTALLY AMERICAN!!
UN-UNLESS YOU'RE NOT--AMERICAN!!

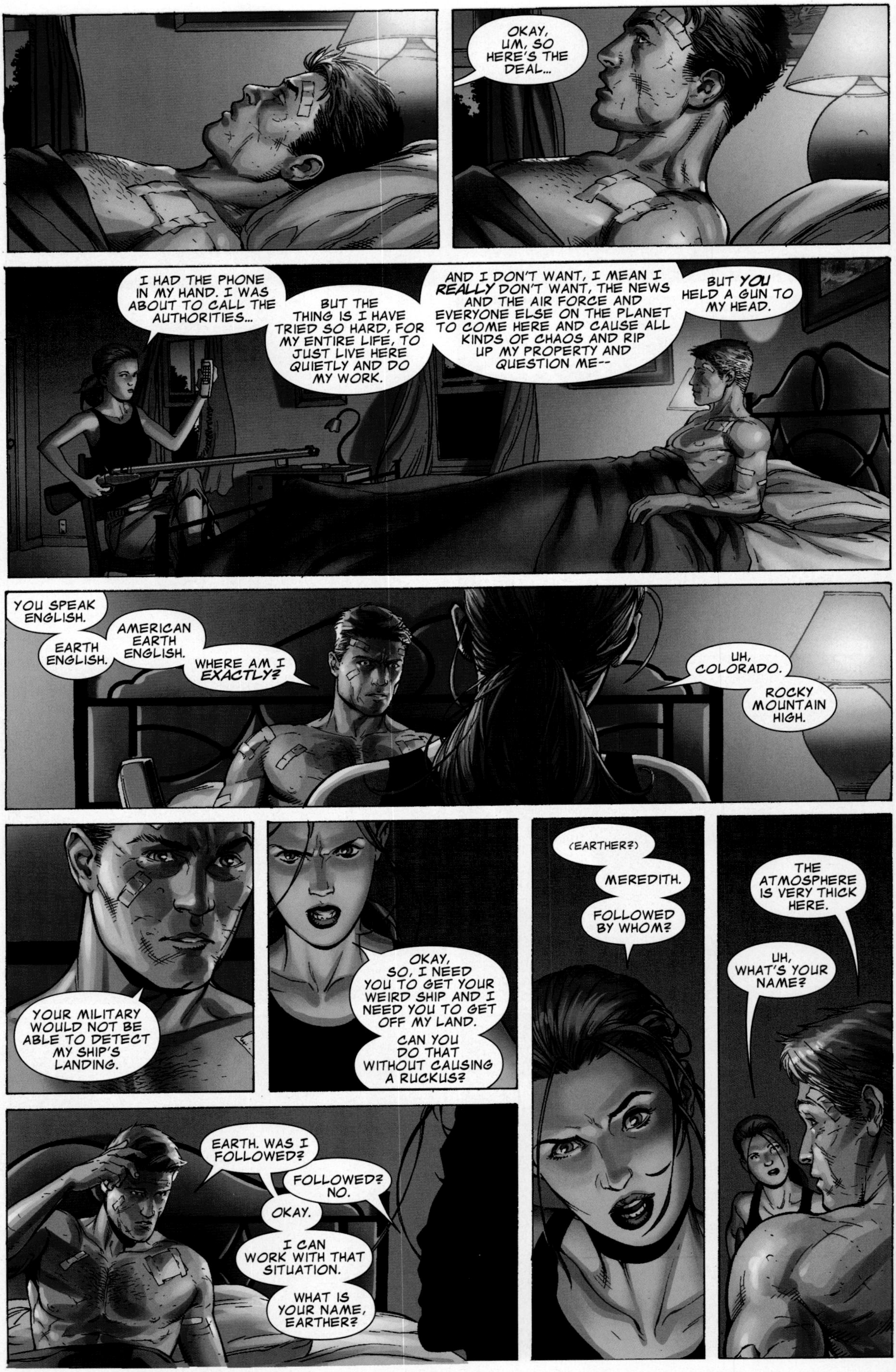
OKAY, UM, SO HERE'S THE DEAL...
I HAD THE PHONE IN MY HAND. I WAS ABOUT TO CALL THE AUTHORITIES...
BUT THE THING IS I HAVE TRIED SO HARD, FOR MY ENTIRE LIFE, TO JUST LIVE HERE QUIETLY AND DO MY WORK.
AND I DON'T WANT, I MEAN I REALLY DON'T WANT, THE NEWS AND THE AIR FORCE AND EVERYONE ELSE ON THE PLANET TO COME HERE AND CAUSE ALL KINDS OF CHAOS AND RIP UP MY PROPERTY AND QUESTION ME--
BUT YOU HELD A GUN TO MY HEAD.
YOU SPEAK ENGLISH.
EARTH ENGLISH.
AMERICAN EARTH ENGLISH.
WHERE AM I EXACTLY?
UH, COLORADO.
ROCKY MOUNTAIN HIGH.
YOUR MILITARY WOULD NOT BE ABLE TO DETECT MY SHIP'S LANDING.
OKAY, SO, I NEED YOU TO GET YOUR WEIRD SHIP AND I NEED YOU TO GET OFF MY LAND.
CAN YOU DO THAT WITHOUT CAUSING A RUCKUS?
EARTH. WAS I FOLLOWED?
FOLLOWED? NO.
OKAY.
I CAN WORK WITH THAT SITUATION.
WHAT IS YOUR NAME, EARTHER?
(EARTHER?)
MEREDITH.
FOLLOWED BY WHOM?
THE ATMOSPHERE IS VERY THICK HERE.
UH, WHAT'S YOUR NAME?

MY NAME IS J'SON OF SPARTAX.

YOUR KINDNESS IS APPRECIATED.

I HOPE I WILL BE ABLE TO RETURN IT.

ARE YOU A PILOT?

IS THAT-- WHAT IS THAT?

I'M FROM SPARTAX. I AM OF THE THRONE.

I WILL NEED TO FIX MY SHIP AND GET BACK TO MY PEOPLE. I WILL TRY TO DO SO AS QUICKLY AS I CAN.

OH MY GOD. ARE YOU KIDDING ME?

ARE YOU FROM--ARE YOU FROM SPACE?

I'M FROM SPARTAX.

I'VE TOLD YOU THIS A FEW TIMES.

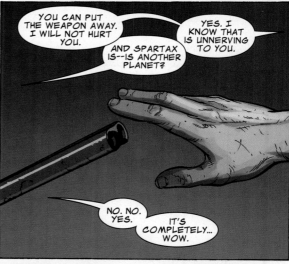

YOU CAN PUT THE WEAPON AWAY. I WILL NOT HURT YOU.

AND SPARTAX IS--IS ANOTHER PLANET?

YES. I KNOW THAT IS UNNERVING TO YOU.

NO. NO. YES.

IT'S COMPLETELY... WOW.

DO YOU-- DO YOU NEED A TOOLBOX OR--?

YOU'RE A FUNNY EARTHER.

NO. I HAVE THE TOOLS. BUT IT MAY TAKE SOME TIME.

EARTHER?

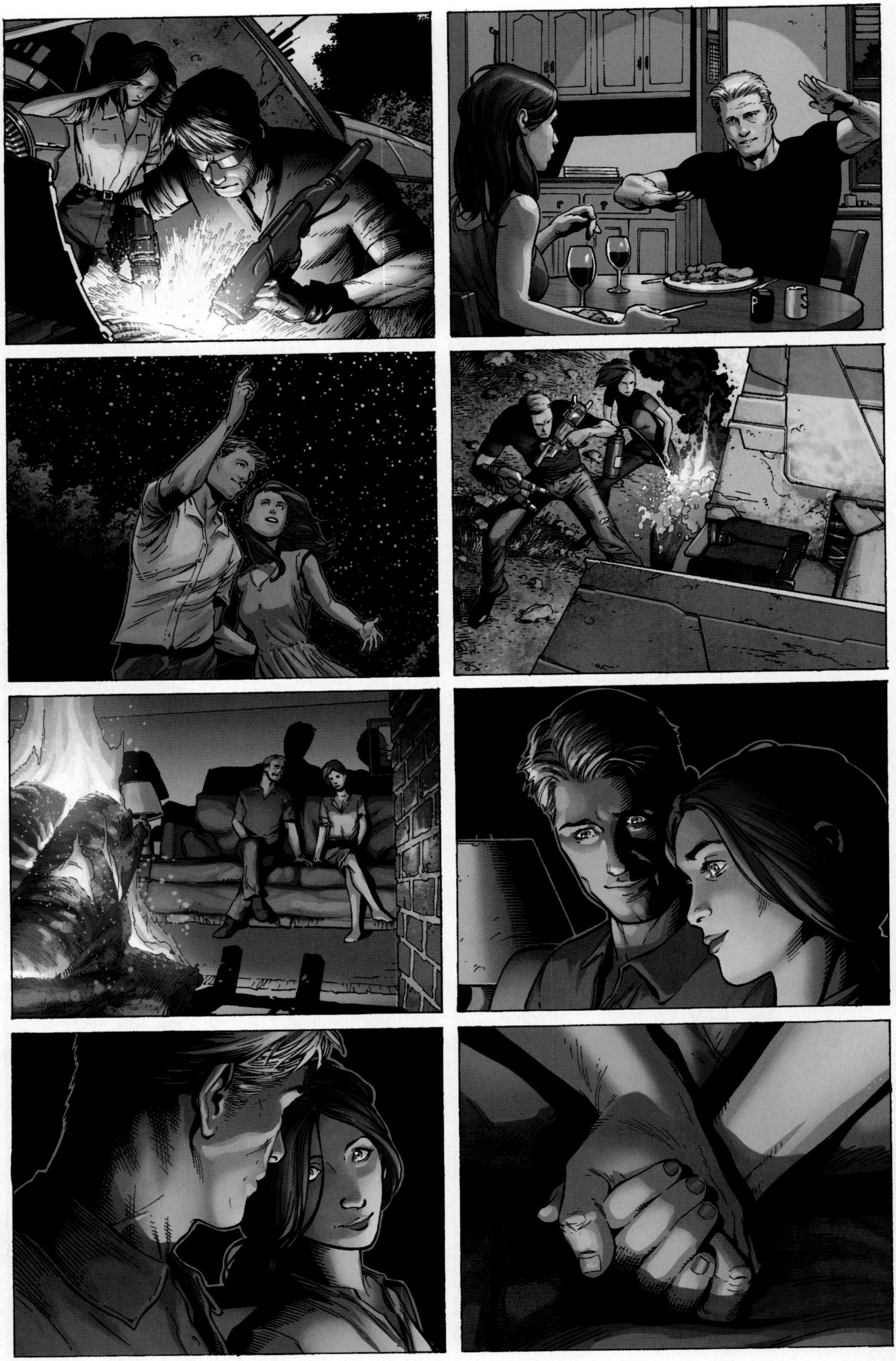

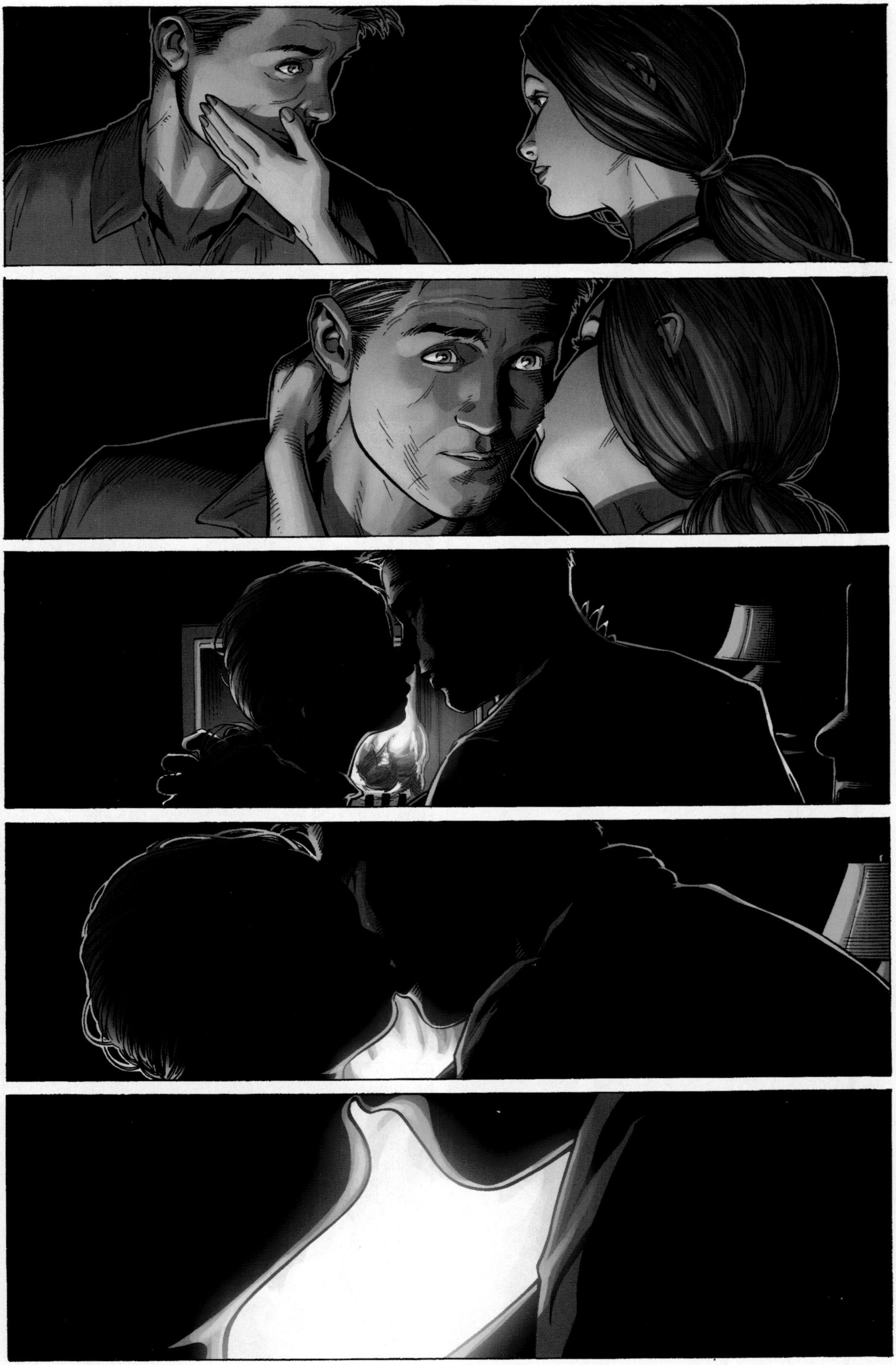

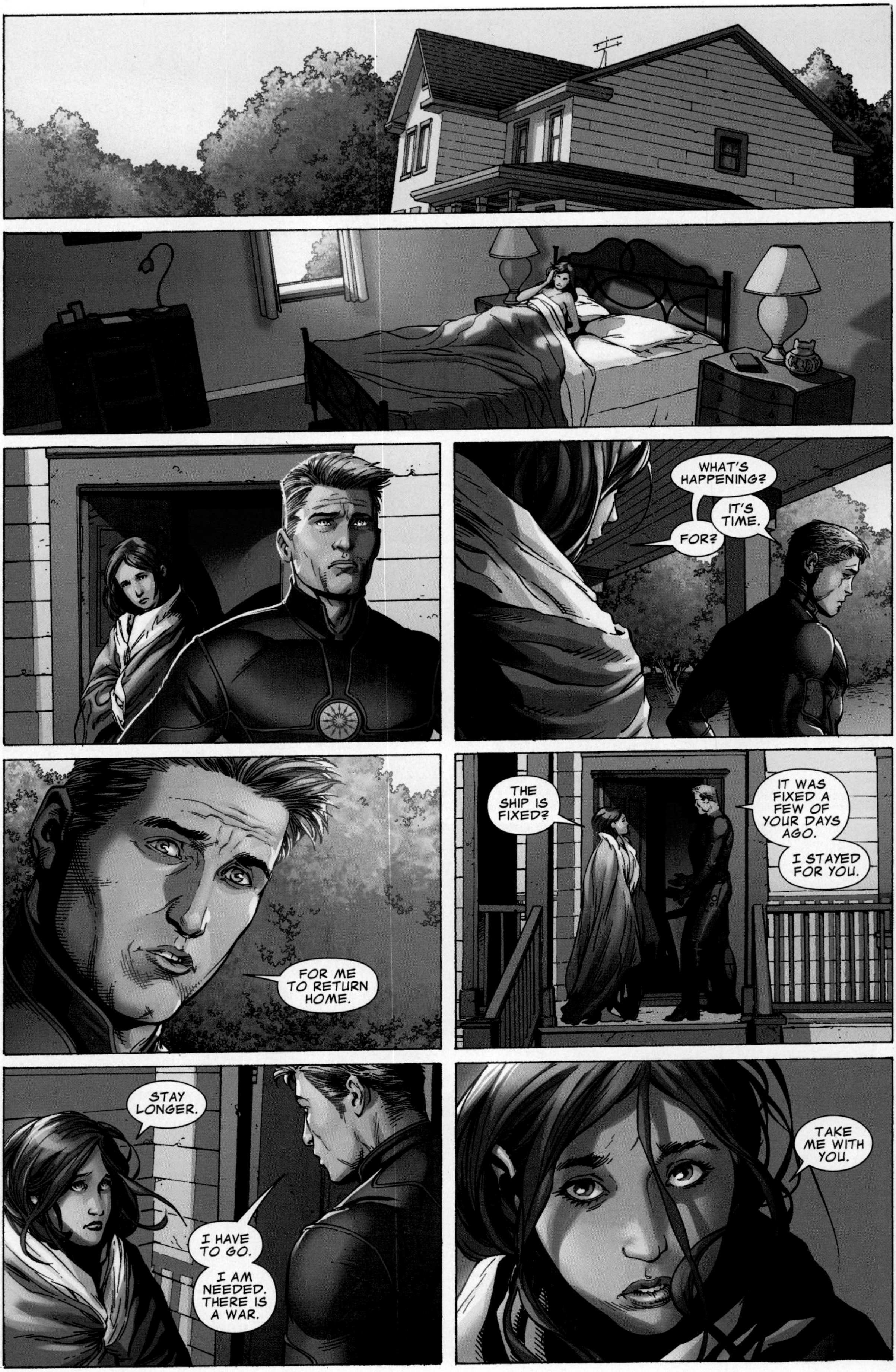
WHAT'S HAPPENING?
IT'S TIME.
FOR?
FOR ME TO RETURN HOME.
THE SHIP IS FIXED?
IT WAS FIXED A FEW OF YOUR DAYS AGO.
I STAYED FOR YOU.
STAY LONGER.
I HAVE TO GO.
I AM NEEDED. THERE IS A WAR.
TAKE ME WITH YOU.

I HAVE THOUGHT ABOUT NOTHING ELSE.

BUT IT WOULD BE CRUEL AND SELFISH.

BECAUSE?

I AM...MY PEOPLE ARE... FIGHTING A WAR WITH A TERRIBLE ENEMY

YOU WOULD NOT BE SAFE AND I CANNOT PUT YOU IN A SITUATION WHERE I *KNOW* THAT TO BE TRUE.

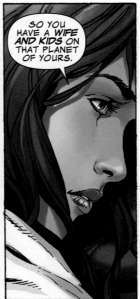

SO YOU HAVE A *WIFE AND KIDS* ON THAT PLANET OF YOURS.

I DO NOT.

YOU ARE NOT READY FOR-- NO ONE ON EARTH IS READY FOR WHAT IS GOING ON IN THE REST OF THIS GALAXY.

I BADLY WANT TO STAY HERE.

BUT YOU CAN'T.

I WILL TRY TO COME BACK TO YOU.

DO YOU WANT YOUR GUN I HID FROM YOU?

YOU KEEP IT.

HOW ROMANTIC.

IT IS.

IT WAS MADE FOR ME.

THERE IS NO OTHER LIKE IT.

I CAN'T BELIEVE THIS.

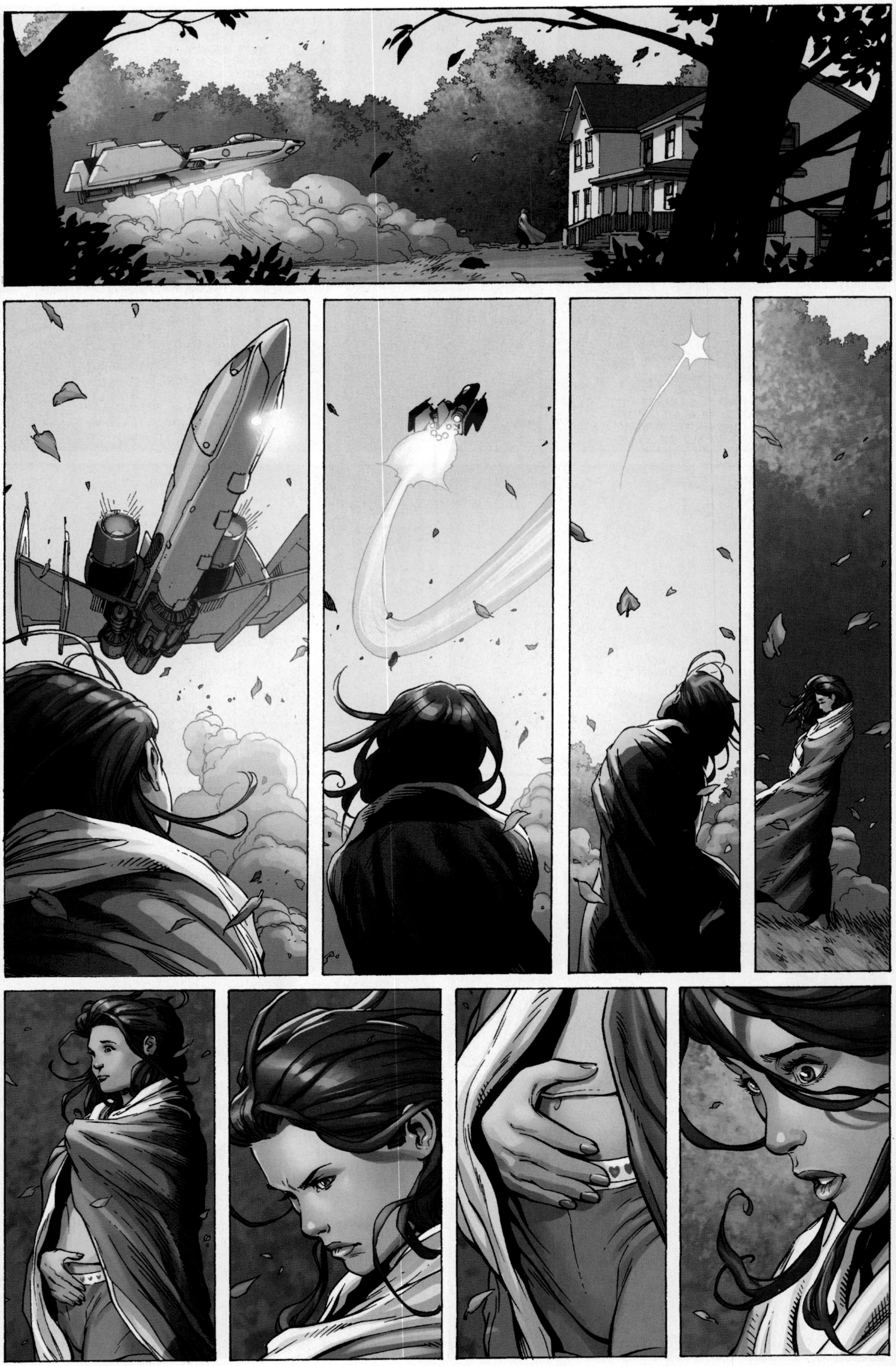

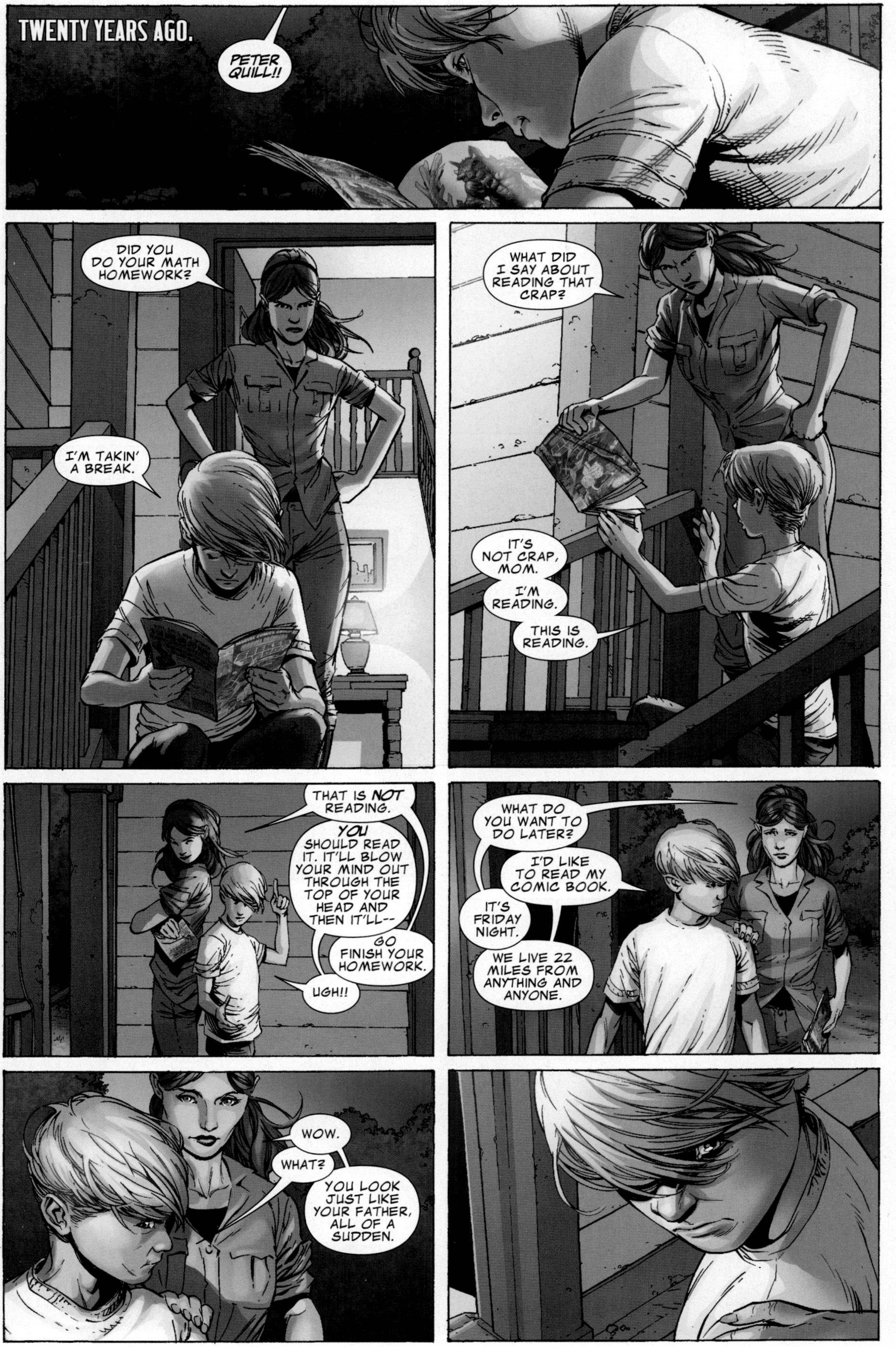
TWENTY YEARS AGO.
PETER QUILL!!
DID YOU DO YOUR MATH HOMEWORK?
I'M TAKIN' A BREAK.
WHAT DID I SAY ABOUT READING THAT CRAP?
IT'S NOT CRAP, MOM.
I'M READING.
THIS IS READING.
THAT IS NOT READING.
YOU SHOULD READ IT. IT'LL BLOW YOUR MIND OUT THROUGH THE TOP OF YOUR HEAD AND THEN IT'LL--
GO FINISH YOUR HOMEWORK.
UGH!!
WHAT DO YOU WANT TO DO LATER?
I'D LIKE TO READ MY COMIC BOOK.
IT'S FRIDAY NIGHT.
WE LIVE 22 MILES FROM ANYTHING AND ANYONE.
WOW.
WHAT?
YOU LOOK JUST LIKE YOUR FATHER, ALL OF A SUDDEN.

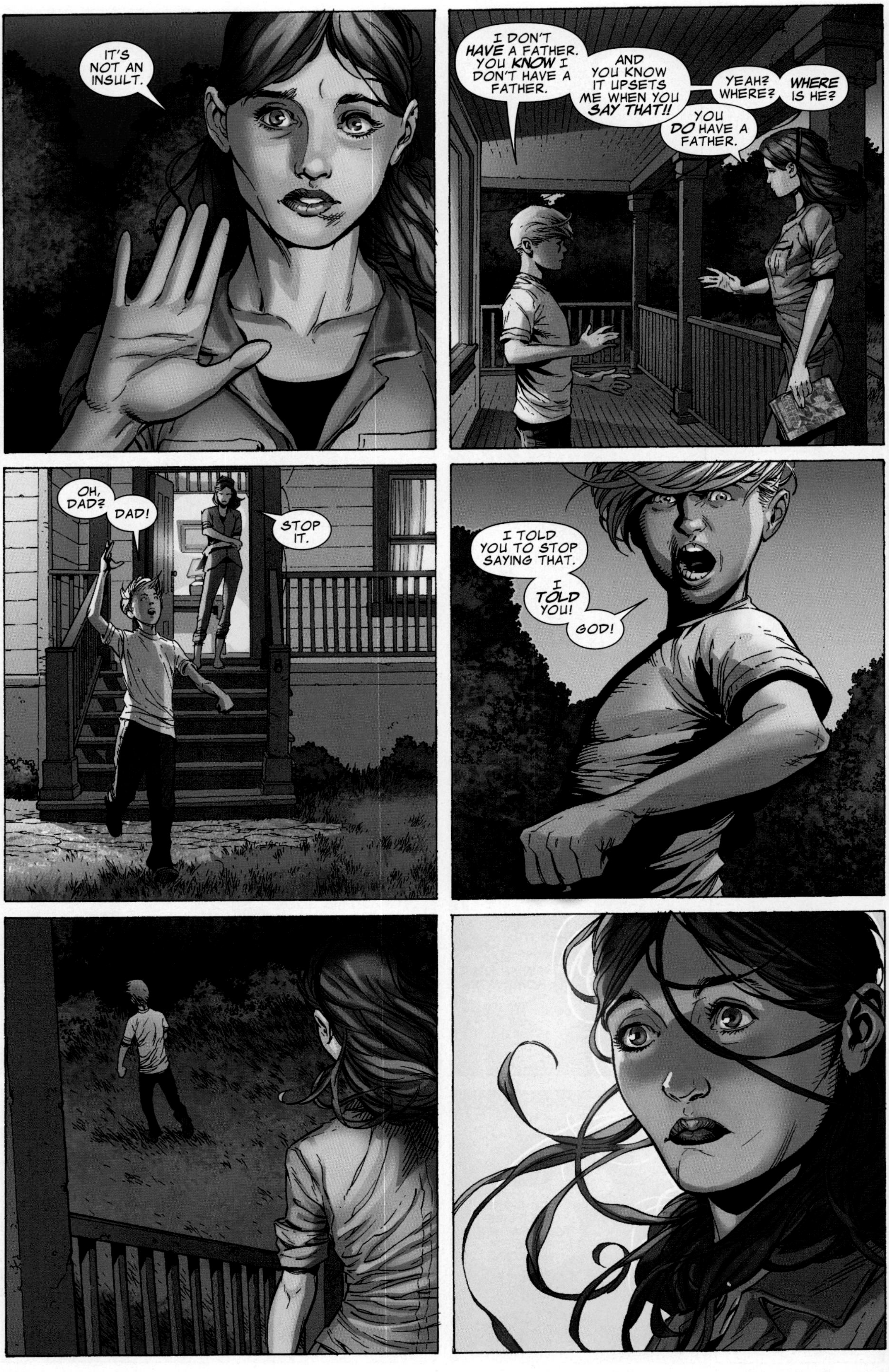
IT'S NOT AN INSULT.
I DON'T HAVE A FATHER. YOU KNOW I DON'T HAVE A FATHER.
AND YOU KNOW IT UPSETS ME WHEN YOU SAY THAT!!
YOU DO HAVE A FATHER.
YEAH? WHERE?
WHERE IS HE?
OH, DAD?
DAD!
STOP IT.
I TOLD YOU TO STOP SAYING THAT.
I TOLD YOU!
GOD!

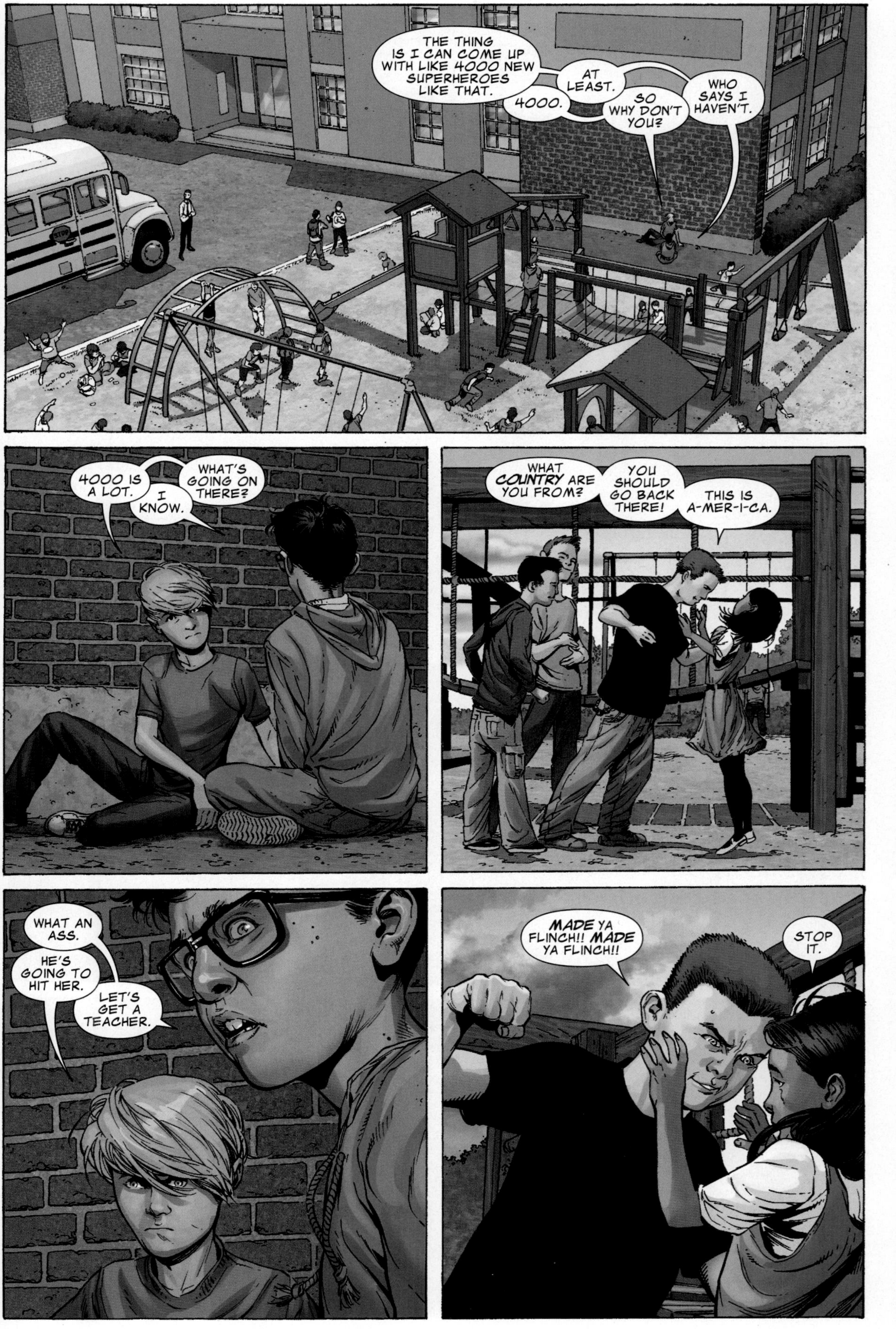

THE THING IS I CAN COME UP WITH LIKE 4000 NEW SUPERHEROES LIKE THAT.
4000.
AT LEAST.
SO WHY DON'T YOU?
WHO SAYS I HAVEN'T.
4000 IS A LOT.
I KNOW.
WHAT'S GOING ON THERE?
WHAT COUNTRY ARE YOU FROM?
YOU SHOULD GO BACK THERE!
THIS IS A-MER-I-CA.
WHAT AN ASS.
HE'S GOING TO HIT HER.
LET'S GET A TEACHER.
MADE YA FLINCH!! MADE YA FLINCH!!
STOP IT.

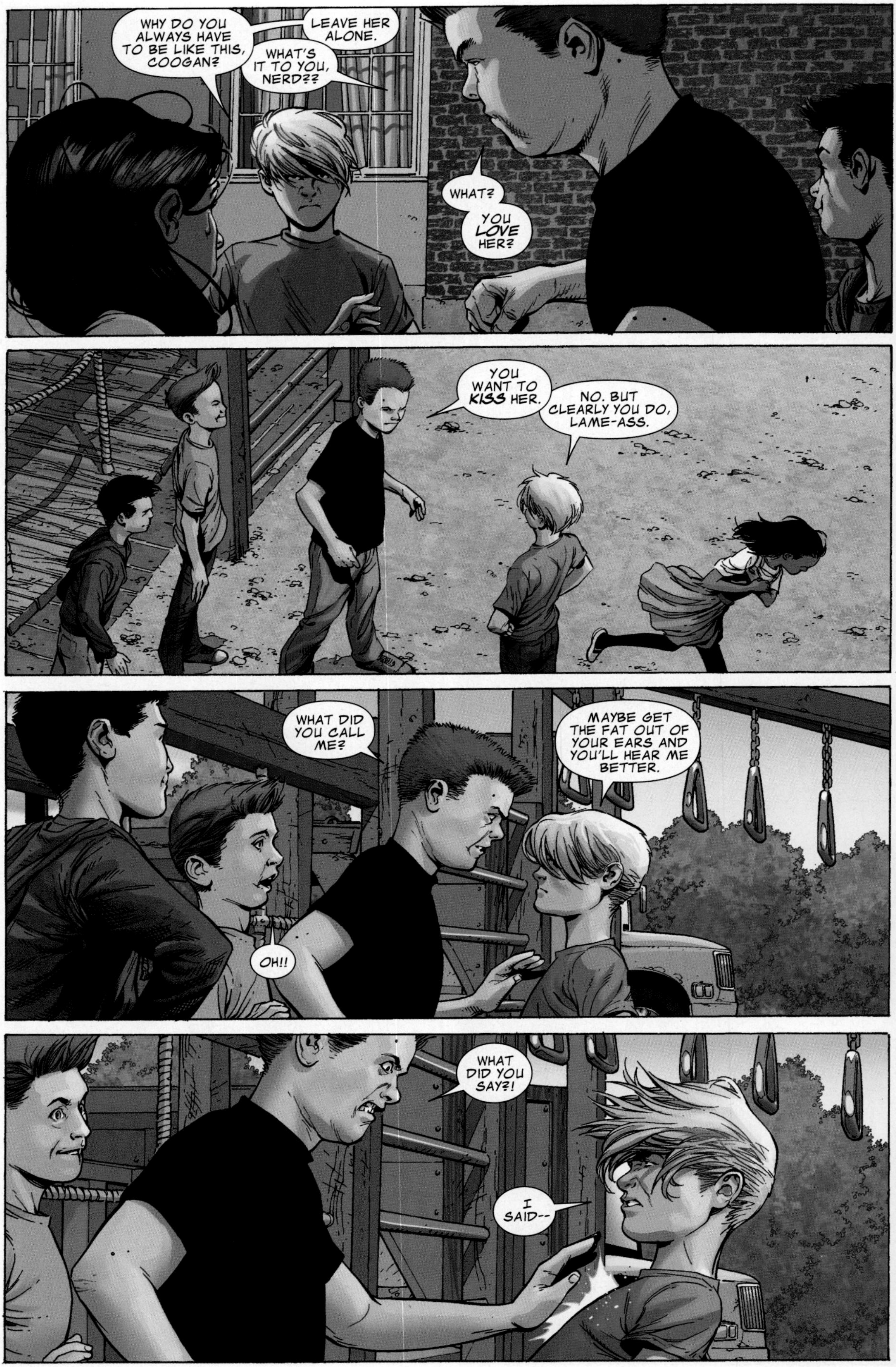
WHY DO YOU ALWAYS HAVE TO BE LIKE THIS, COOGAN?
LEAVE HER ALONE.
WHAT'S IT TO YOU, NERD??
WHAT? YOU LOVE HER?
YOU WANT TO KISS HER.
NO. BUT CLEARLY YOU DO, LAME-ASS.
WHAT DID YOU CALL ME?
MAYBE GET THE FAT OUT OF YOUR EARS AND YOU'LL HEAR ME BETTER.
OH!!
WHAT DID YOU SAY?!
I SAID--

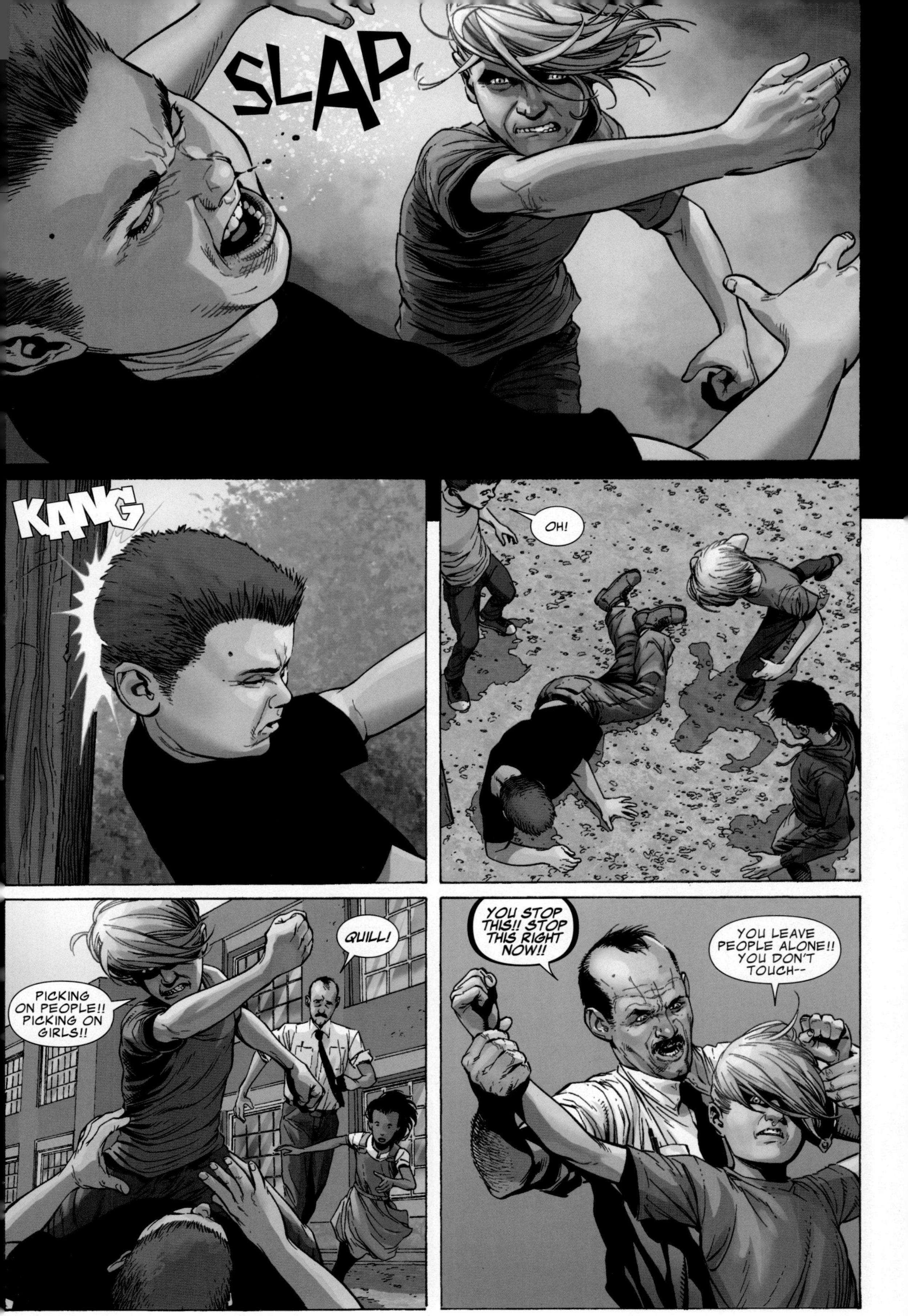
SLAP
KANG
OH!
QUILL!
PICKING ON PEOPLE!! PICKING ON GIRLS!!
YOU STOP THIS!! STOP THIS RIGHT NOW!!
YOU LEAVE PEOPLE ALONE!! YOU DON'T TOUCH--

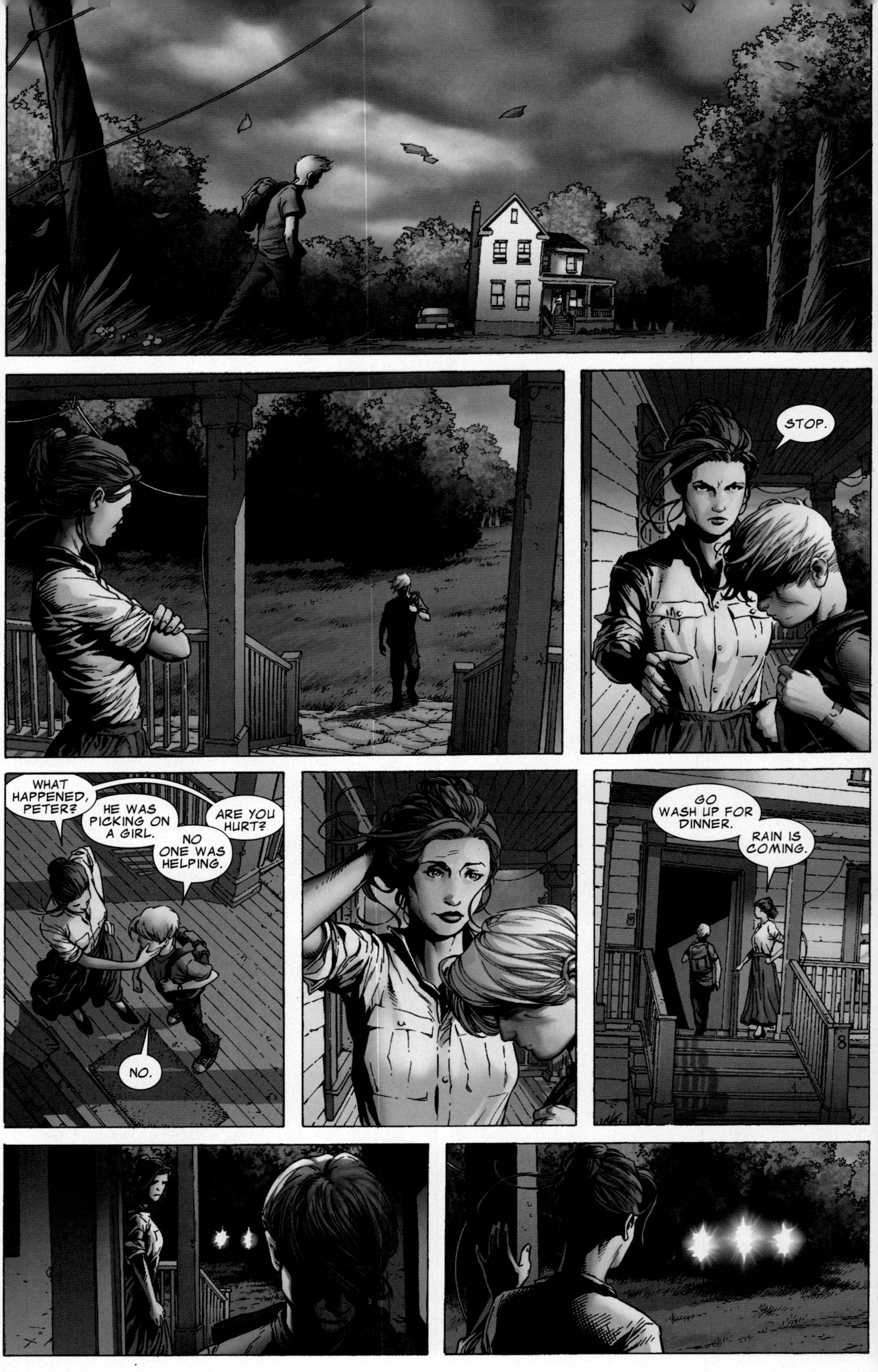
STOP.
WHAT HAPPENED, PETER?
HE WAS PICKING ON A GIRL.
NO ONE WAS HELPING.
ARE YOU HURT?
NO.
GO WASH UP FOR DINNER.
RAIN IS COMING.

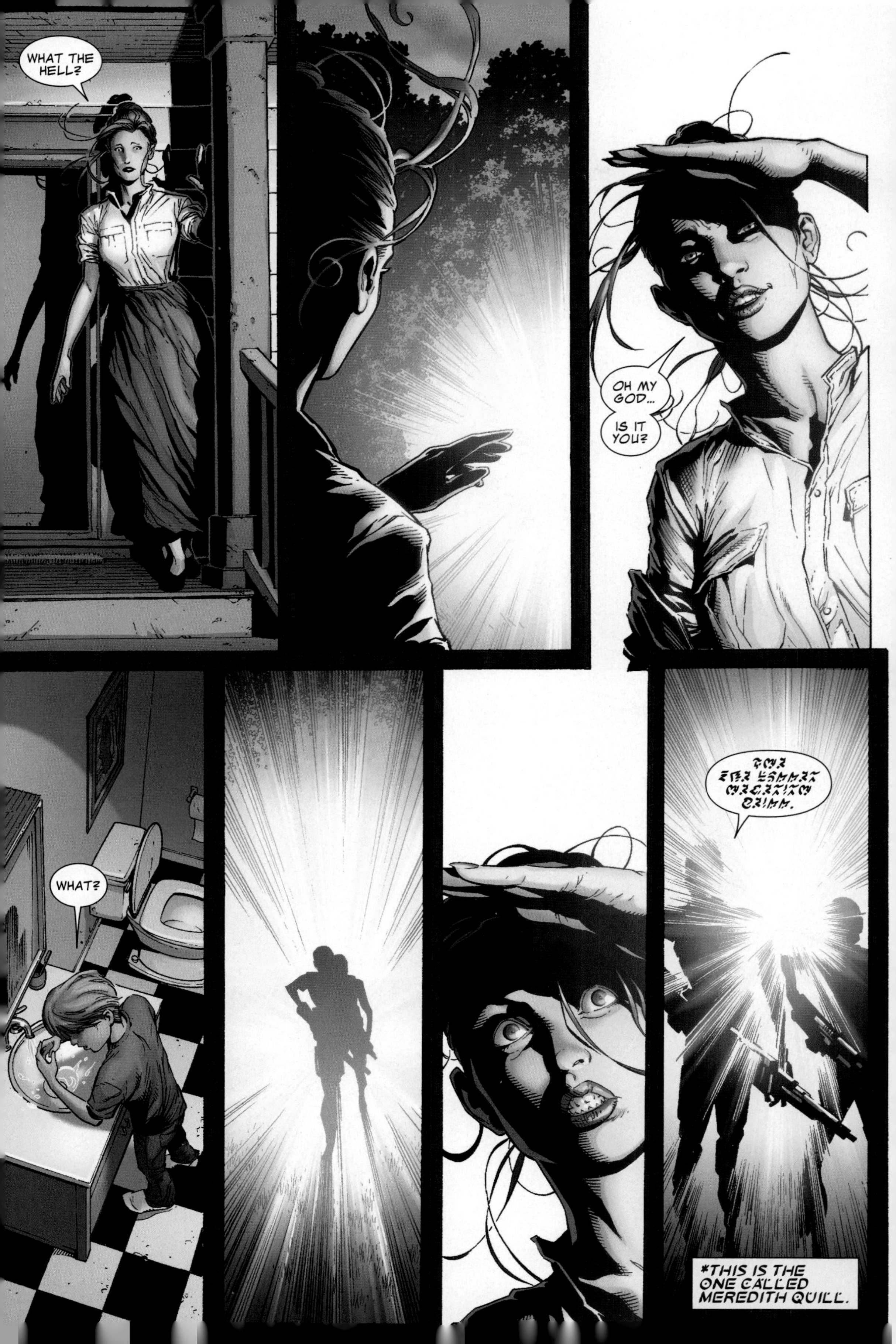
WHAT THE HELL?
OH MY GOD...
IS IT YOU?
WHAT?
*THIS IS THE ONE CALLED MEREDITH QUILL.

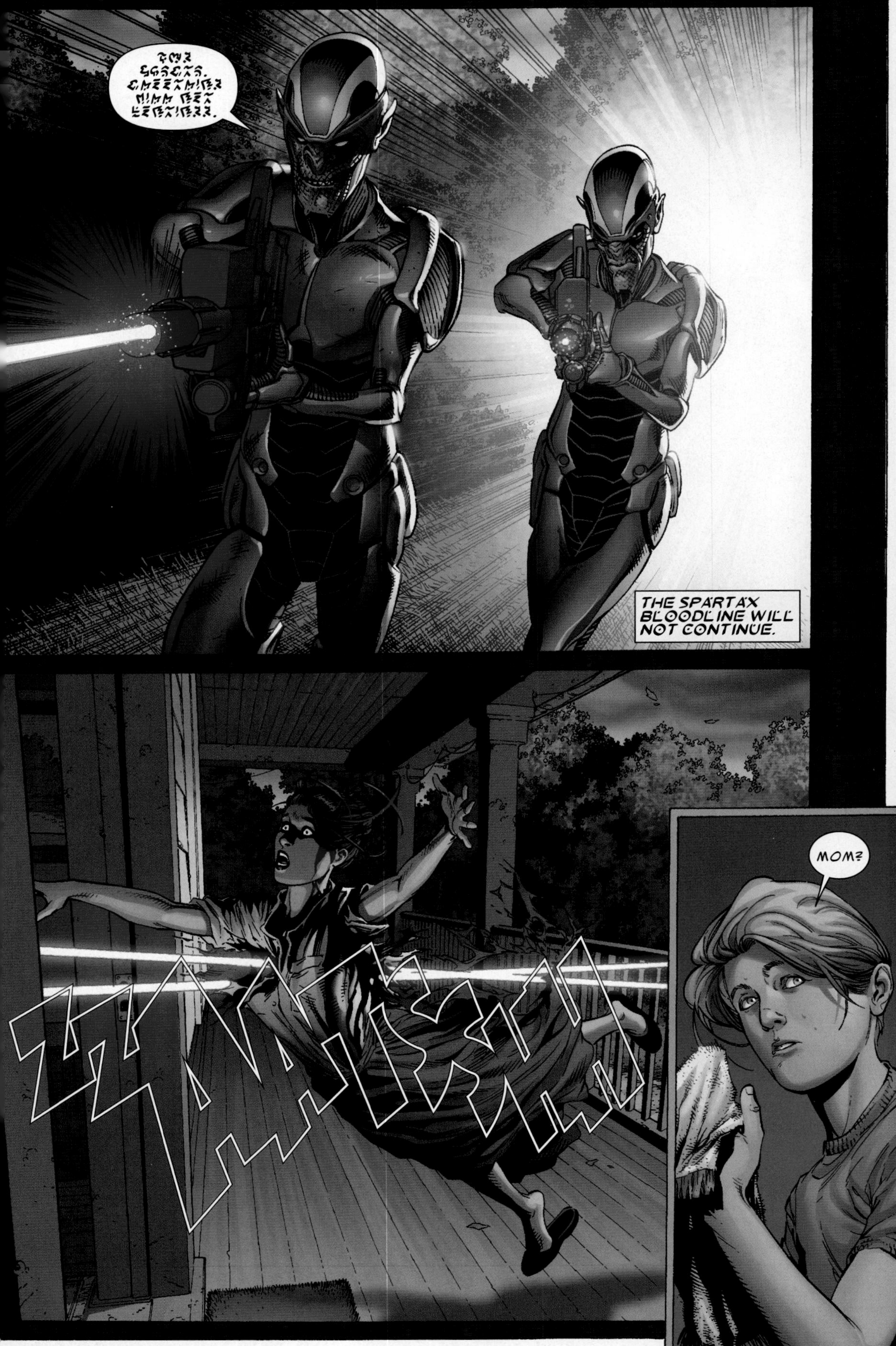
THE SPARTAX BLOODLINE WILL NOT CONTINUE.
MOM?

SHEE THE GUN.

MOMZZ

AAGH!!

ZZAATISHH
ZZAATISHH

ZZAATISHH

HEY!!

ZZAATISHH

WHAT THE HELL?

WHAT THE--?

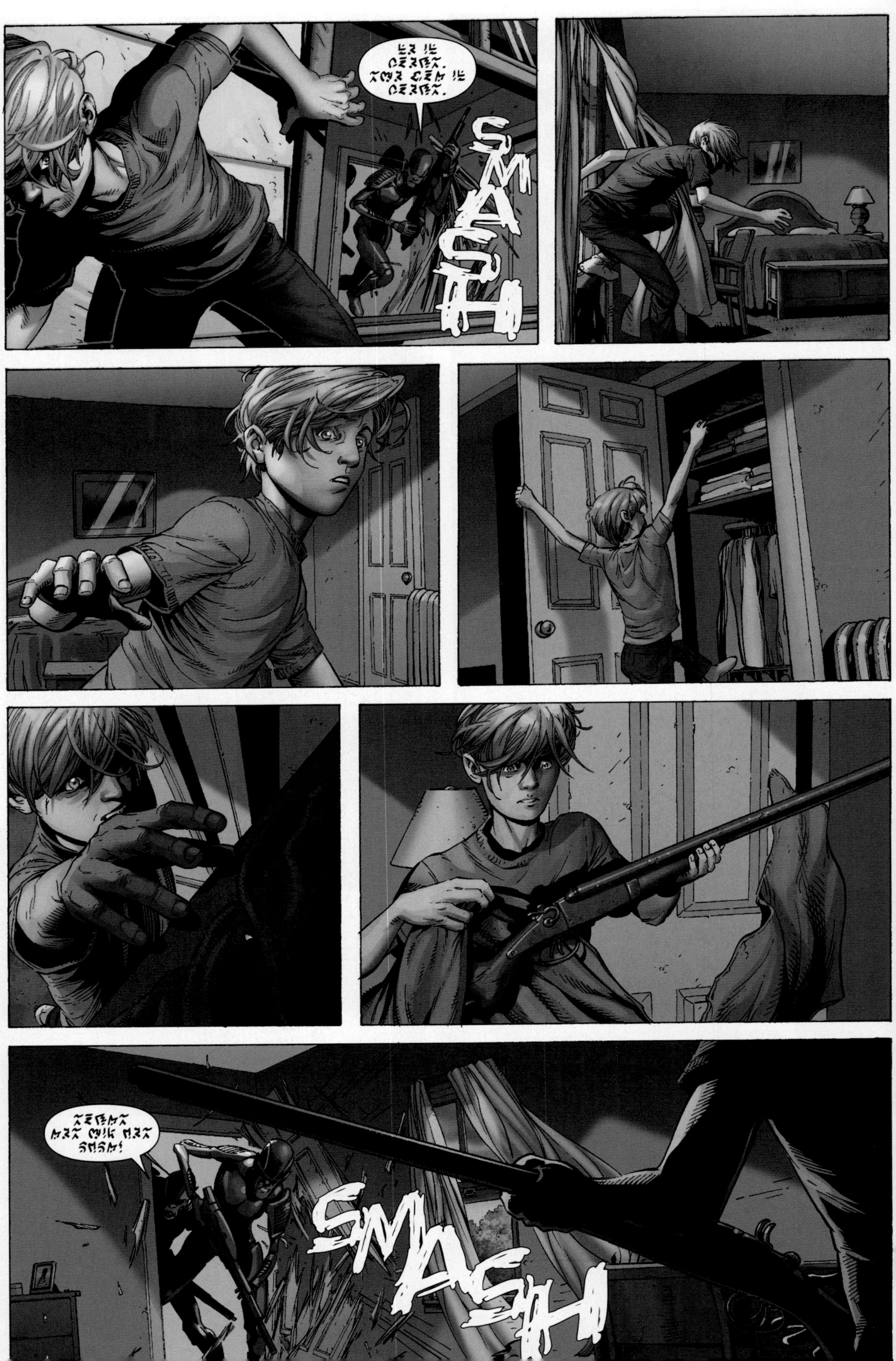
SMASH
SMASH

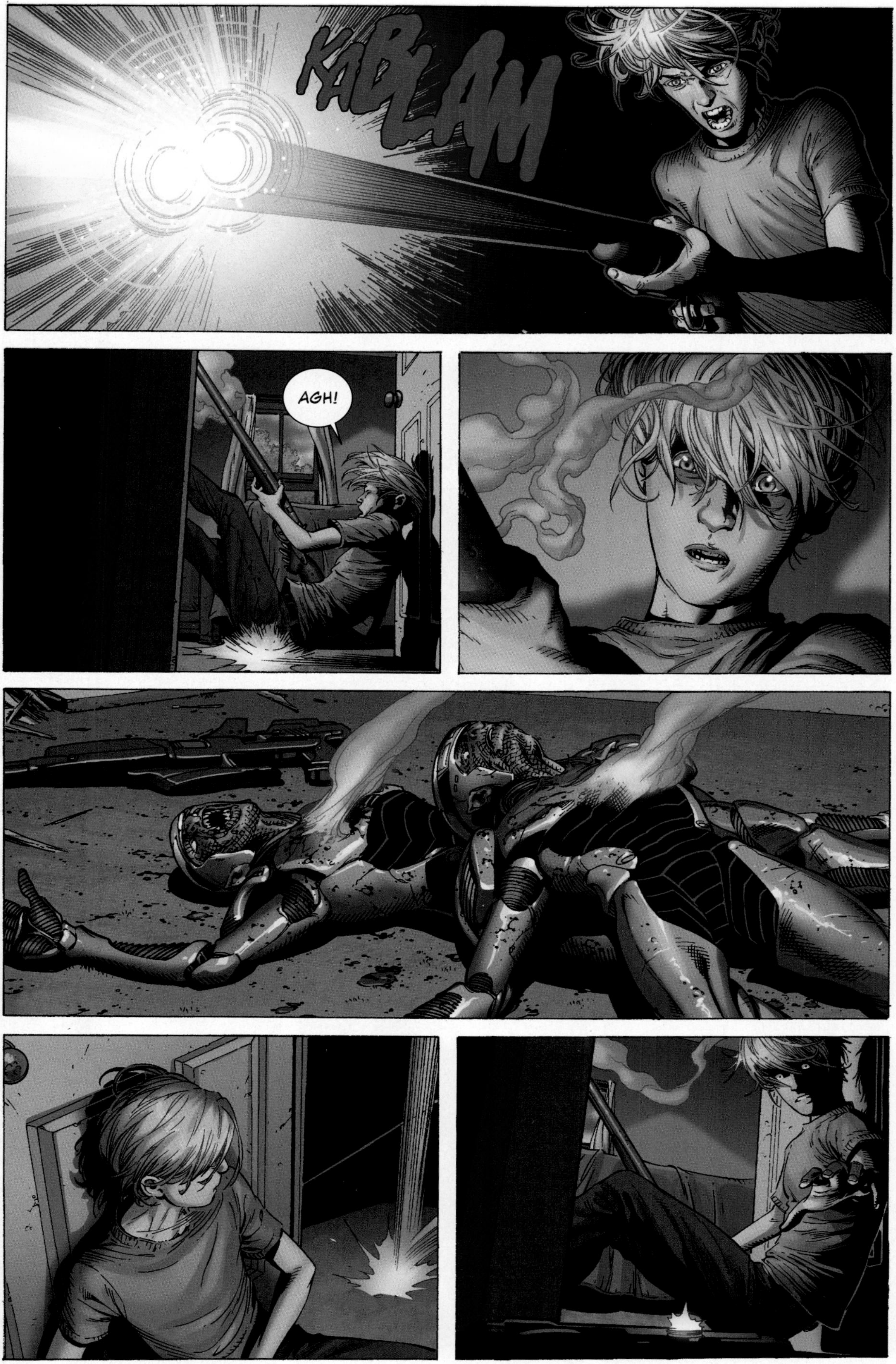
KABLAM
AGH!

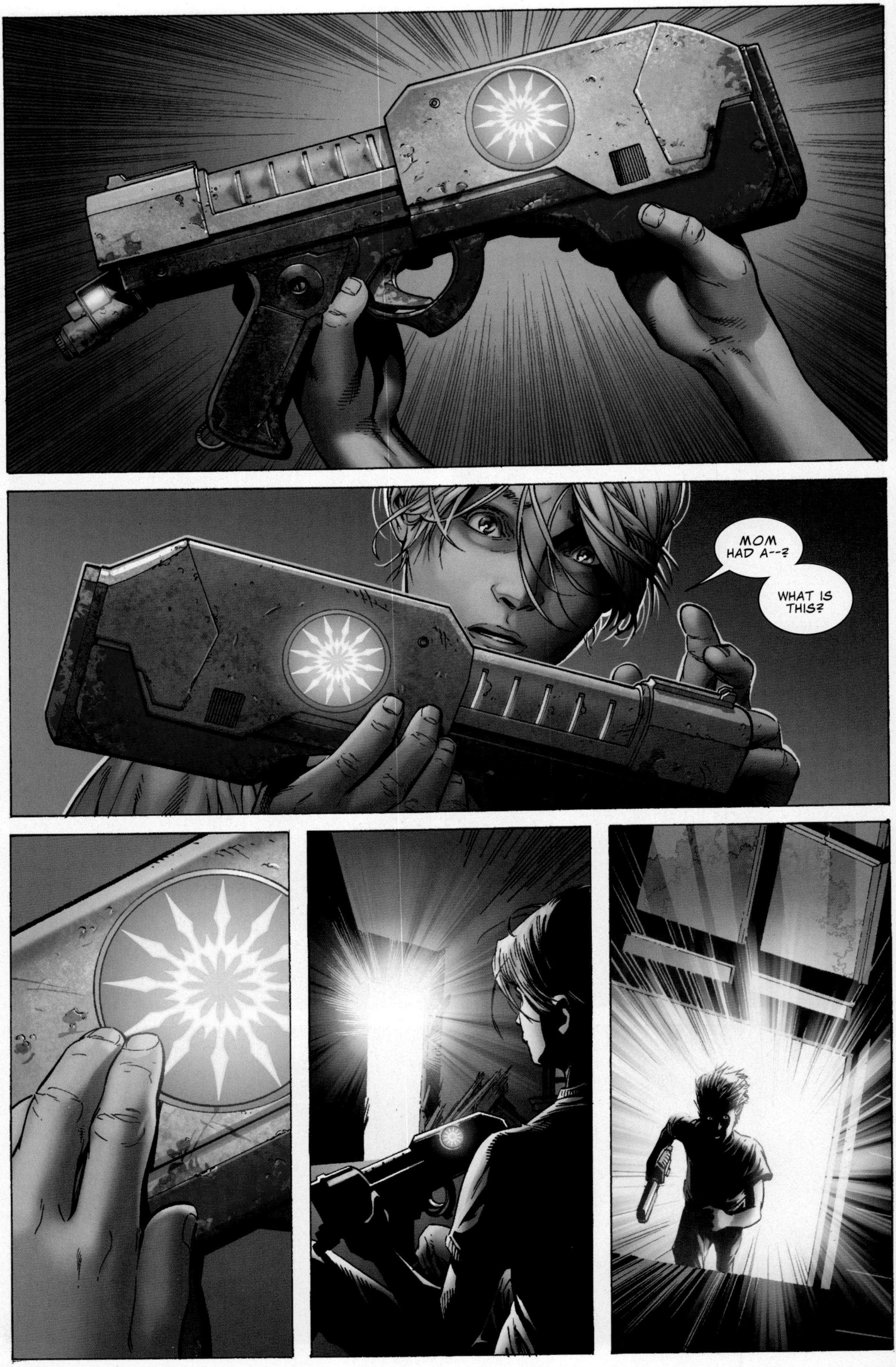
MOM HAD A--?
WHAT IS THIS?

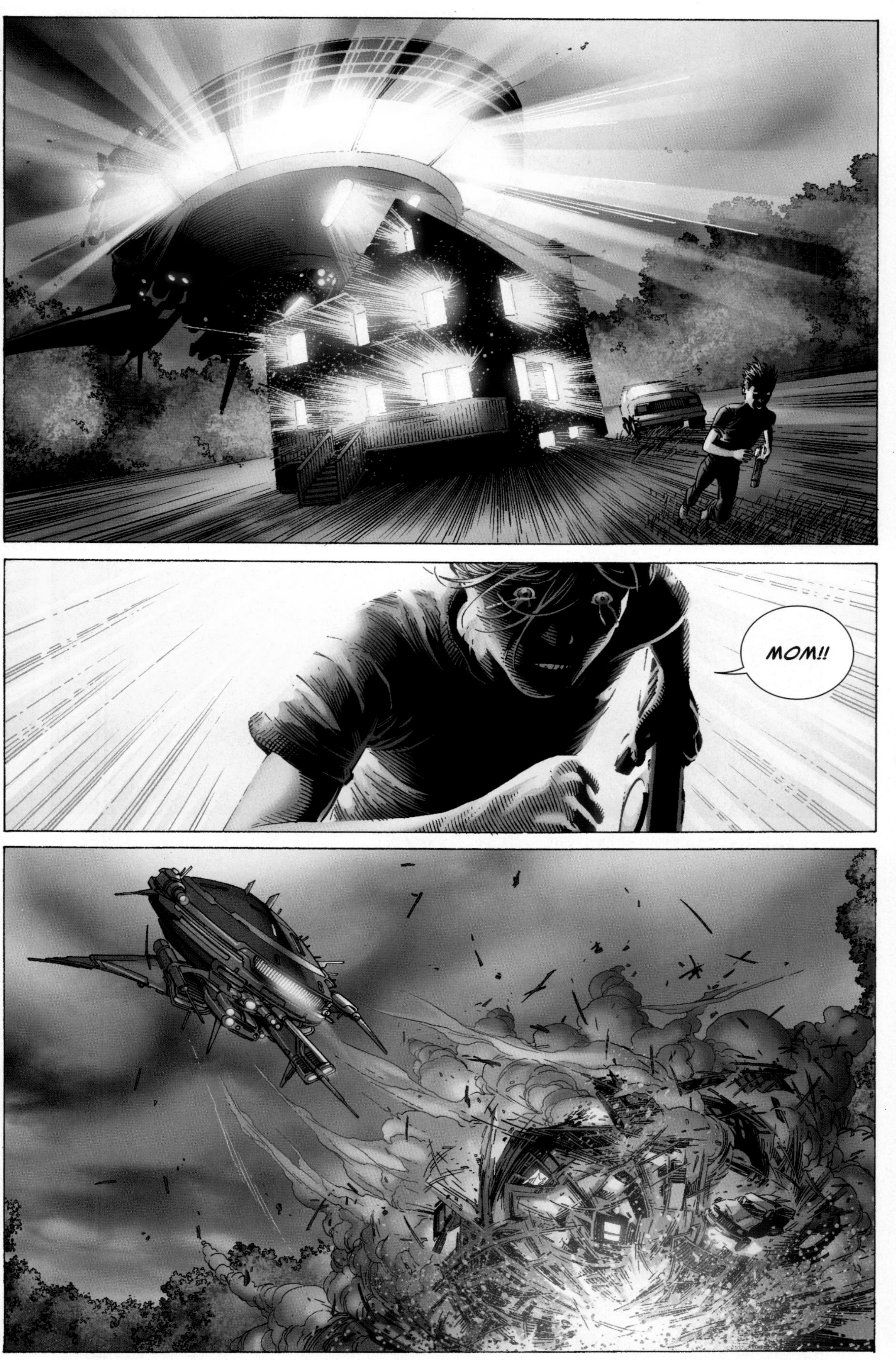
MOM!!

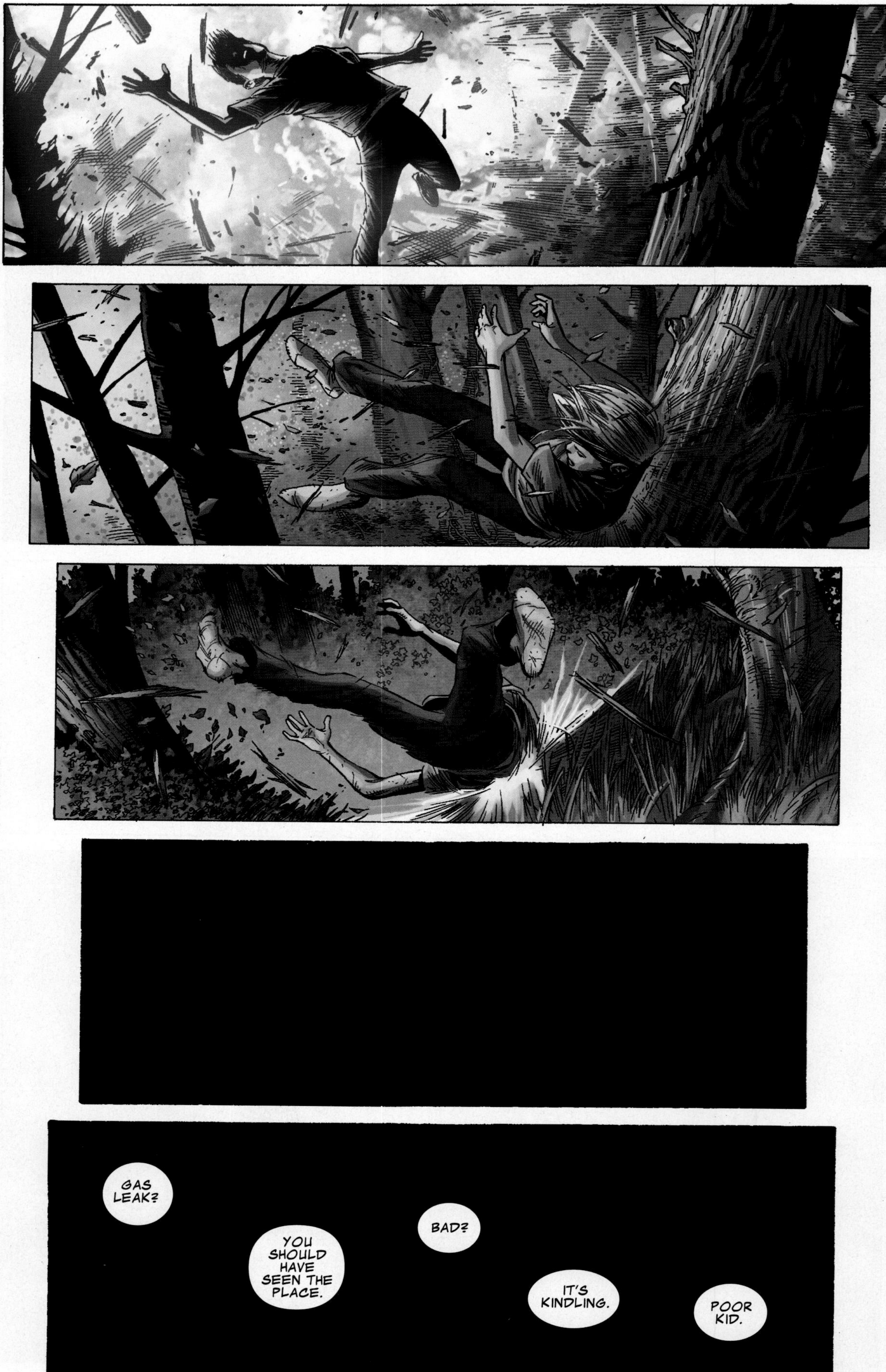
GAS LEAK?
YOU SHOULD HAVE SEEN THE PLACE.
BAD?
IT'S KINDLING.
POOR KID.

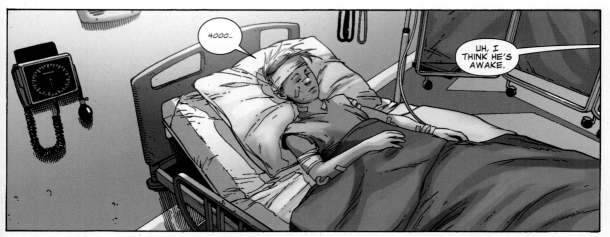

4000...

UH, I THINK HE'S AWAKE.

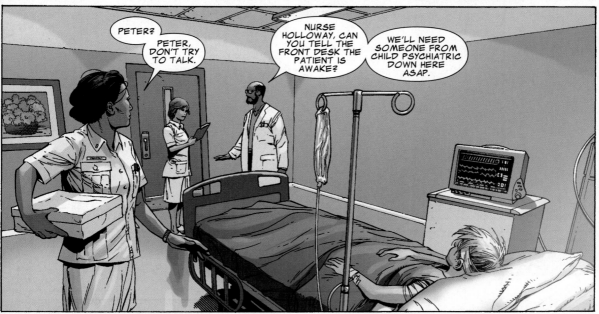

PETER?

PETER, DON'T TRY TO TALK.

NURSE HOLLOWAY, CAN YOU TELL THE FRONT DESK THE PATIENT IS AWAKE?

WE'LL NEED SOMEONE FROM CHILD PSYCHIATRIC DOWN HERE ASAP.

PETER, DO YOU REMEMBER MEETING ME YESTERDAY?

NO.

THAT'S OKAY.

YOU WERE PRETTY OUT OF IT.

DO YOU REMEMBER WHAT HAPPENED TO YOU?

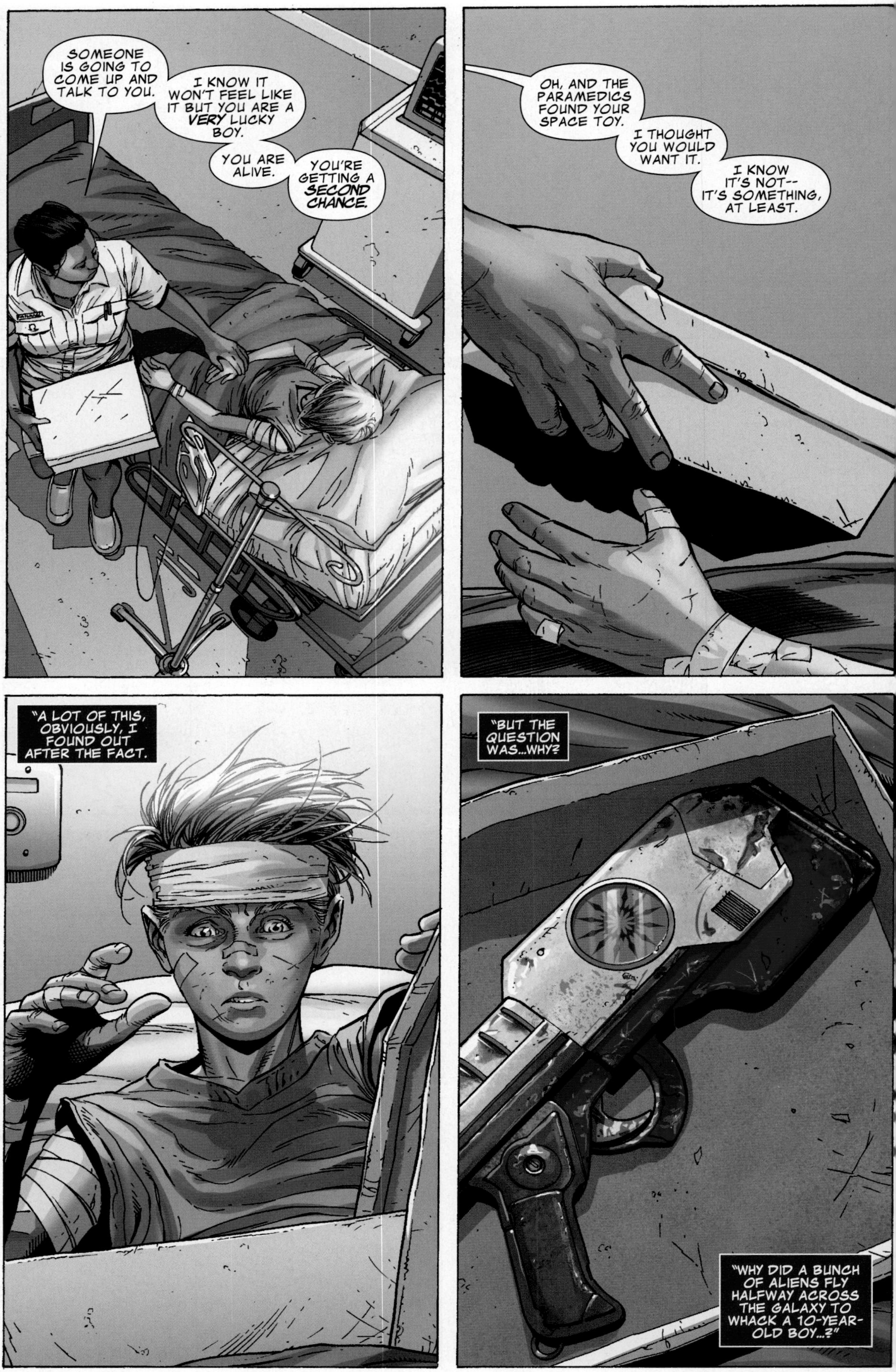
SOMEONE IS GOING TO COME UP AND TALK TO YOU.
I KNOW IT WON'T FEEL LIKE IT BUT YOU ARE A VERY LUCKY BOY.
YOU ARE ALIVE.
YOU'RE GETTING A SECOND CHANCE.
OH, AND THE PARAMEDICS FOUND YOUR SPACE TOY.
I THOUGHT YOU WOULD WANT IT.
I KNOW IT'S NOT-- IT'S SOMETHING, AT LEAST.
"A LOT OF THIS, OBVIOUSLY, I FOUND OUT AFTER THE FACT.
"BUT THE QUESTION WAS...WHY?
"WHY DID A BUNCH OF ALIENS FLY HALFWAY ACROSS THE GALAXY TO WHACK A 10-YEAR-OLD BOY...?"

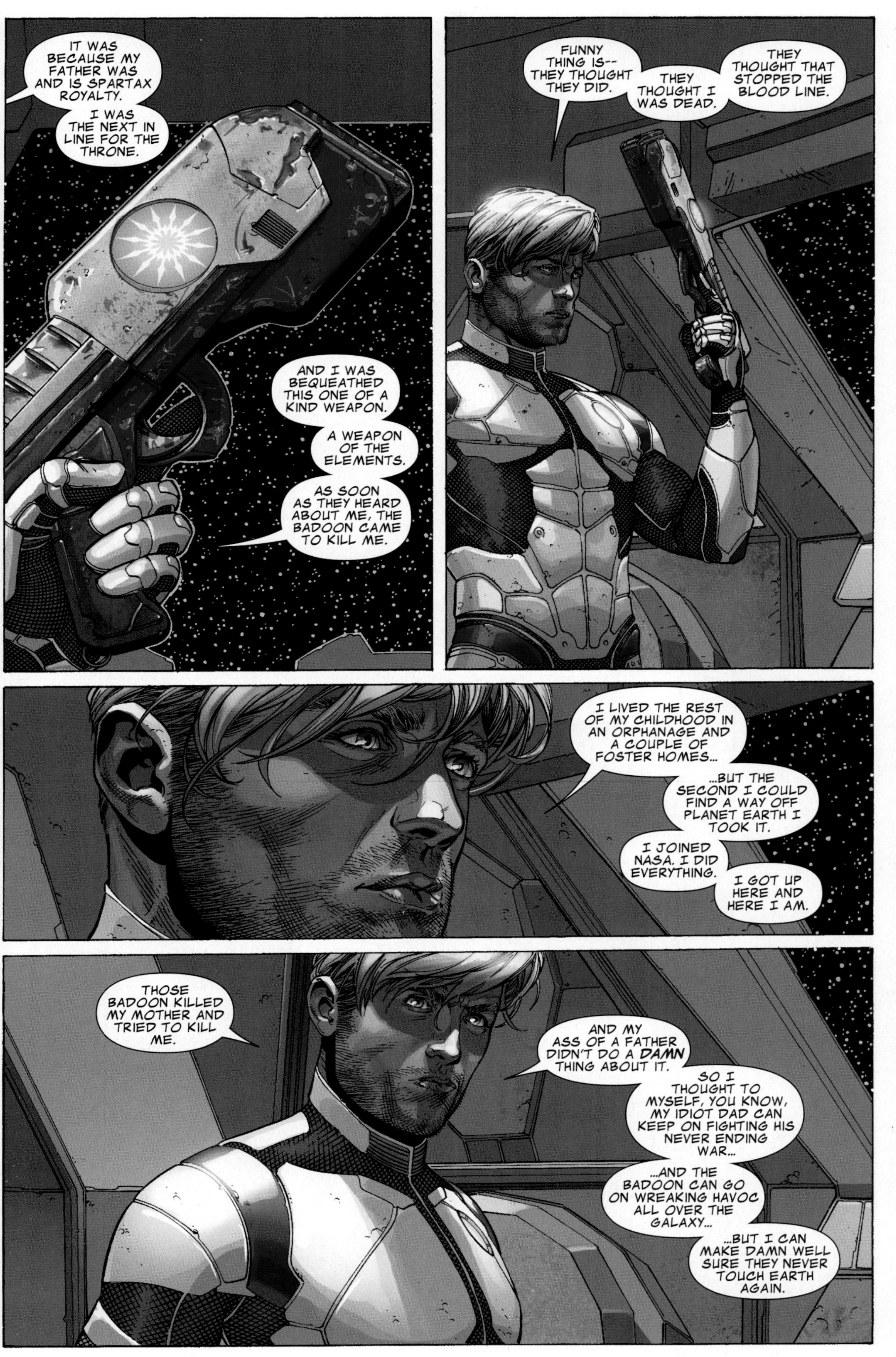

IT WAS BECAUSE MY FATHER WAS AND IS SPARTAX ROYALTY.
I WAS THE NEXT IN LINE FOR THE THRONE.
AND I WAS BEQUEATHED THIS ONE OF A KIND WEAPON.
A WEAPON OF THE ELEMENTS.
AS SOON AS THEY HEARD ABOUT ME, THE BADOON CAME TO KILL ME.
FUNNY THING IS-- THEY THOUGHT THEY DID.
THEY THOUGHT I WAS DEAD.
THEY THOUGHT THAT STOPPED THE BLOOD LINE.
I LIVED THE REST OF MY CHILDHOOD IN AN ORPHANAGE AND A COUPLE OF FOSTER HOMES...
...BUT THE SECOND I COULD FIND A WAY OFF PLANET EARTH I TOOK IT.
I JOINED NASA. I DID EVERYTHING.
I GOT UP HERE AND HERE I AM.
THOSE BADOON KILLED MY MOTHER AND TRIED TO KILL ME.
AND MY ASS OF A FATHER DIDN'T DO A DAMN THING ABOUT IT.
SO I THOUGHT TO MYSELF, YOU KNOW, MY IDIOT DAD CAN KEEP ON FIGHTING HIS NEVER ENDING WAR...
...AND THE BADOON CAN GO ON WREAKING HAVOC ALL OVER THE GALAXY...
...BUT I CAN MAKE DAMN WELL SURE THEY NEVER TOUCH EARTH AGAIN.

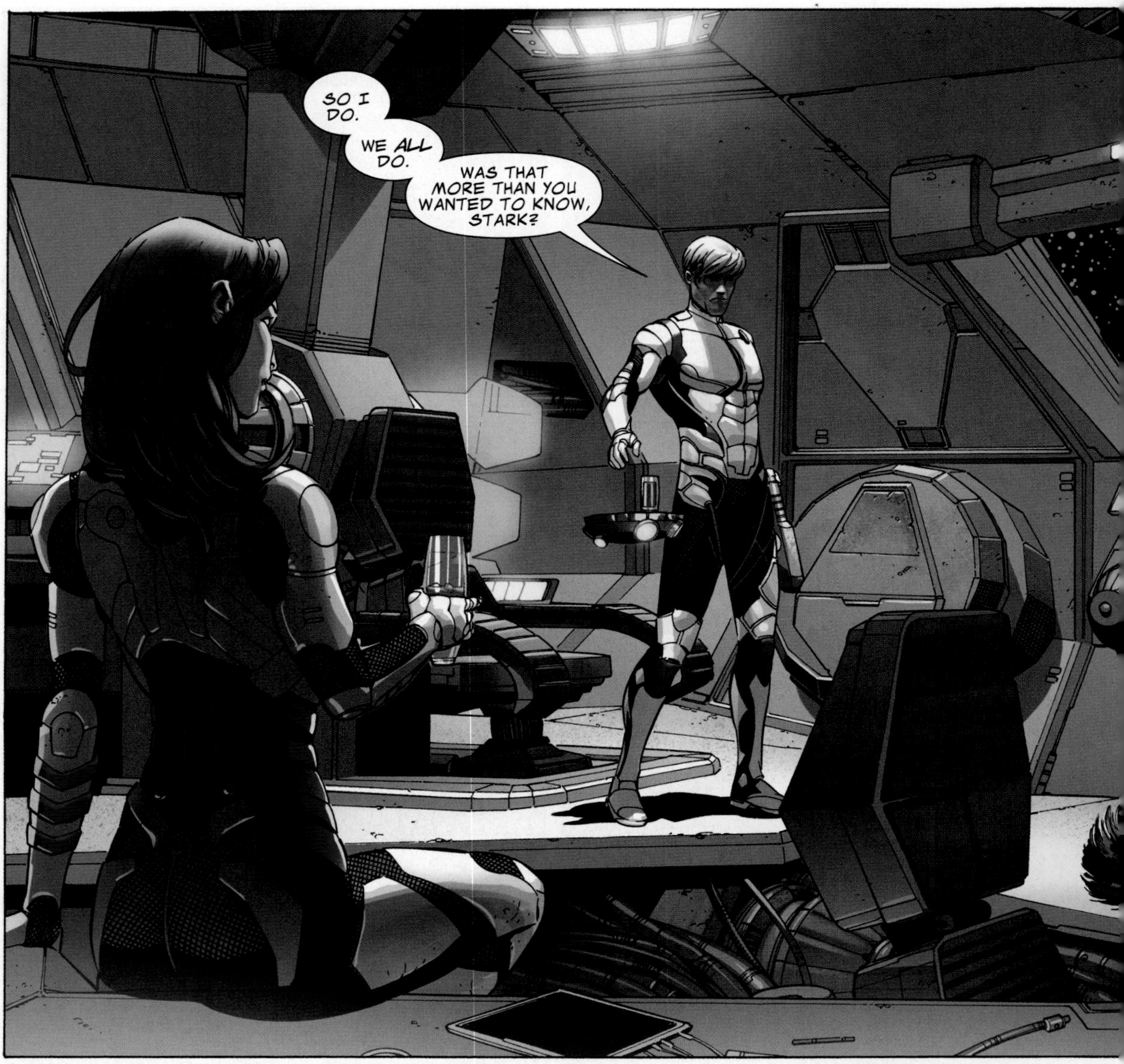
SO I DO.
WE *ALL* DO.
WAS THAT MORE THAN YOU WANTED TO KNOW, STARK?

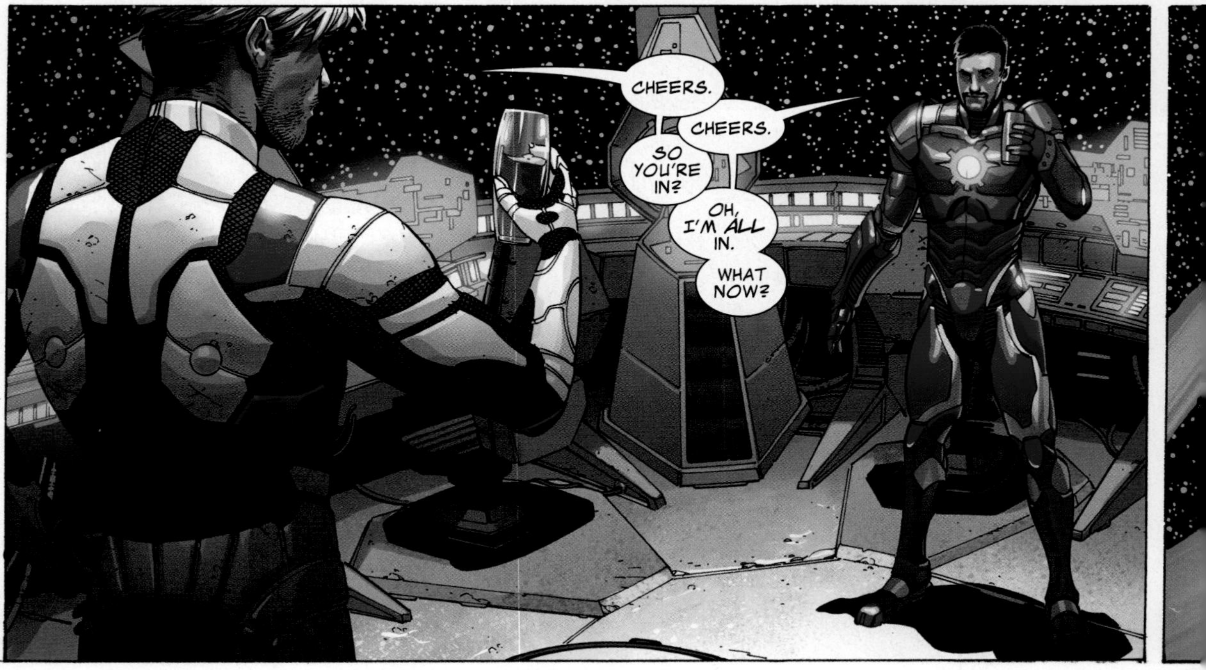
CHEERS.
CHEERS.
SO YOU'RE IN?
OH, I'M *ALL* IN.
WHAT NOW?

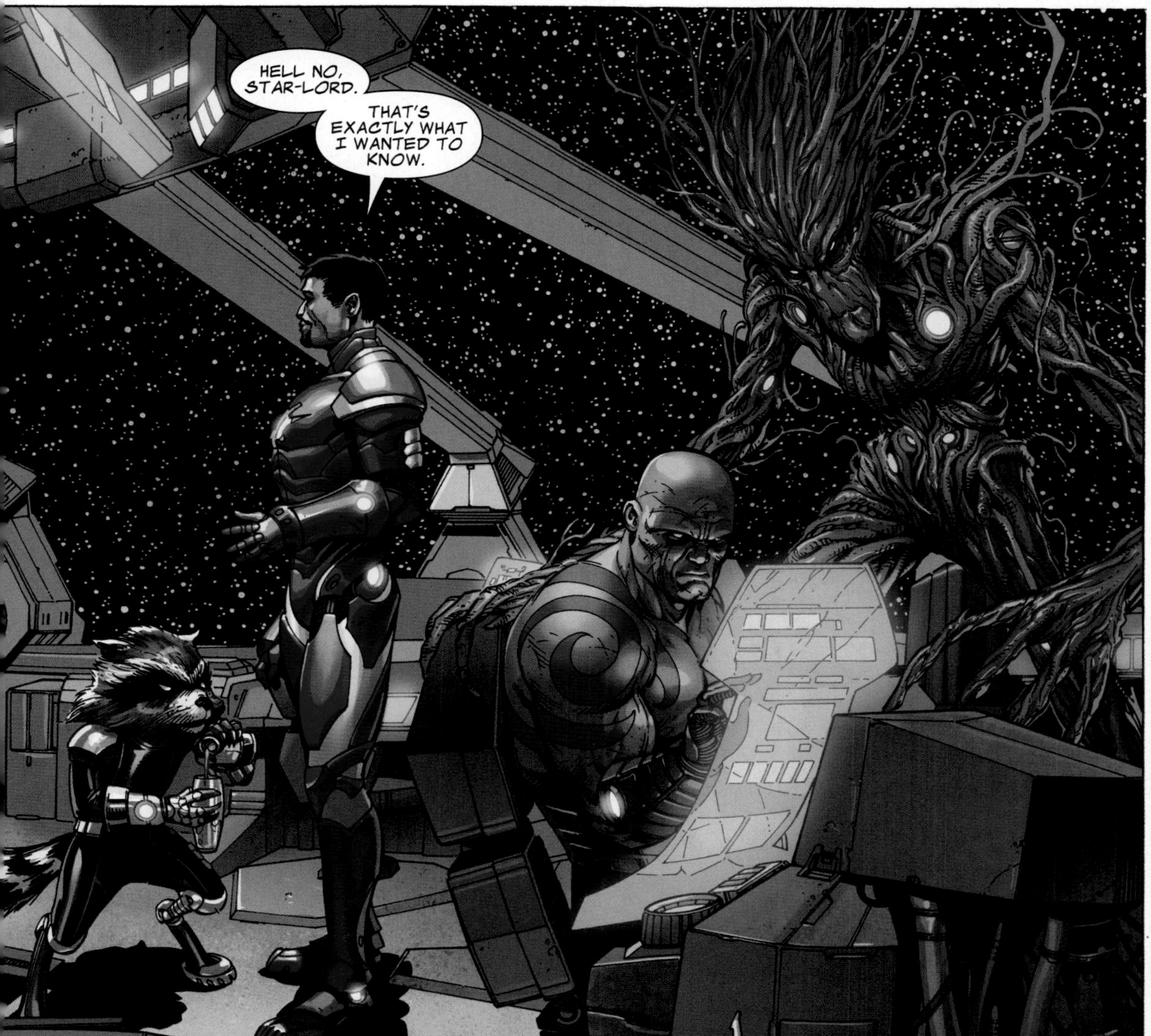
HELL NO, STAR-LORD.
THAT'S EXACTLY WHAT I WANTED TO KNOW.

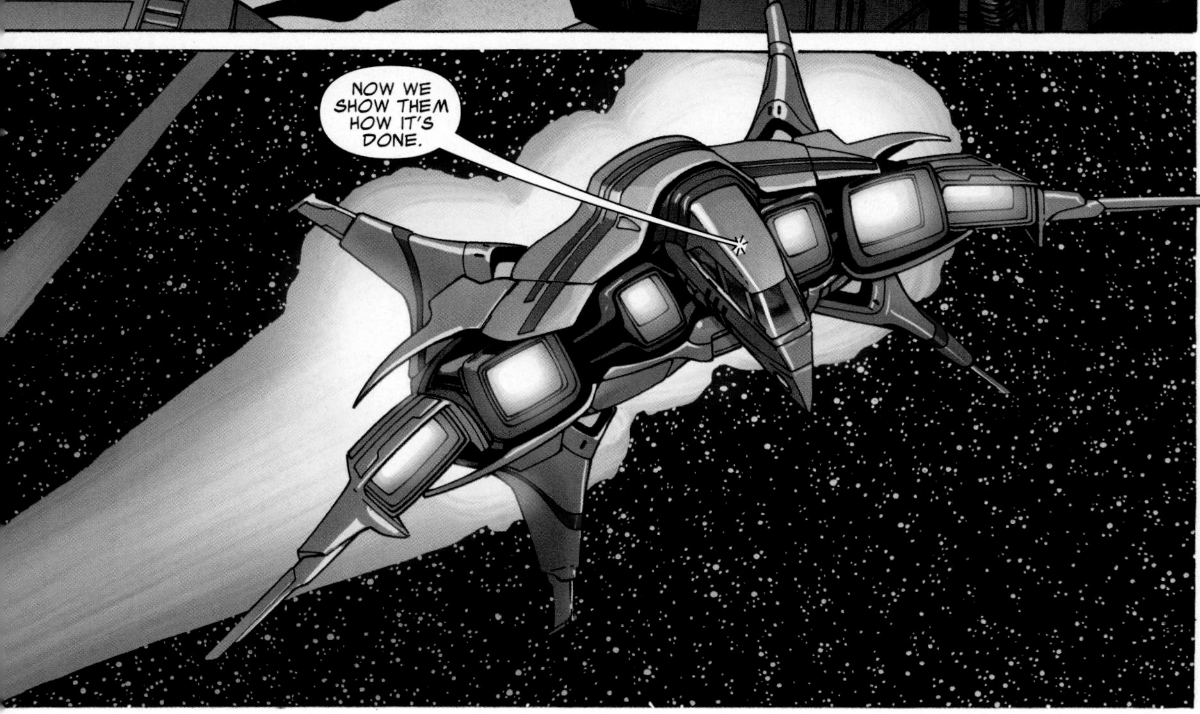
NOW WE SHOW THEM HOW IT'S DONE.

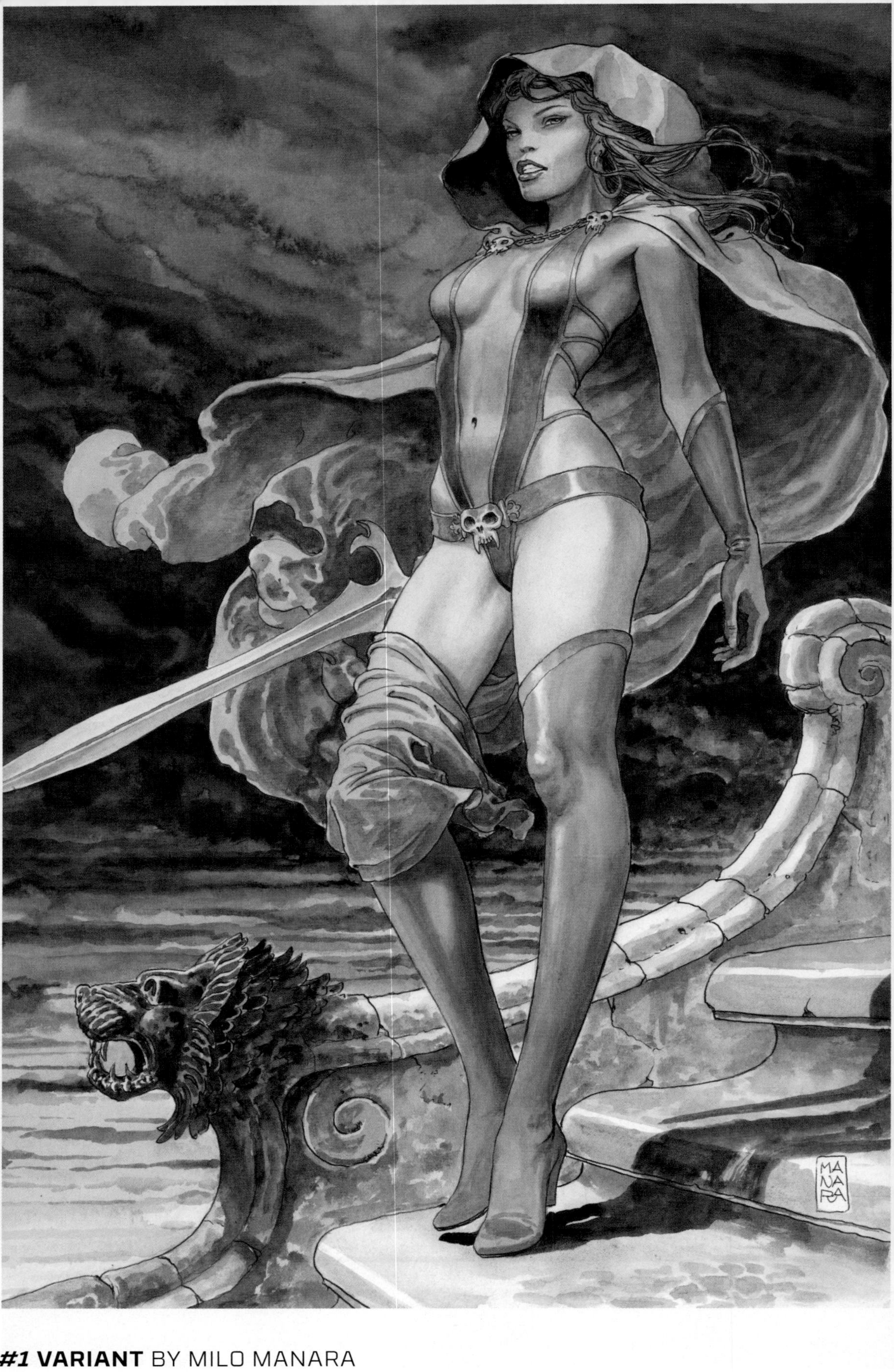
MANARA

***#1* VARIANT** BY MILO MANARA

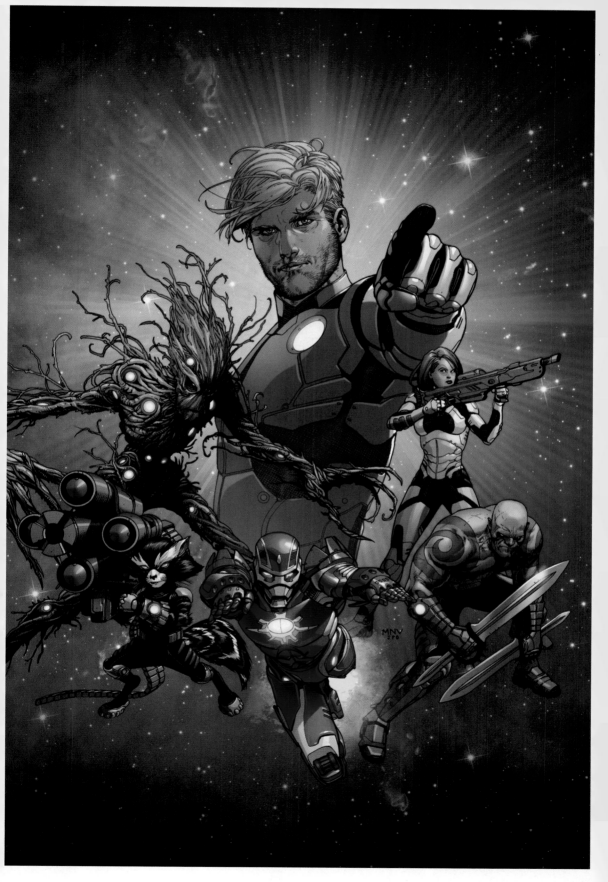

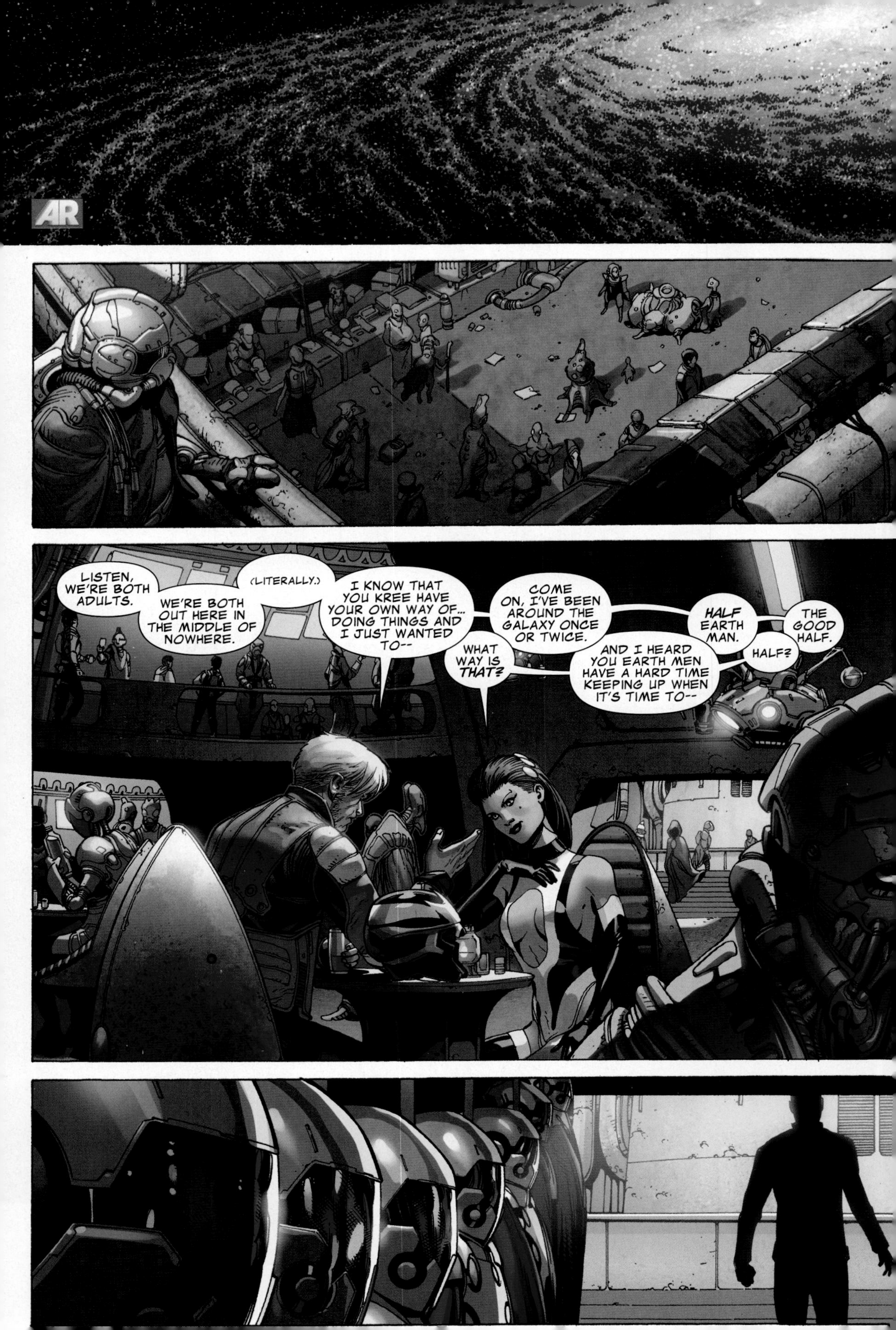
LISTEN, WE'RE BOTH ADULTS.
WE'RE BOTH OUT HERE IN THE MIDDLE OF NOWHERE.
(LITERALLY.)
I KNOW THAT YOU KREE HAVE YOUR OWN WAY OF... DOING THINGS AND I JUST WANTED TO--
WHAT WAY IS *THAT?*
COME ON, I'VE BEEN AROUND THE GALAXY ONCE OR TWICE.
AND I HEARD YOU EARTH MEN HAVE A HARD TIME KEEPING UP WHEN IT'S TIME TO--
HALF?
HALF EARTH MAN.
THE GOOD HALF.

WHAT EXACTLY DO YOU THINK YOU'RE DOING, MISTER QUILL?

AND, TRUST ME, I KNOW HOW...

YOU...

YOU SHOULD GET OUT OF HERE.

WHAT ARE YOU TALKING ABOUT?

YOU SHOULD GET OUT OF HERE *NOW*.

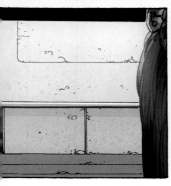

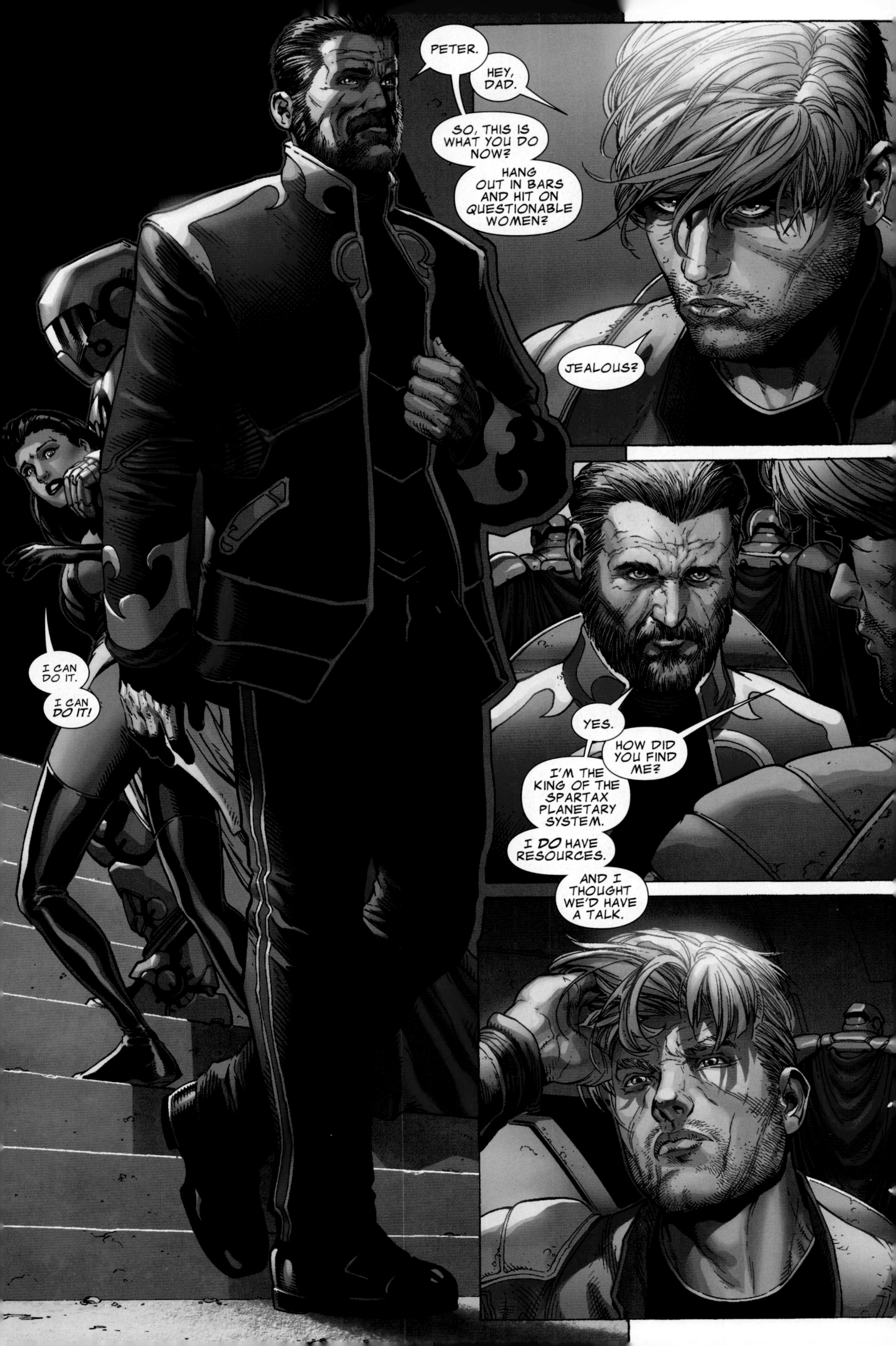
PETER.
HEY, DAD.
SO, THIS IS WHAT YOU DO NOW?
HANG OUT IN BARS AND HIT ON QUESTIONABLE WOMEN?
JEALOUS?
I CAN DO IT.
I CAN *DO* IT!
YES.
HOW DID YOU FIND ME?
I'M THE KING OF THE SPARTAX PLANETARY SYSTEM.
I *DO* HAVE RESOURCES.
AND I THOUGHT WE'D HAVE A TALK.

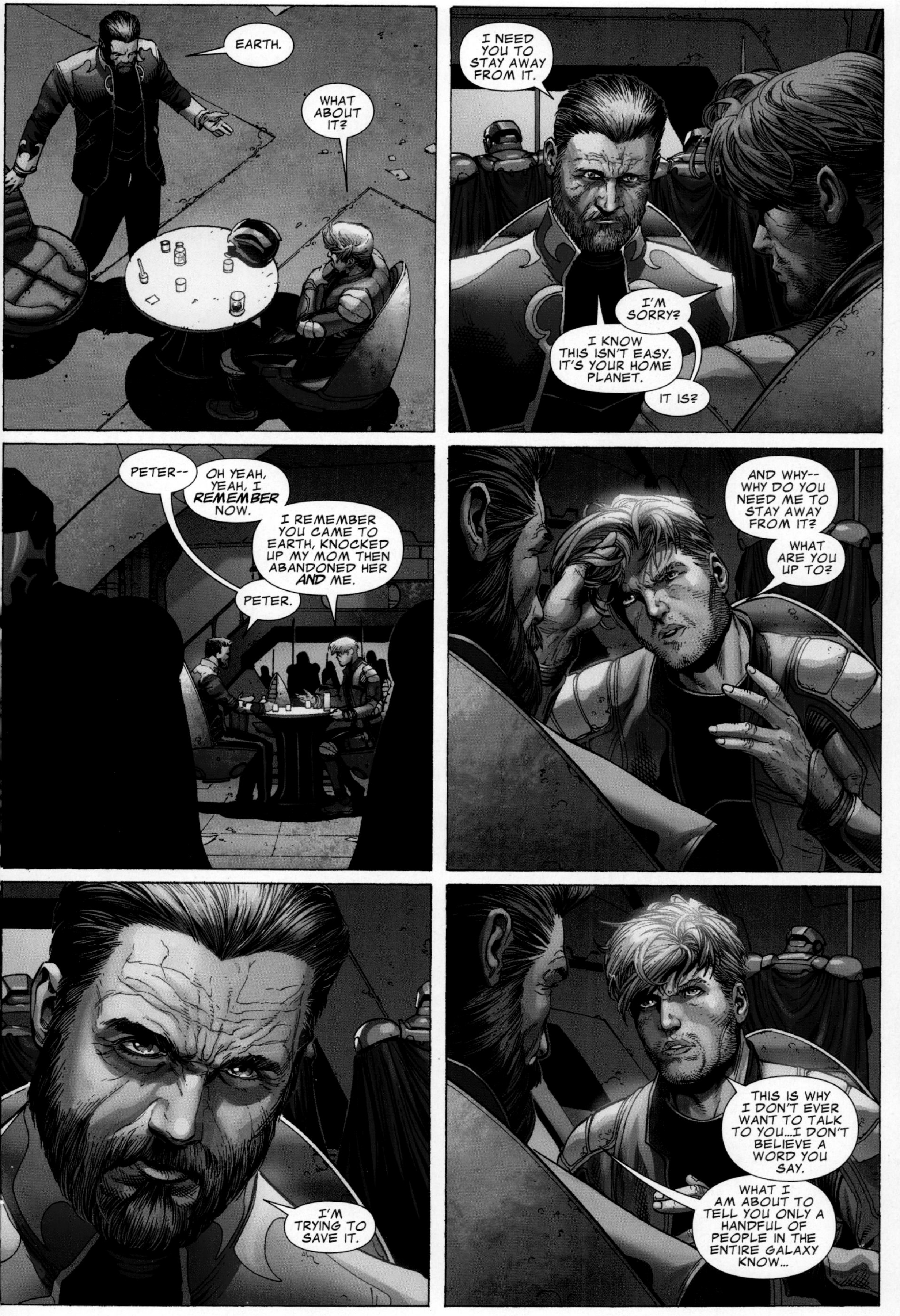

EARTH.
WHAT ABOUT IT?
I NEED YOU TO STAY AWAY FROM IT.
I'M SORRY?
I KNOW THIS ISN'T EASY. IT'S YOUR HOME PLANET.
IT IS?
PETER--
OH YEAH, YEAH, I REMEMBER NOW.
I REMEMBER YOU CAME TO EARTH, KNOCKED UP MY MOM THEN ABANDONED HER AND ME.
PETER.
AND WHY-- WHY DO YOU NEED ME TO STAY AWAY FROM IT?
WHAT ARE YOU UP TO?
I'M TRYING TO SAVE IT.
THIS IS WHY I DON'T EVER WANT TO TALK TO YOU...I DON'T BELIEVE A WORD YOU SAY.
WHAT I AM ABOUT TO TELL YOU ONLY A HANDFUL OF PEOPLE IN THE ENTIRE GALAXY KNOW...

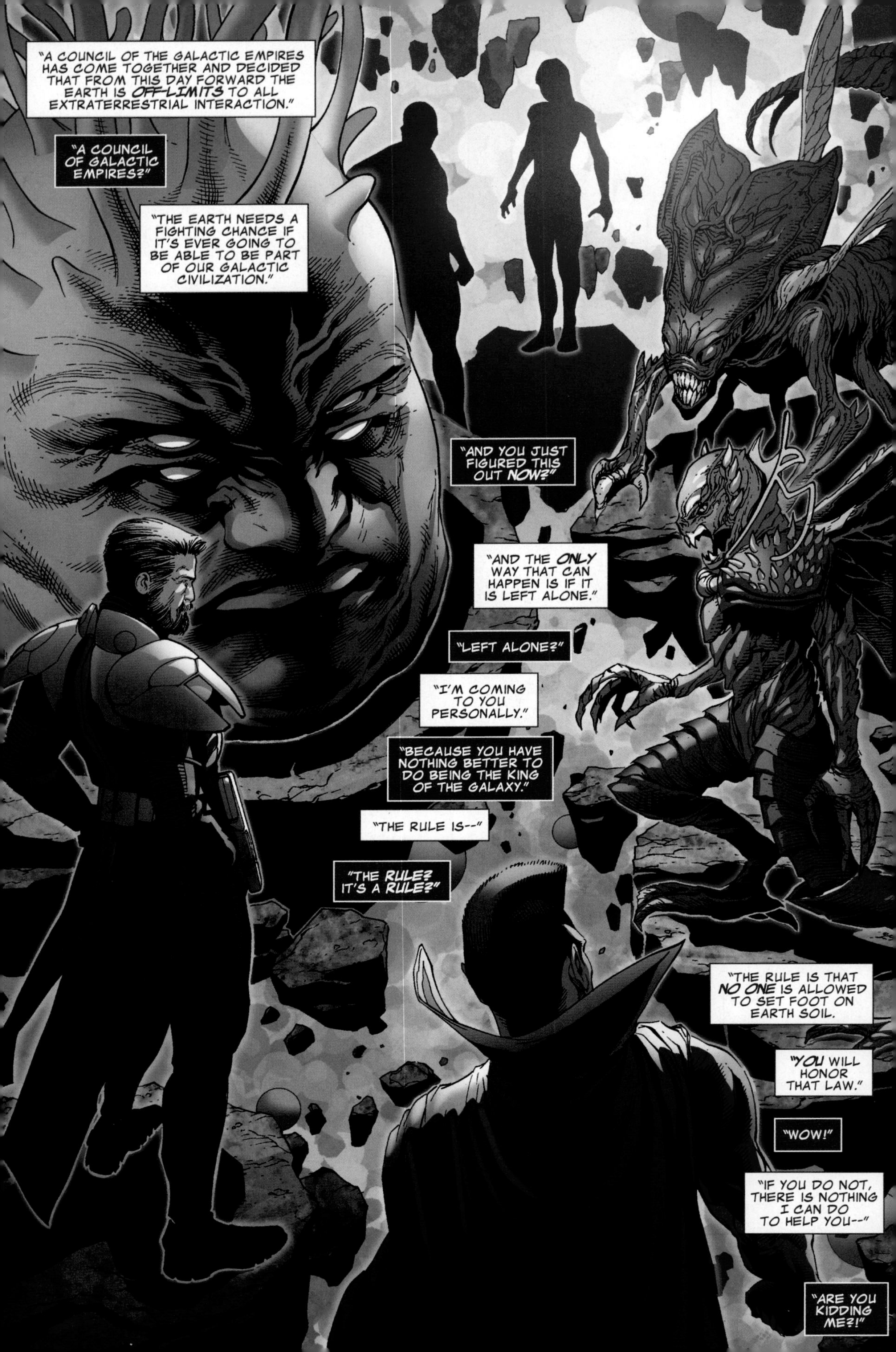
"A COUNCIL OF THE GALACTIC EMPIRES HAS COME TOGETHER AND DECIDED THAT FROM THIS DAY FORWARD THE EARTH IS OFF-LIMITS TO ALL EXTRATERRESTRIAL INTERACTION."
"A COUNCIL OF GALACTIC EMPIRES?"
"THE EARTH NEEDS A FIGHTING CHANCE IF IT'S EVER GOING TO BE ABLE TO BE PART OF OUR GALACTIC CIVILIZATION."
"AND YOU JUST FIGURED THIS OUT NOW?"
"AND THE ONLY WAY THAT CAN HAPPEN IS IF IT IS LEFT ALONE."
"LEFT ALONE?"
"I'M COMING TO YOU PERSONALLY."
"BECAUSE YOU HAVE NOTHING BETTER TO DO BEING THE KING OF THE GALAXY."
"THE RULE IS--"
"THE RULE? IT'S A RULE?"
"THE RULE IS THAT NO ONE IS ALLOWED TO SET FOOT ON EARTH SOIL.
"YOU WILL HONOR THAT LAW."
"WOW!"
"IF YOU DO NOT, THERE IS NOTHING I CAN DO TO HELP YOU--"
"ARE YOU KIDDING ME?!"

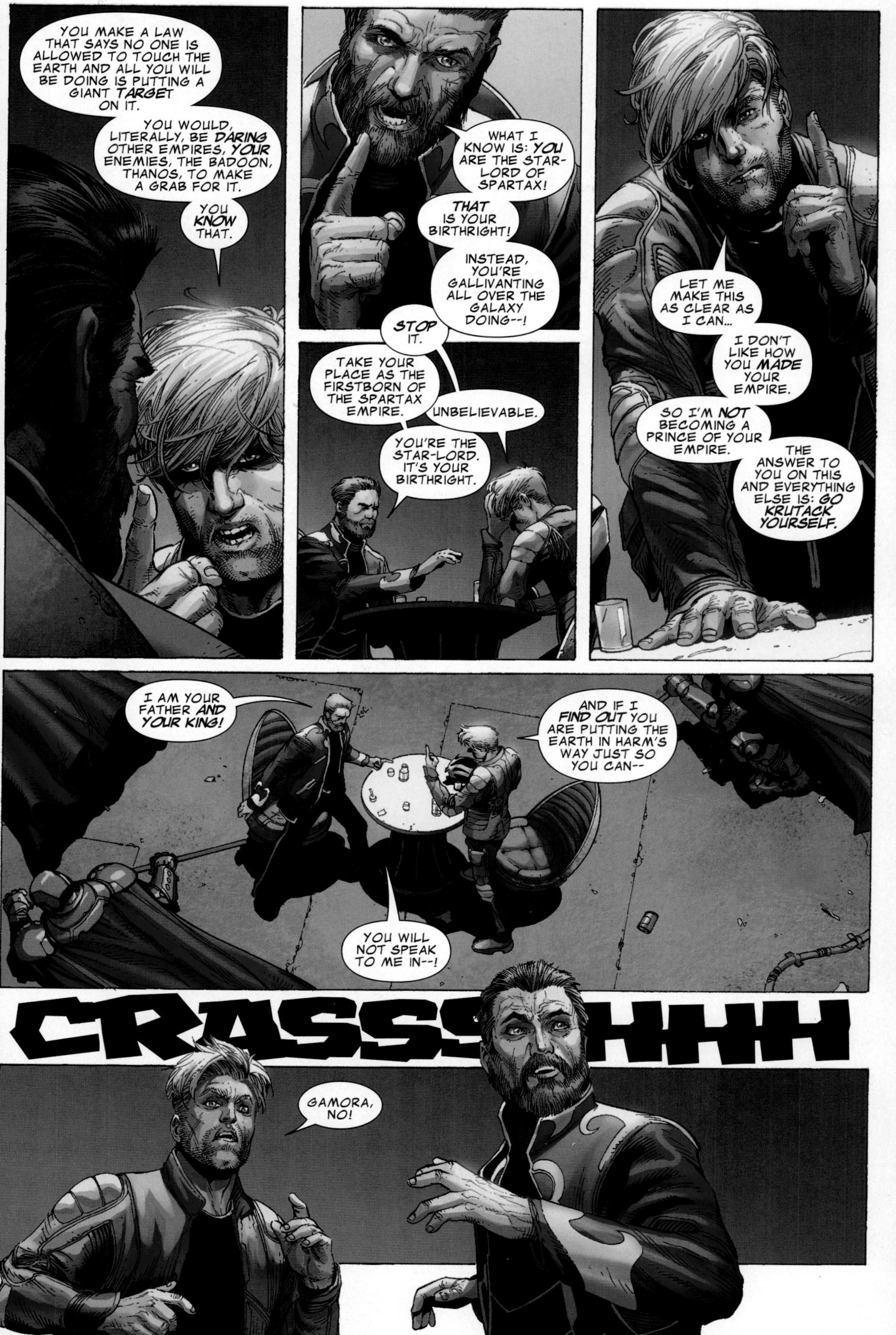
YOU MAKE A LAW THAT SAYS NO ONE IS ALLOWED TO TOUCH THE EARTH AND ALL YOU WILL BE DOING IS PUTTING A GIANT TARGET ON IT.
YOU WOULD, LITERALLY, BE DARING OTHER EMPIRES, YOUR ENEMIES, THE BADOON, THANOS, TO MAKE A GRAB FOR IT.
YOU KNOW THAT.
WHAT I KNOW IS: YOU ARE THE STAR-LORD OF SPARTAX!
THAT IS YOUR BIRTHRIGHT!
INSTEAD, YOU'RE GALLIVANTING ALL OVER THE GALAXY DOING--!
STOP IT.
TAKE YOUR PLACE AS THE FIRSTBORN OF THE SPARTAX EMPIRE.
UNBELIEVABLE.
YOU'RE THE STAR-LORD. IT'S YOUR BIRTHRIGHT.
LET ME MAKE THIS AS CLEAR AS I CAN...
I DON'T LIKE HOW YOU MADE YOUR EMPIRE.
SO I'M NOT BECOMING A PRINCE OF YOUR EMPIRE.
THE ANSWER TO YOU ON THIS AND EVERYTHING ELSE IS: GO KRUTACK YOURSELF.
I AM YOUR FATHER AND YOUR KING!
AND IF I FIND OUT YOU ARE PUTTING THE EARTH IN HARM'S WAY JUST SO YOU CAN--
YOU WILL NOT SPEAK TO ME IN--!
CRASSSHHHH
GAMORA, NO!

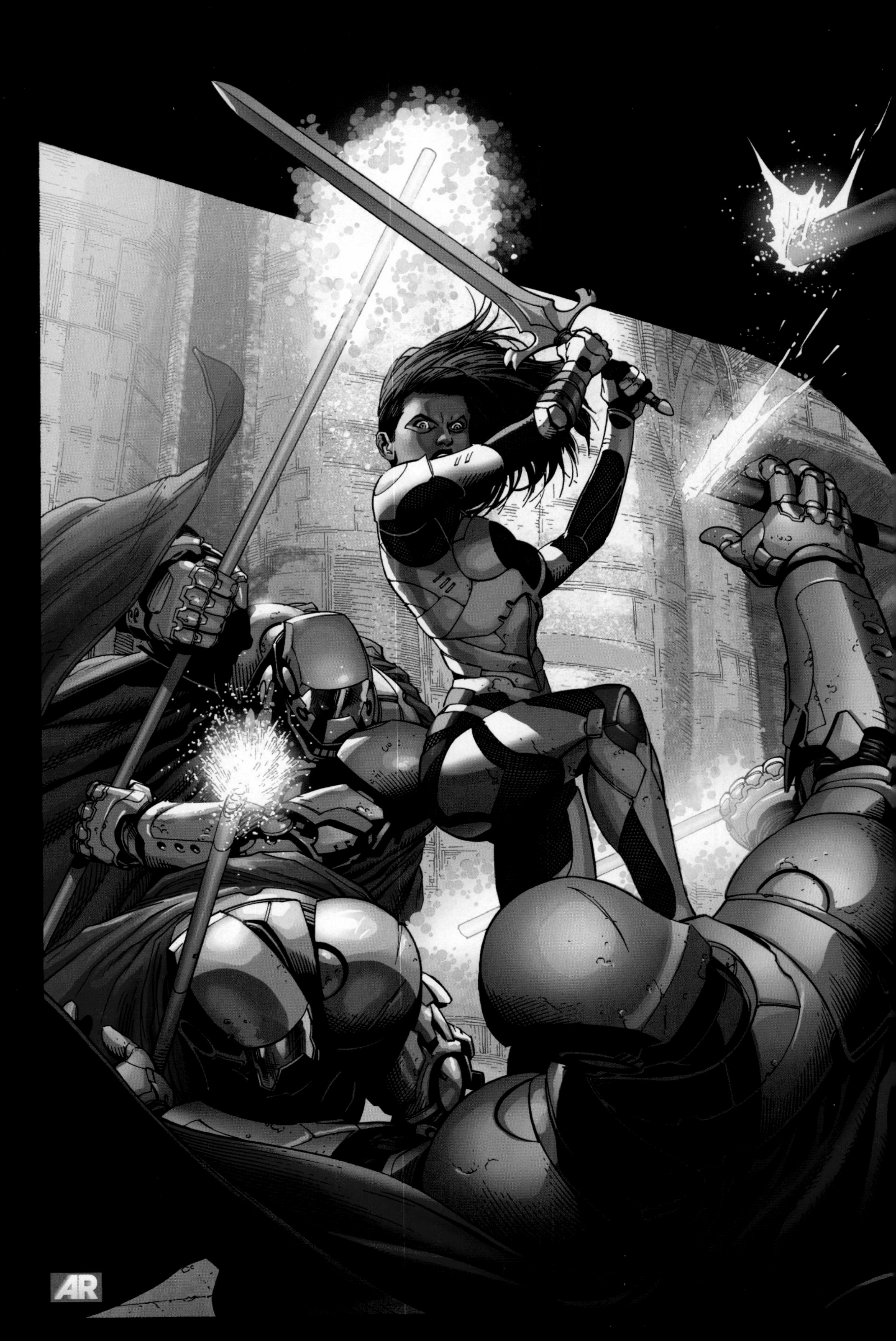

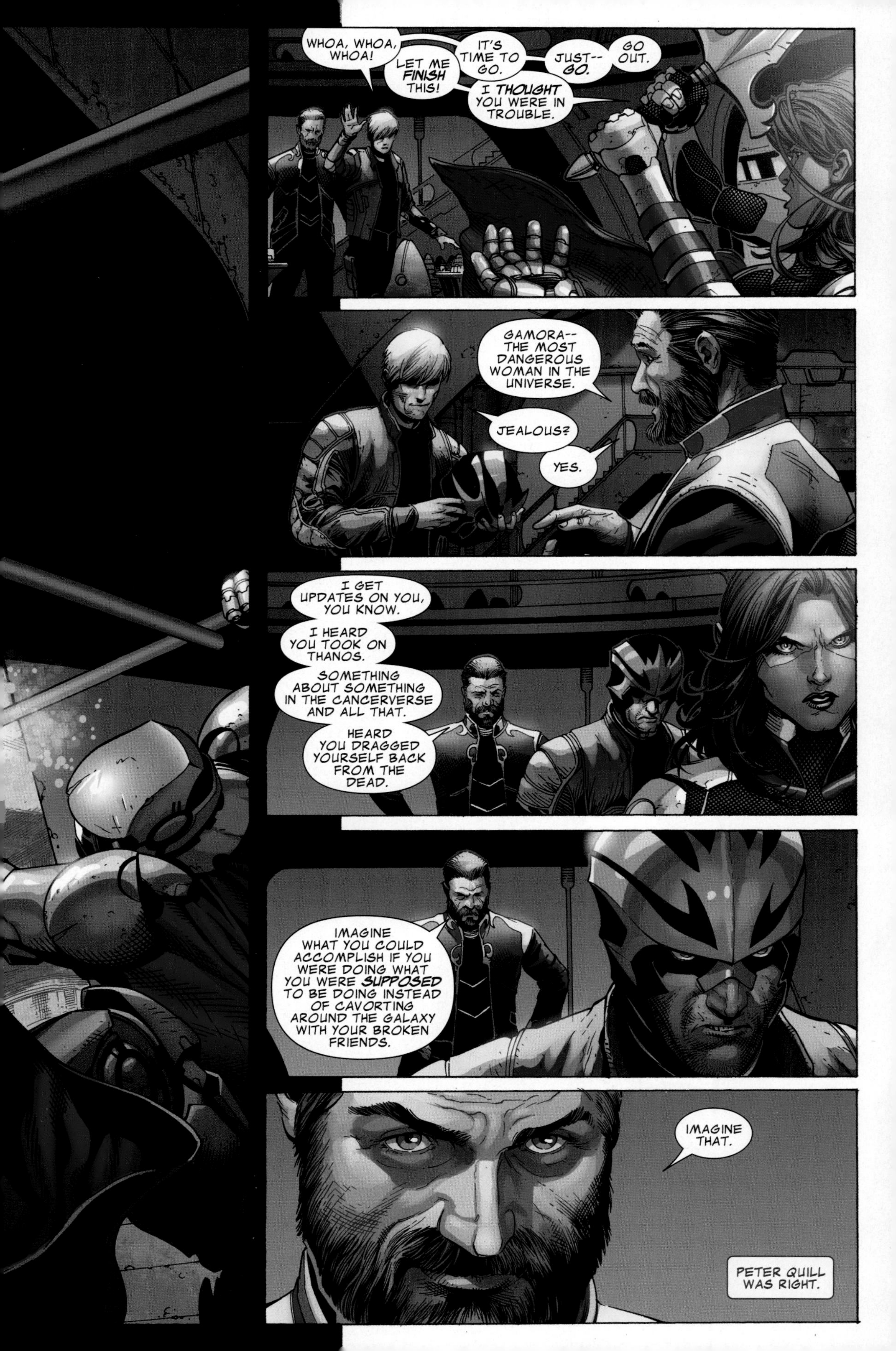
WHOA, WHOA, WHOA!
LET ME FINISH THIS!
IT'S TIME TO GO.
JUST-- GO.
GO OUT.
I THOUGHT YOU WERE IN TROUBLE.
GAMORA-- THE MOST DANGEROUS WOMAN IN THE UNIVERSE.
JEALOUS?
YES.
I GET UPDATES ON YOU, YOU KNOW.
I HEARD YOU TOOK ON THANOS.
SOMETHING ABOUT SOMETHING IN THE CANCERVERSE AND ALL THAT.
HEARD YOU DRAGGED YOURSELF BACK FROM THE DEAD.
IMAGINE WHAT YOU COULD ACCOMPLISH IF YOU WERE DOING WHAT YOU WERE SUPPOSED TO BE DOING INSTEAD OF CAVORTING AROUND THE GALAXY WITH YOUR BROKEN FRIENDS.
IMAGINE THAT.
PETER QUILL WAS RIGHT.

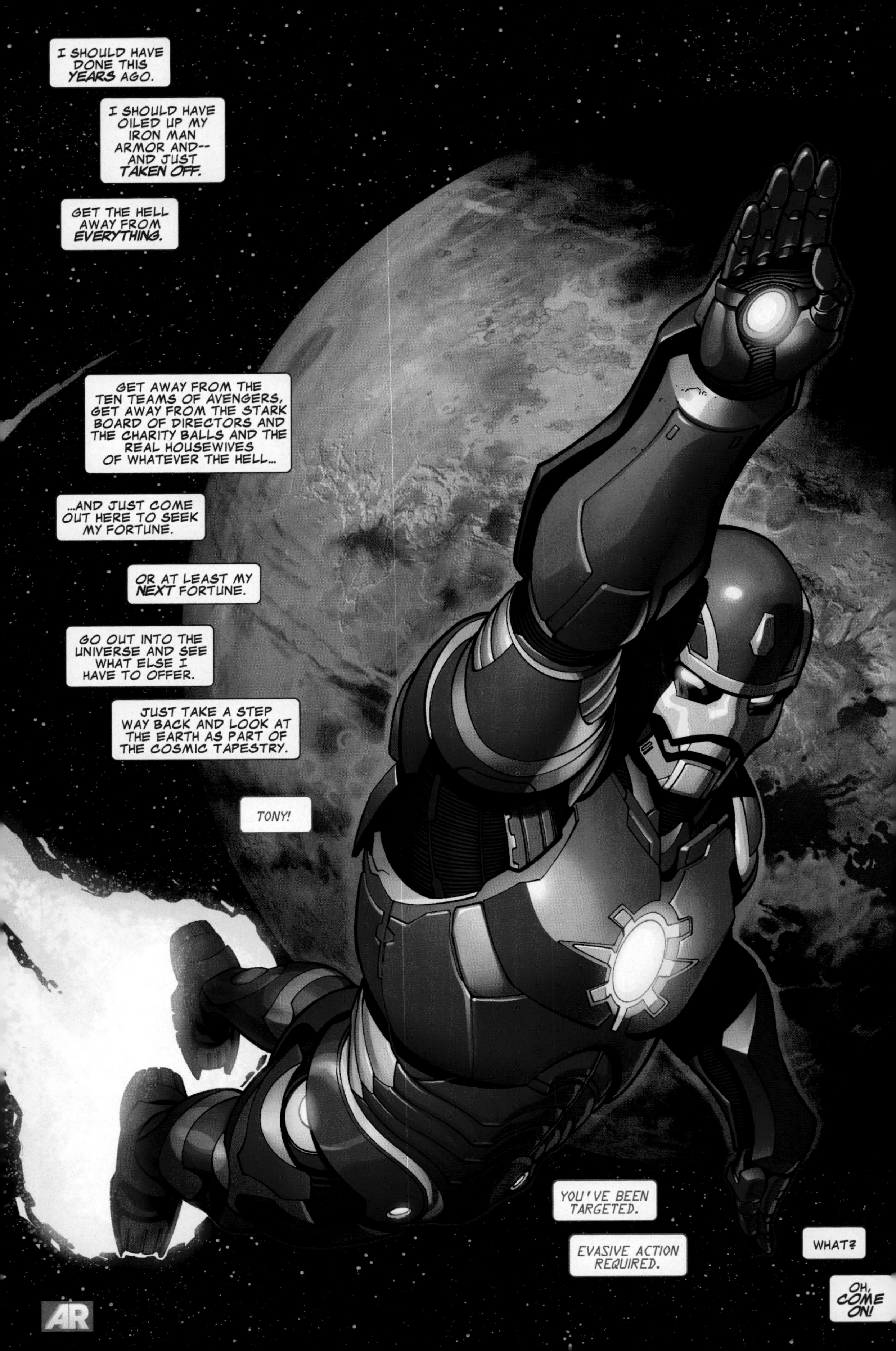
I SHOULD HAVE DONE THIS YEARS AGO.
I SHOULD HAVE OILED UP MY IRON MAN ARMOR AND-- AND JUST TAKEN OFF.
GET THE HELL AWAY FROM EVERYTHING.
GET AWAY FROM THE TEN TEAMS OF AVENGERS, GET AWAY FROM THE STARK BOARD OF DIRECTORS AND THE CHARITY BALLS AND THE REAL HOUSEWIVES OF WHATEVER THE HELL...
...AND JUST COME OUT HERE TO SEEK MY FORTUNE.
OR AT LEAST MY NEXT FORTUNE.
GO OUT INTO THE UNIVERSE AND SEE WHAT ELSE I HAVE TO OFFER.
JUST TAKE A STEP WAY BACK AND LOOK AT THE EARTH AS PART OF THE COSMIC TAPESTRY.
TONY!
YOU'VE BEEN TARGETED.
EVASIVE ACTION REQUIRED.
WHAT?
OH, COME ON!

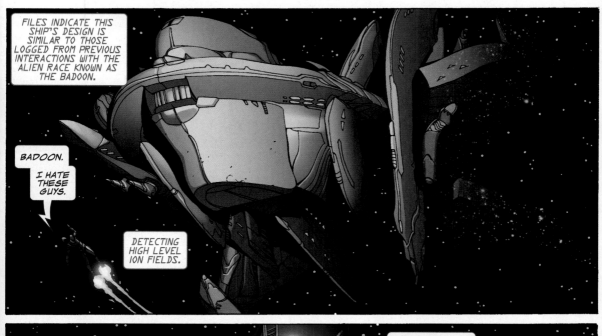

FILES INDICATE THIS SHIP'S DESIGN IS SIMILAR TO THOSE LOGGED FROM PREVIOUS INTERACTIONS WITH THE ALIEN RACE KNOWN AS THE BADOON.

BADOON.

I HATE THESE GUYS.

DETECTING HIGH LEVEL ION FIELDS.

P.E.P.P.E.R., ALL ENERGY TO FRONT SHIELD AND MAIN REPULSOR RAYS. LET'S END THIS FAST.

DETECTING ENERGY FLUCTUATIONS FROM THE NORTH AND SOUTH QUADRANTS...

THEY'VE GOT SHIELDS.

YEP. THEY DO.

FABOOM

BAD NEWS. UNIDENTIFIED SPACECRAFT HAS ENTERED THE PERIMETER.

UH-OH! OH WAIT...

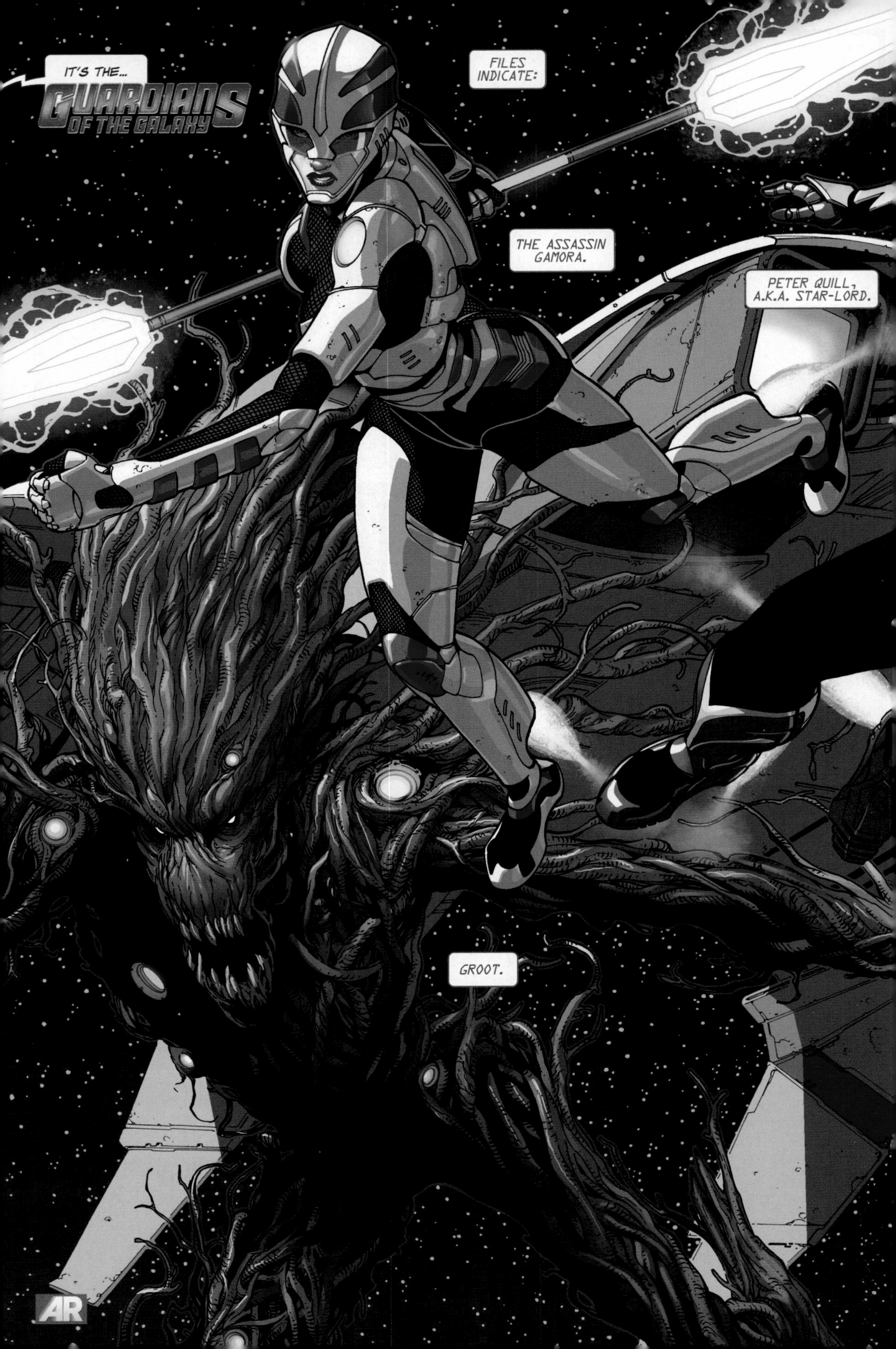
IT'S THE...
GUARDIANS OF THE GALAXY
FILES INDICATE:
THE ASSASSIN GAMORA.
PETER QUILL, A.K.A. STAR-LORD.
GROOT.
AR

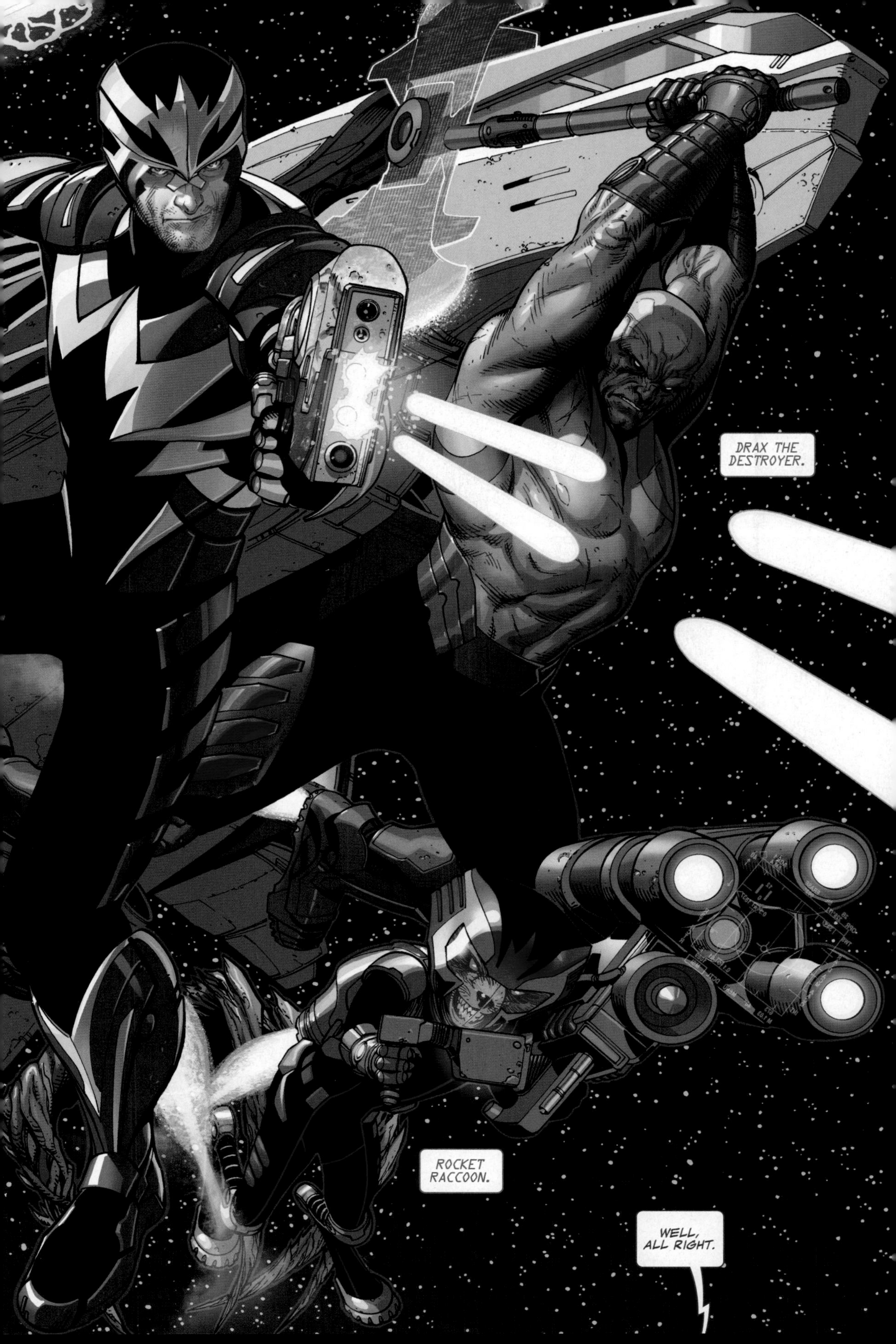
DRAX THE DESTROYER.
ROCKET RACCOON.
WELL, ALL RIGHT.

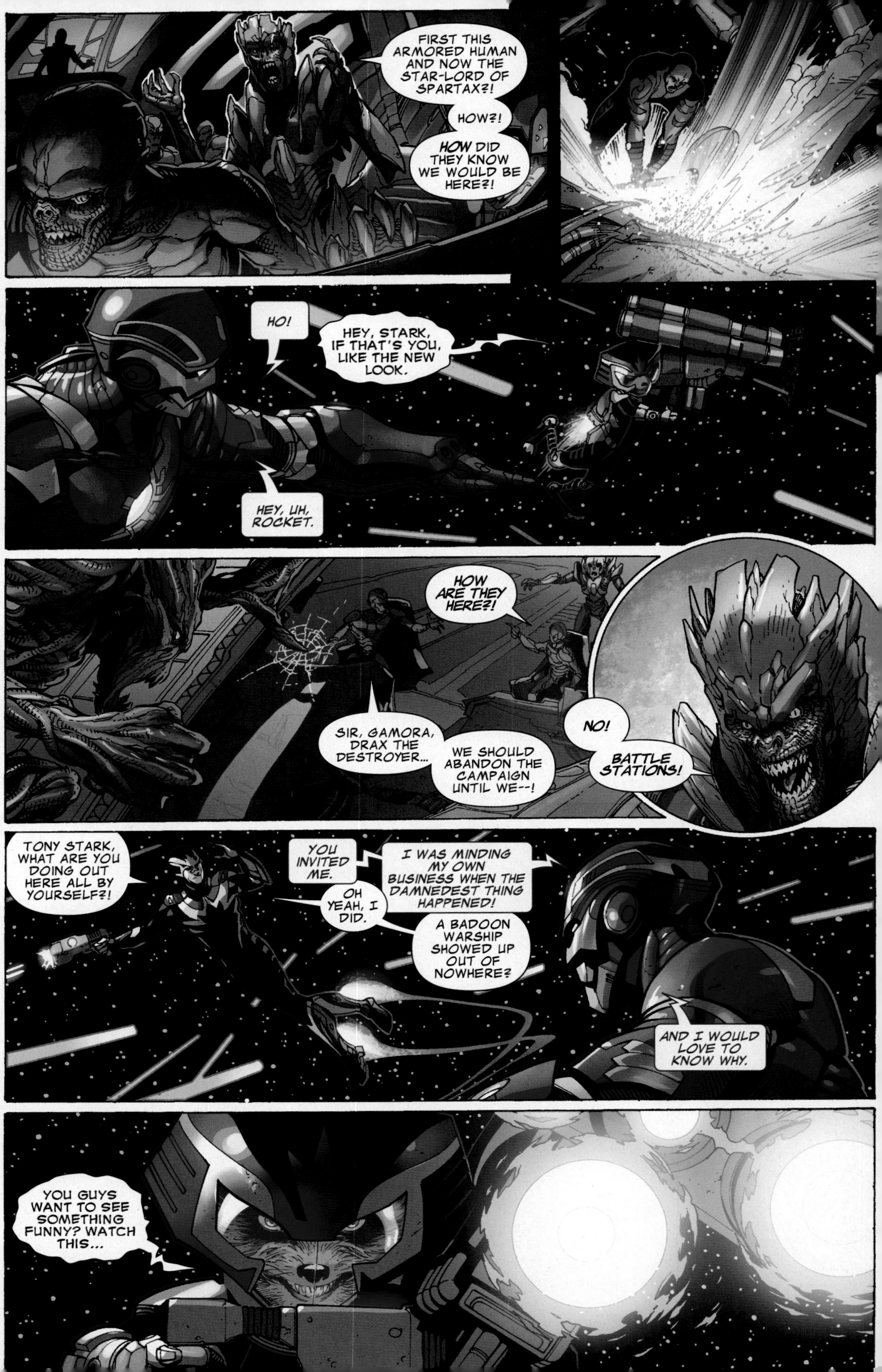
FIRST THIS ARMORED HUMAN AND NOW THE STAR-LORD OF SPARTAX?!
HOW?!
HOW DID THEY KNOW WE WOULD BE HERE?!
HO!
HEY, STARK, IF THAT'S YOU, LIKE THE NEW LOOK.
HEY, UH, ROCKET.
HOW ARE THEY HERE?!
SIR, GAMORA, DRAX THE DESTROYER...
WE SHOULD ABANDON THE CAMPAIGN UNTIL WE--!
NO!
BATTLE STATIONS!
TONY STARK, WHAT ARE YOU DOING OUT HERE ALL BY YOURSELF?!
YOU INVITED ME.
OH YEAH, I DID.
I WAS MINDING MY OWN BUSINESS WHEN THE DAMNEDEST THING HAPPENED!
A BADOON WARSHIP SHOWED UP OUT OF NOWHERE?
AND I WOULD LOVE TO KNOW WHY.
YOU GUYS WANT TO SEE SOMETHING FUNNY? WATCH THIS...

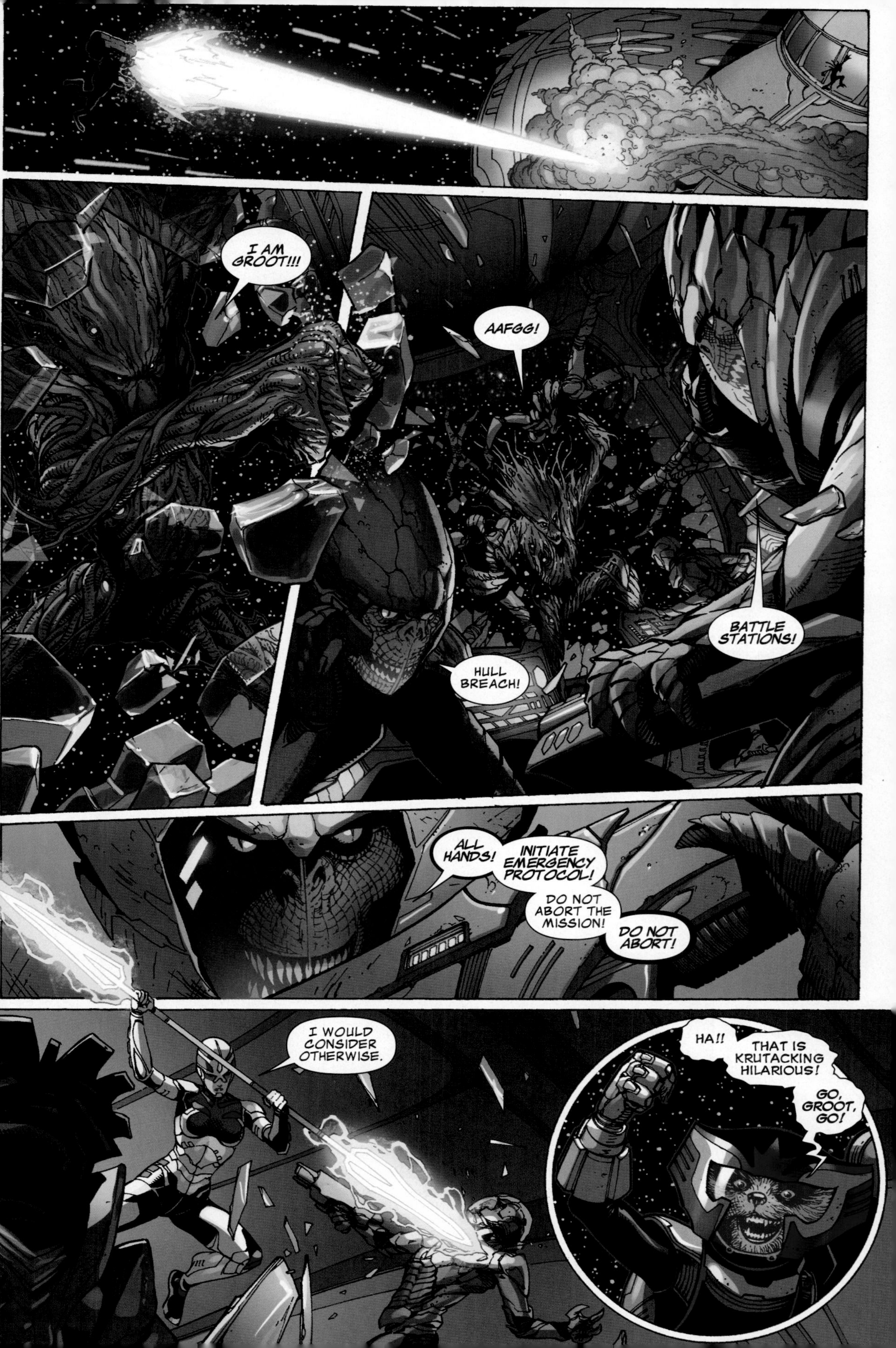
I AM GROOT!!!
AAFGG!
HULL BREACH!
BATTLE STATIONS!
ALL HANDS!
INITIATE EMERGENCY PROTOCOL!
DO NOT ABORT THE MISSION!
DO NOT ABORT!
I WOULD CONSIDER OTHERWISE.
HA!!
THAT IS KRUTACKING HILARIOUS!
GO, GROOT, GO!

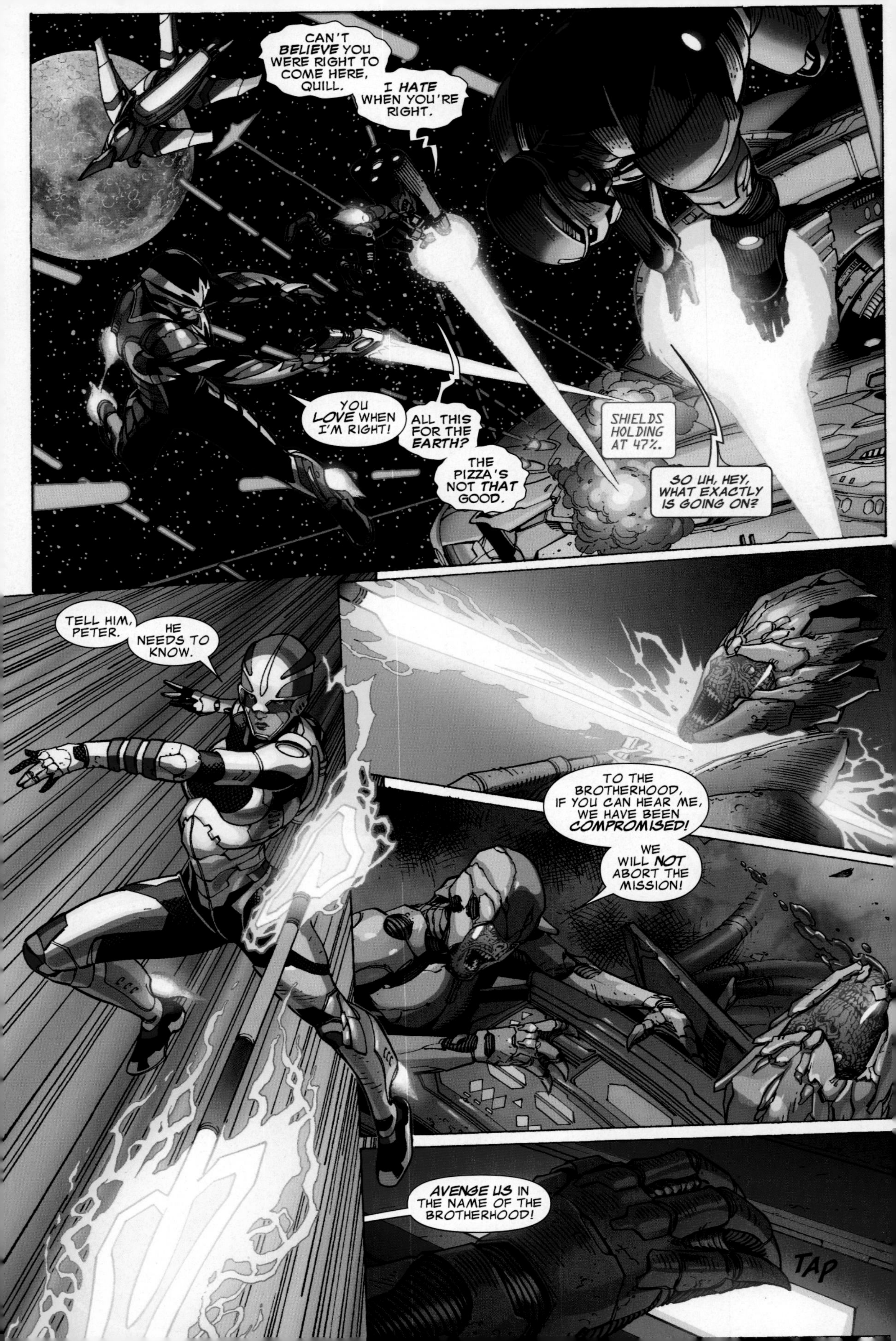
CAN'T BELIEVE YOU WERE RIGHT TO COME HERE, QUILL.
I HATE WHEN YOU'RE RIGHT.
YOU LOVE WHEN I'M RIGHT!
ALL THIS FOR THE EARTH?
THE PIZZA'S NOT THAT GOOD.
SHIELDS HOLDING AT 47%.
SO UH, HEY, WHAT EXACTLY IS GOING ON?
TELL HIM, PETER.
HE NEEDS TO KNOW.
TO THE BROTHERHOOD, IF YOU CAN HEAR ME, WE HAVE BEEN COMPROMISED!
WE WILL NOT ABORT THE MISSION!
AVENGE US IN THE NAME OF THE BROTHERHOOD!
TAP

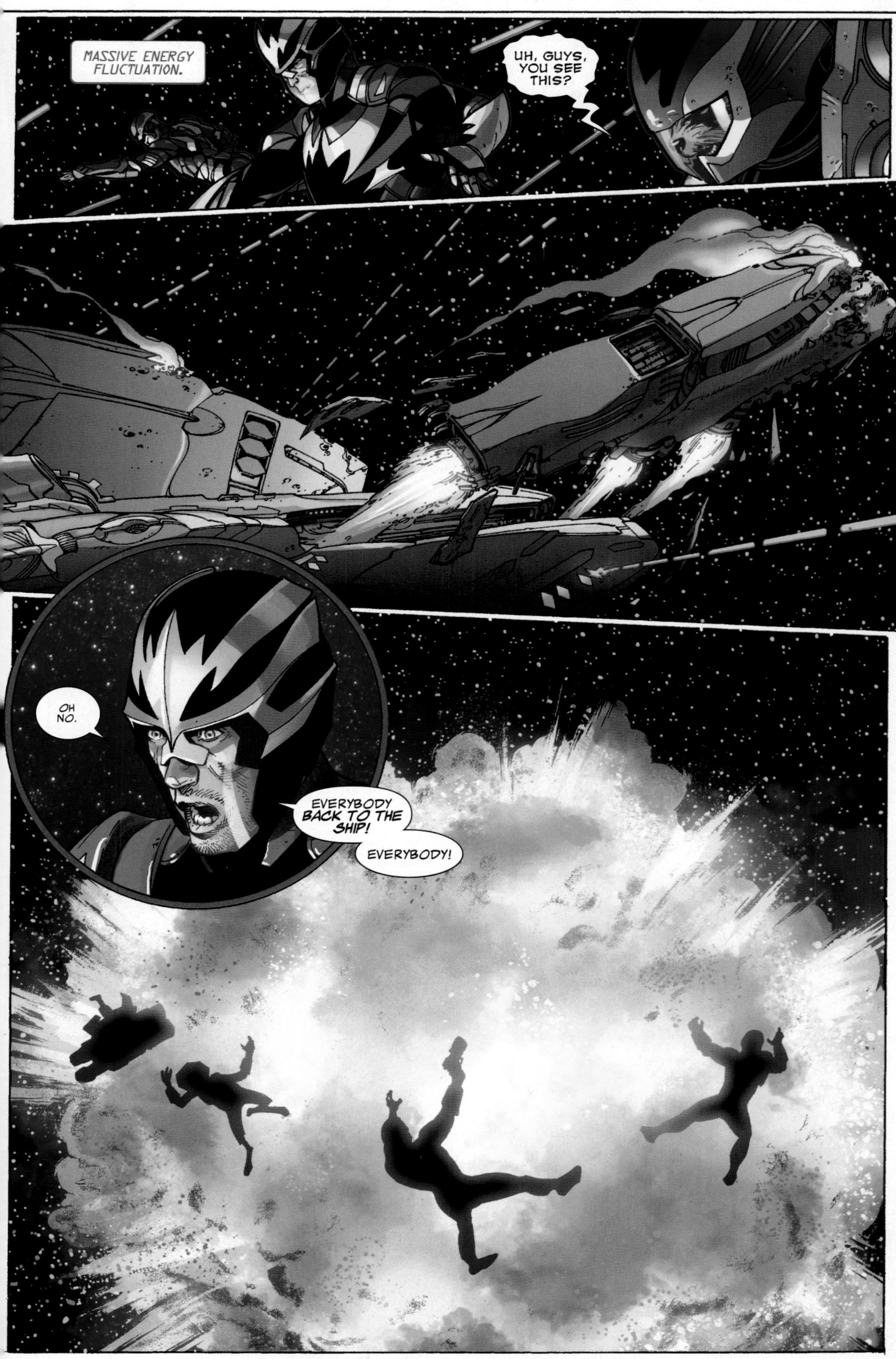
MASSIVE ENERGY FLUCTUATION.
UH, GUYS, YOU SEE THIS?
OH NO.
EVERYBODY BACK TO THE SHIP!
EVERYBODY!

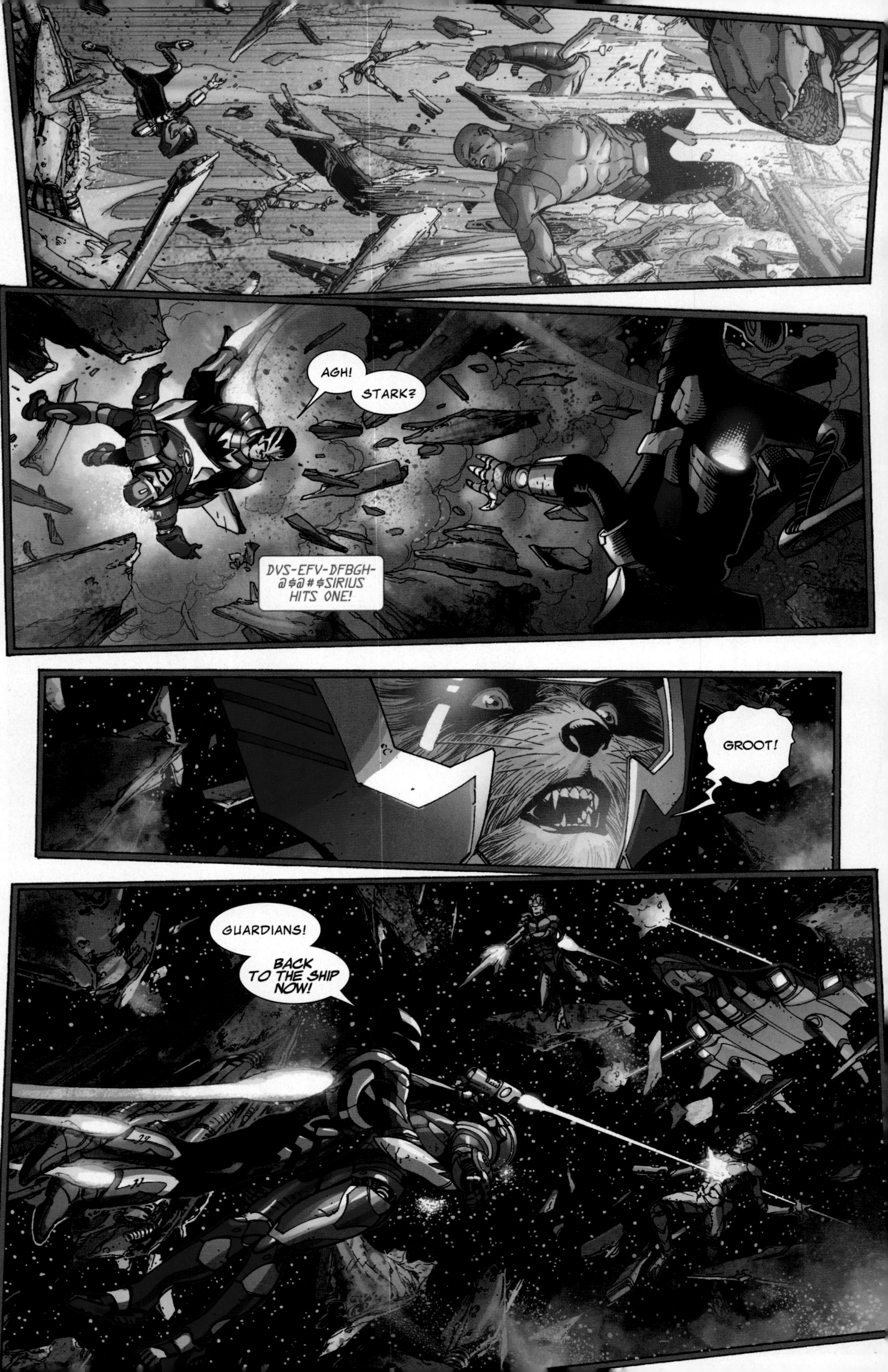
AGH!
STARK?
DVS-EFV-DFBGH-@$@#$SIRIUS HITS ONE!
GROOT!
GUARDIANS!
BACK TO THE SHIP NOW!

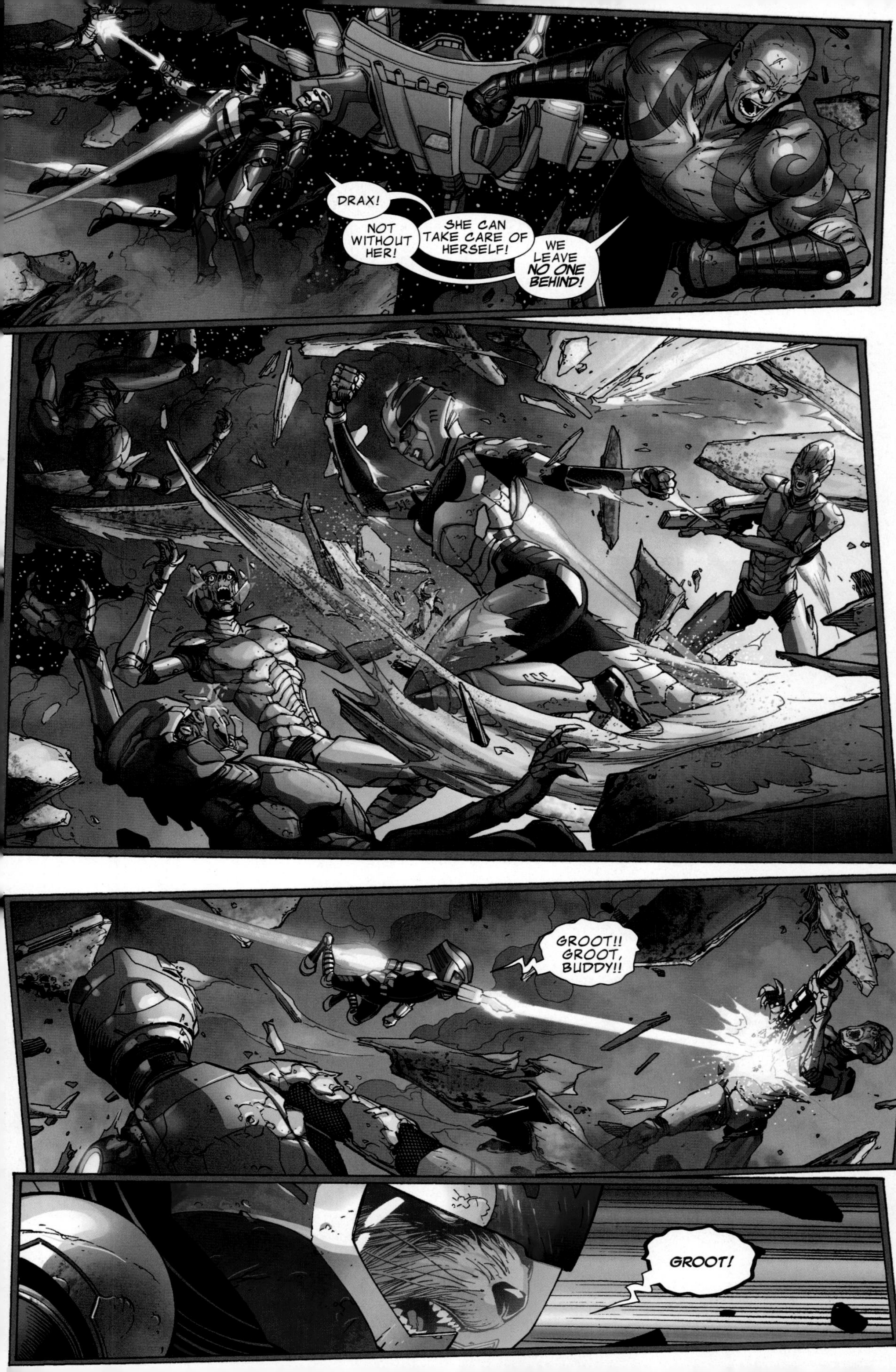
DRAX!
NOT WITHOUT HER!
SHE CAN TAKE CARE OF HERSELF!
WE LEAVE NO ONE BEHIND!
GROOT!! GROOT, BUDDY!!
GROOT!

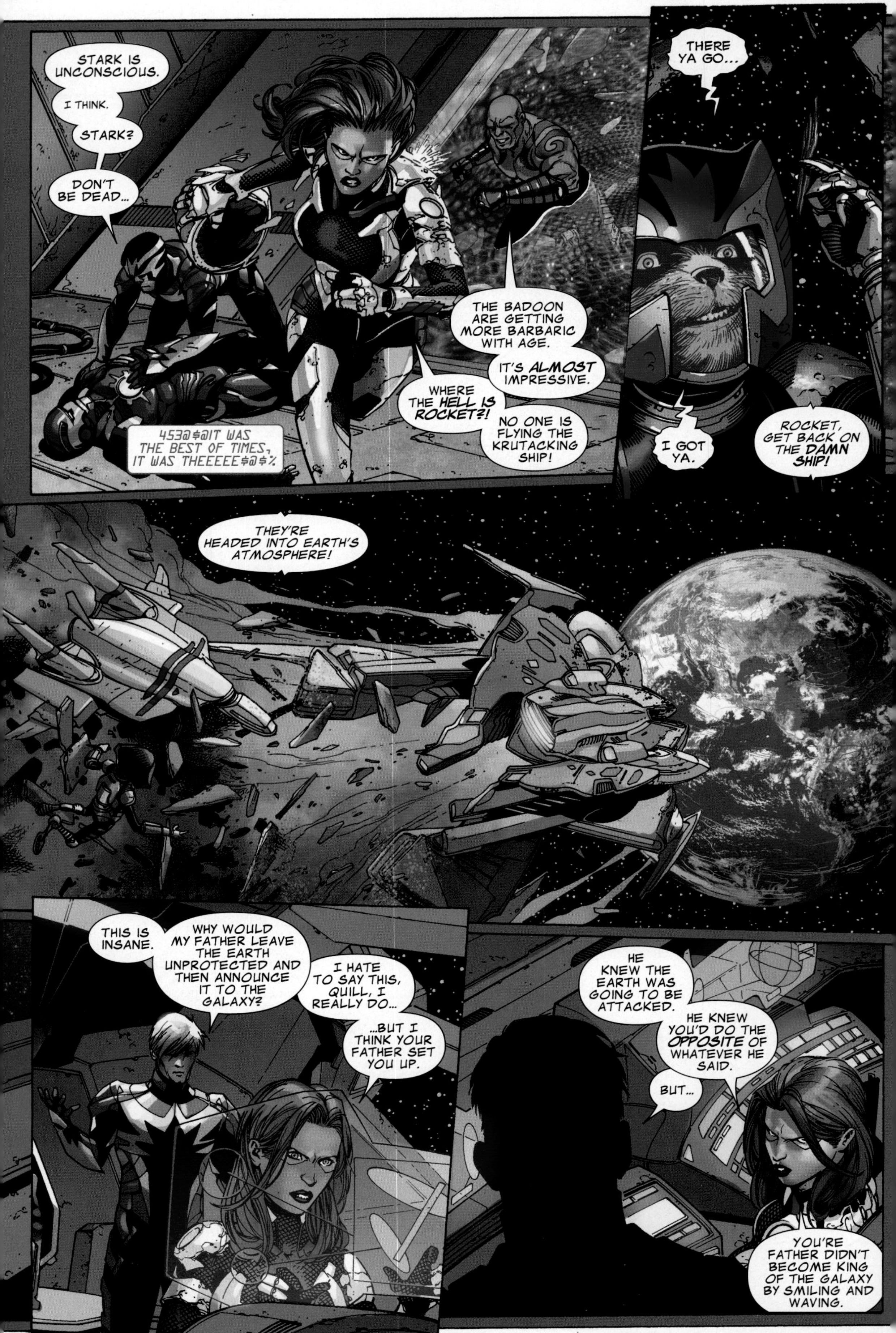
STARK IS UNCONSCIOUS.
I THINK.
STARK?
DON'T BE DEAD...
453@$@IT WAS THE BEST OF TIMES, IT WAS THEEEEE$@$%
THE BADOON ARE GETTING MORE BARBARIC WITH AGE.
IT'S ALMOST IMPRESSIVE.
WHERE THE HELL IS ROCKET?!
NO ONE IS FLYING THE KRUTACKING SHIP!
THERE YA GO...
I GOT YA.
ROCKET, GET BACK ON THE DAMN SHIP!
THEY'RE HEADED INTO EARTH'S ATMOSPHERE!
THIS IS INSANE.
WHY WOULD MY FATHER LEAVE THE EARTH UNPROTECTED AND THEN ANNOUNCE IT TO THE GALAXY?
I HATE TO SAY THIS, QUILL, I REALLY DO...
...BUT I THINK YOUR FATHER SET YOU UP.
HE KNEW THE EARTH WAS GOING TO BE ATTACKED.
HE KNEW YOU'D DO THE OPPOSITE OF WHATEVER HE SAID.
BUT...
YOU'RE FATHER DIDN'T BECOME KING OF THE GALAXY BY SMILING AND WAVING.

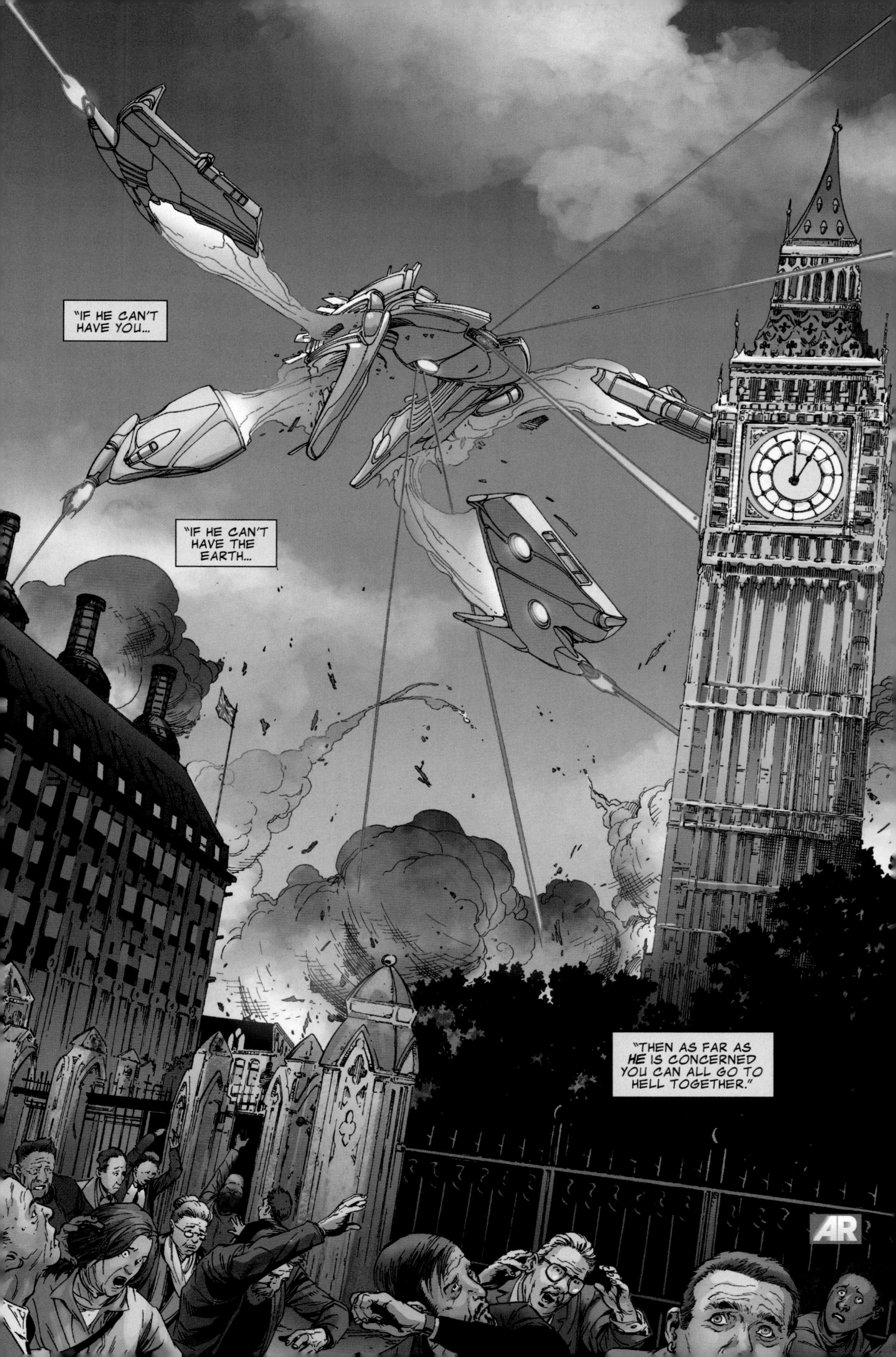
"IF HE CAN'T HAVE YOU...
"IF HE CAN'T HAVE THE EARTH...
"THEN AS FAR AS HE IS CONCERNED YOU CAN ALL GO TO HELL TOGETHER."

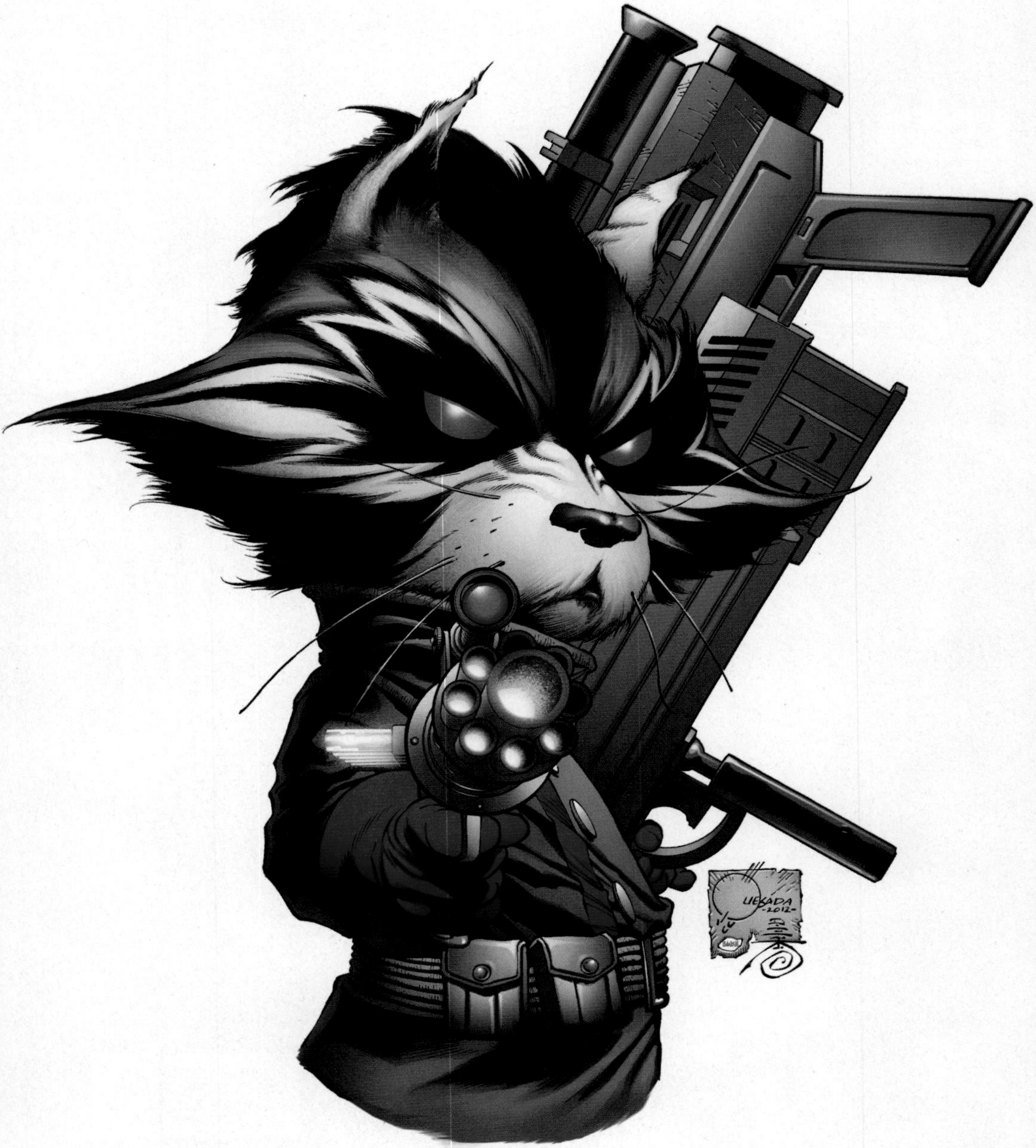

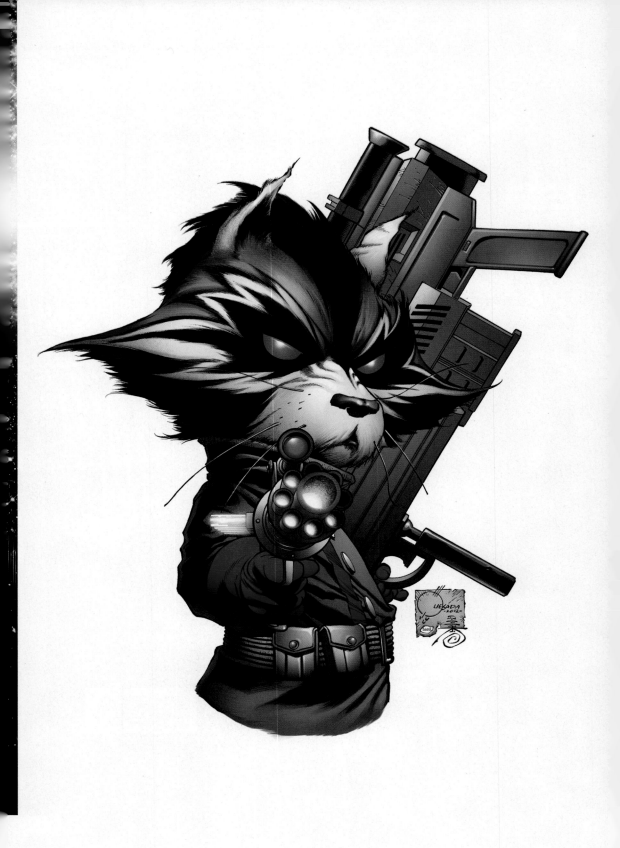

#2 VARIANT BY JOE QUESADA, DANNY MIKI & RICHARD ISANOVE

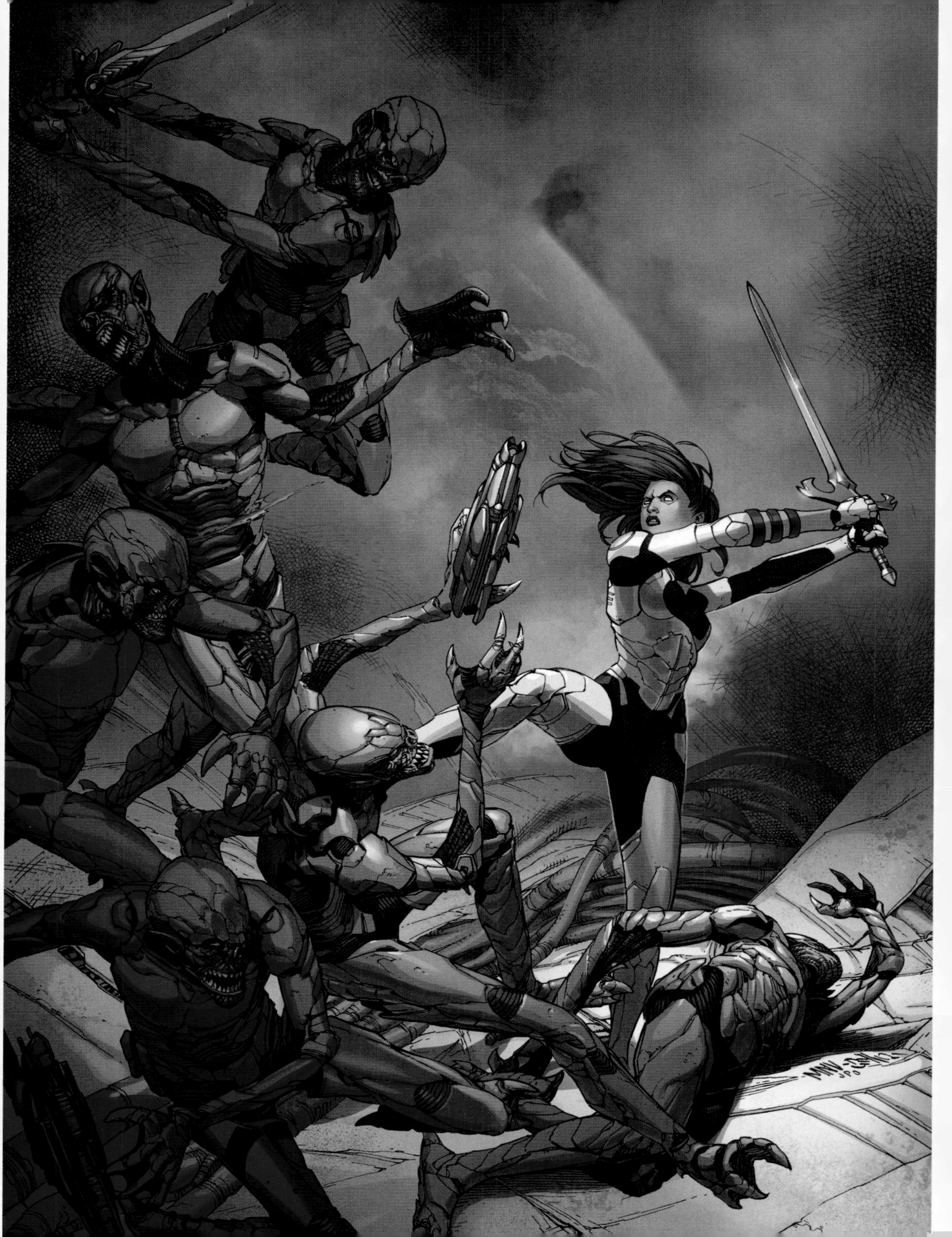

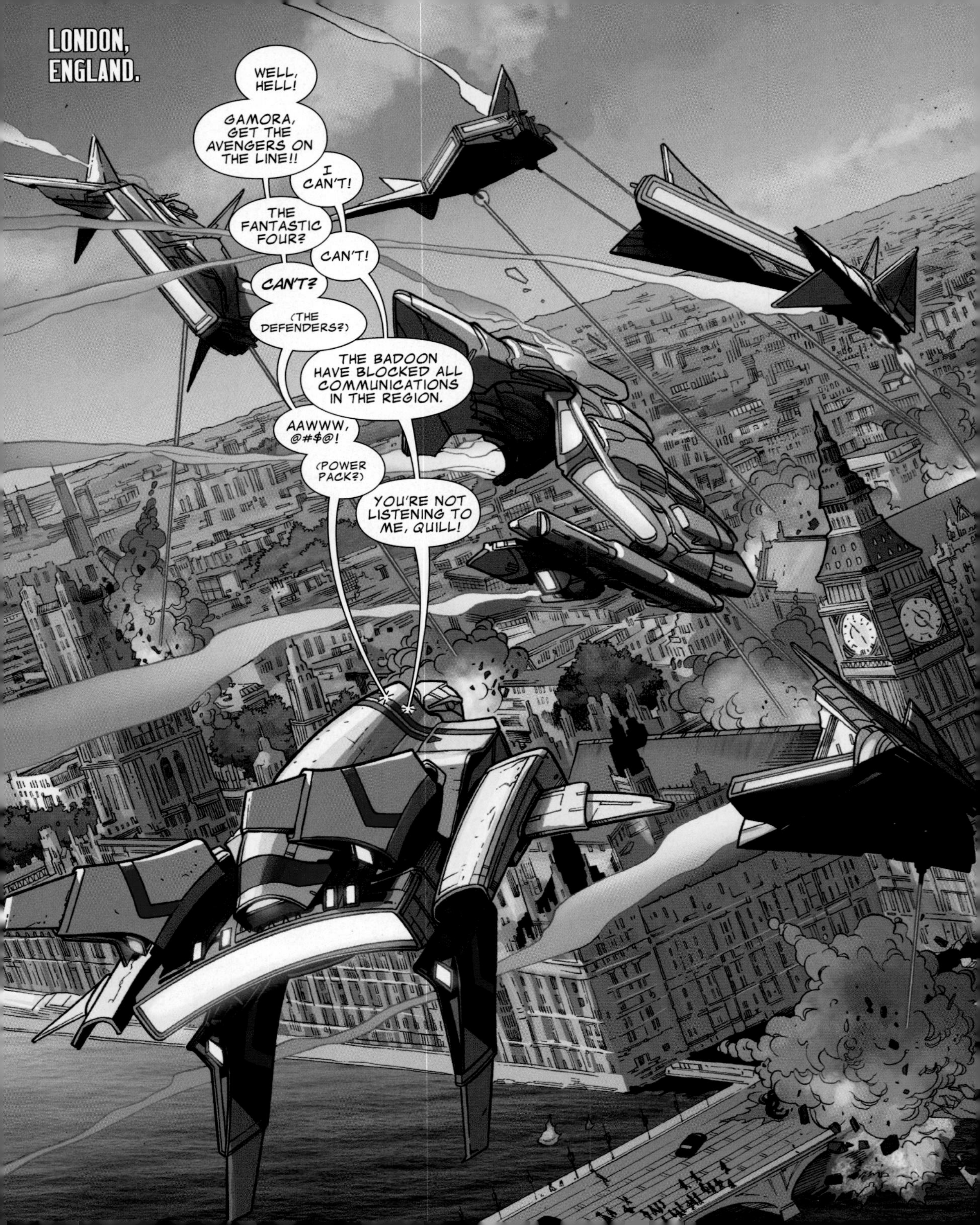
LONDON, ENGLAND.
WELL, HELL!
GAMORA, GET THE AVENGERS ON THE LINE!!
I CAN'T!
THE FANTASTIC FOUR?
CAN'T!
CAN'T?
(THE DEFENDERS?)
THE BADOON HAVE BLOCKED ALL COMMUNICATIONS IN THE REGION.
AAWWW, @#$@!
(POWER PACK?)
YOU'RE NOT LISTENING TO ME, QUILL!

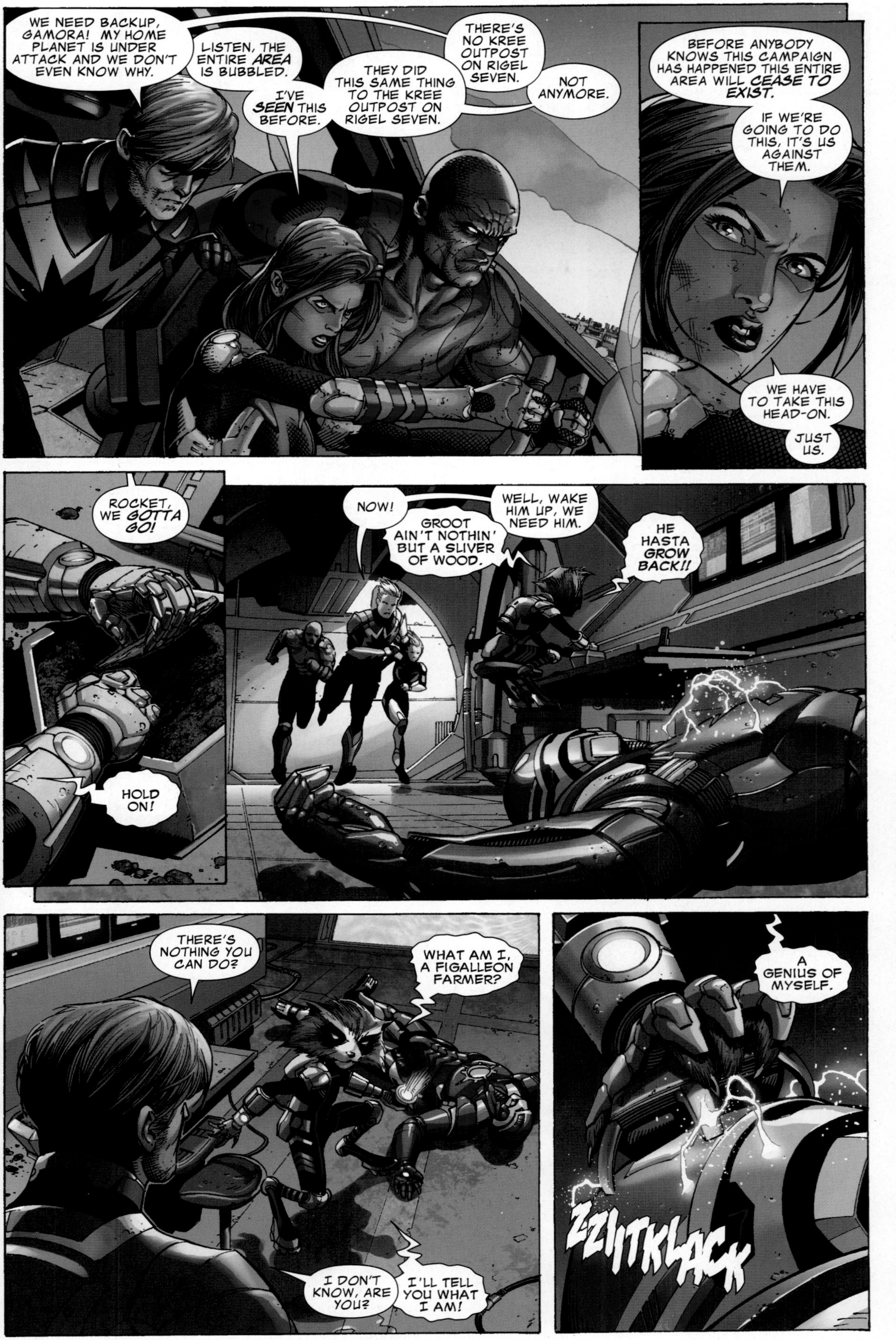

WE NEED BACKUP, GAMORA! MY HOME PLANET IS UNDER ATTACK AND WE DON'T EVEN KNOW WHY.
LISTEN, THE ENTIRE AREA IS BUBBLED.
I'VE SEEN THIS BEFORE.
THEY DID THIS SAME THING TO THE KREE OUTPOST ON RIGEL SEVEN.
THERE'S NO KREE OUTPOST ON RIGEL SEVEN.
NOT ANYMORE.
BEFORE ANYBODY KNOWS THIS CAMPAIGN HAS HAPPENED THIS ENTIRE AREA WILL CEASE TO EXIST.
IF WE'RE GOING TO DO THIS, IT'S US AGAINST THEM.
WE HAVE TO TAKE THIS HEAD-ON.
JUST US.
ROCKET, WE GOTTA GO!
HOLD ON!
NOW!
GROOT AIN'T NOTHIN' BUT A SLIVER OF WOOD.
WELL, WAKE HIM UP, WE NEED HIM.
HE HASTA GROW BACK!!
THERE'S NOTHING YOU CAN DO?
WHAT AM I, A FIGALLEON FARMER?
I DON'T KNOW, ARE YOU?
I'LL TELL YOU WHAT I AM!
A GENIUS OF MYSELF.
ZZIITKLACK

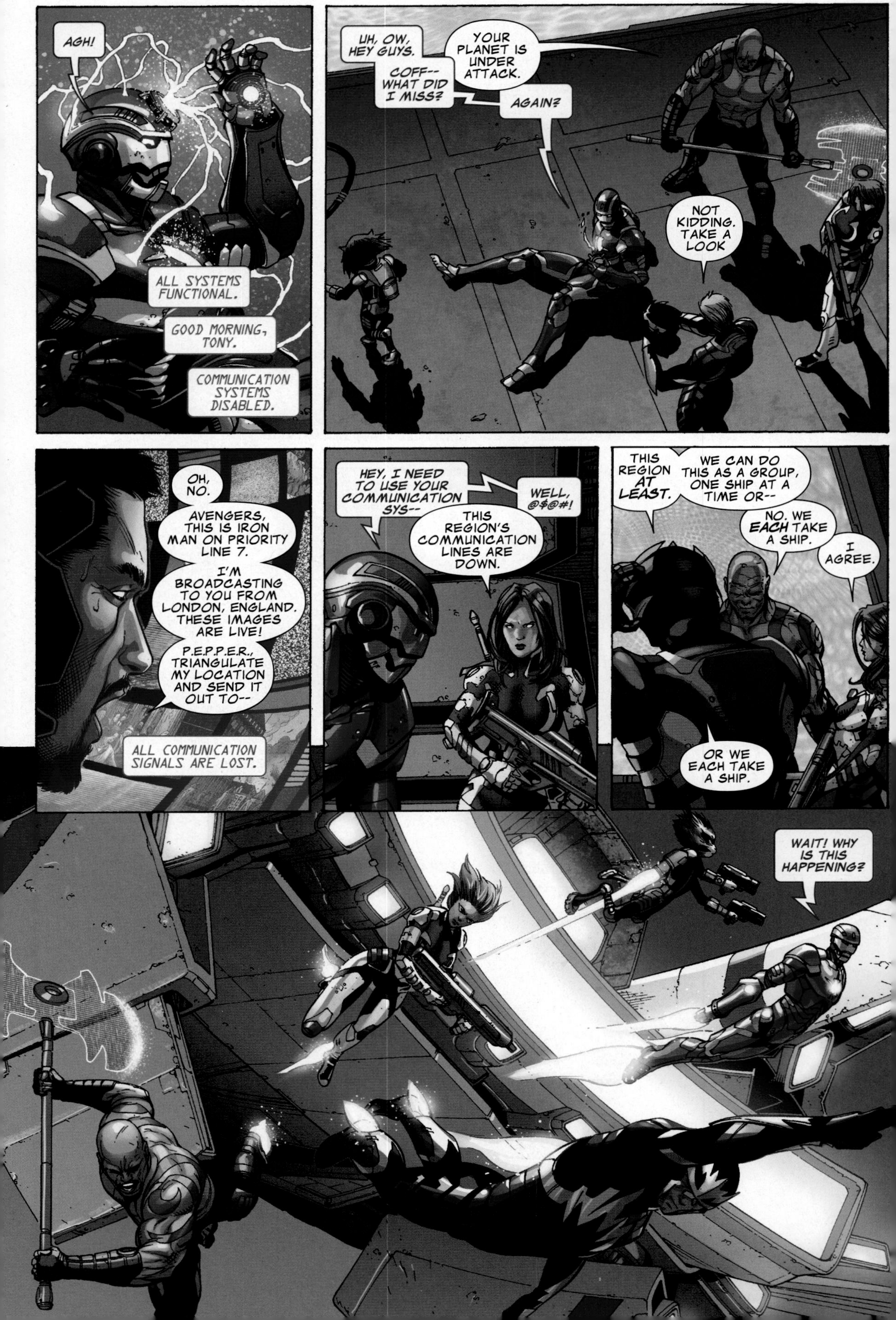
AGH!
ALL SYSTEMS FUNCTIONAL.
GOOD MORNING, TONY.
COMMUNICATION SYSTEMS DISABLED.
UH, OW, HEY GUYS.
COFF-- WHAT DID I MISS?
YOUR PLANET IS UNDER ATTACK.
AGAIN?
NOT KIDDING. TAKE A LOOK
OH, NO.
AVENGERS, THIS IS IRON MAN ON PRIORITY LINE 7.
I'M BROADCASTING TO YOU FROM LONDON, ENGLAND. THESE IMAGES ARE LIVE!
P.E.P.P.E.R., TRIANGULATE MY LOCATION AND SEND IT OUT TO--
ALL COMMUNICATION SIGNALS ARE LOST.
HEY, I NEED TO USE YOUR COMMUNICATION SYS--
WELL, @$@#!
THIS REGION'S COMMUNICATION LINES ARE DOWN.
THIS REGION AT LEAST.
WE CAN DO THIS AS A GROUP, ONE SHIP AT A TIME OR--
NO. WE EACH TAKE A SHIP.
I AGREE.
OR WE EACH TAKE A SHIP.
WAIT! WHY IS THIS HAPPENING?

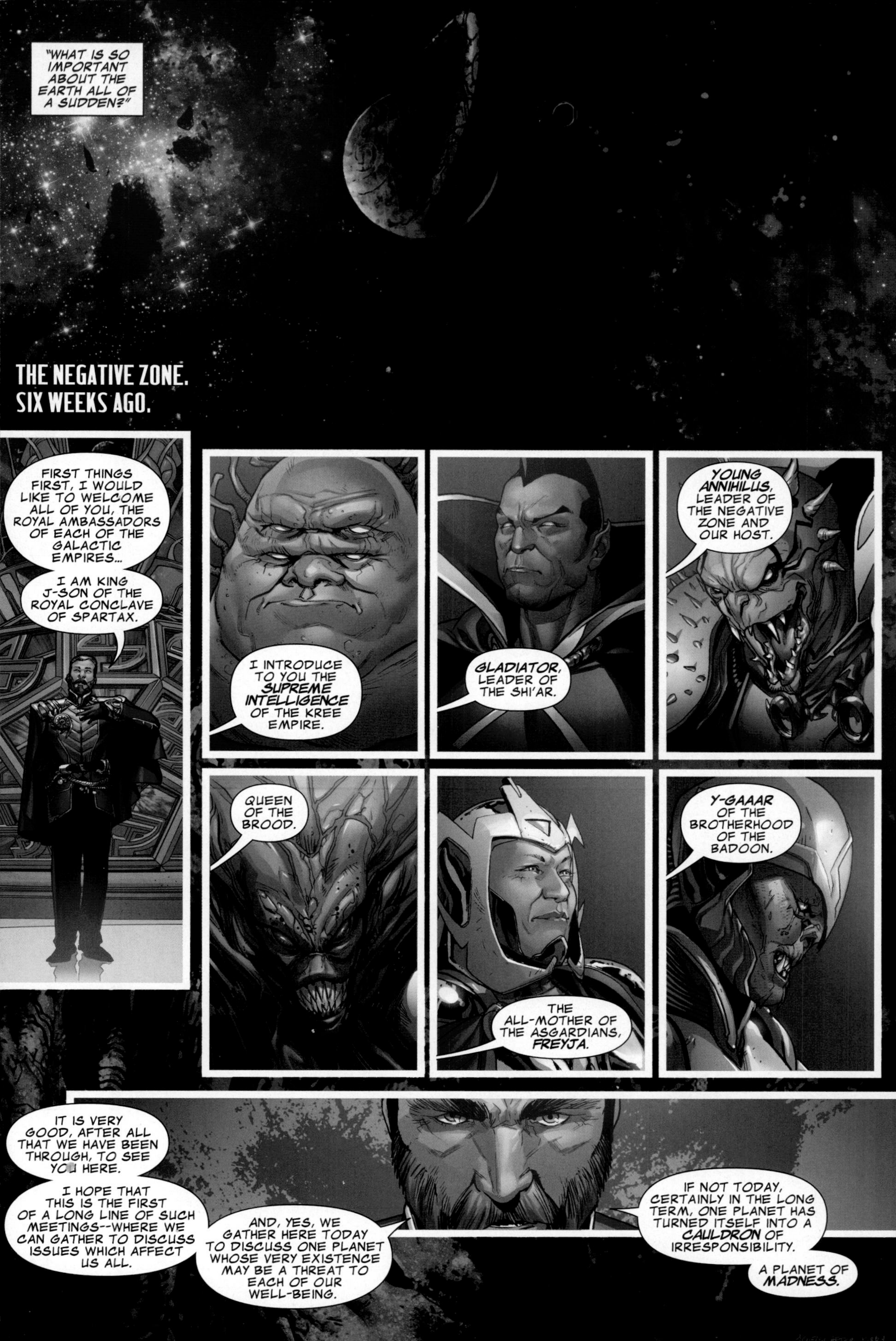

"WHAT IS SO IMPORTANT ABOUT THE EARTH ALL OF A SUDDEN?"
THE NEGATIVE ZONE. SIX WEEKS AGO.
FIRST THINGS FIRST, I WOULD LIKE TO WELCOME ALL OF YOU, THE ROYAL AMBASSADORS OF EACH OF THE GALACTIC EMPIRES...
I AM KING J-SON OF THE ROYAL CONCLAVE OF SPARTAX.
I INTRODUCE TO YOU THE SUPREME INTELLIGENCE OF THE KREE EMPIRE.
GLADIATOR, LEADER OF THE SHI'AR.
YOUNG ANNIHILUS, LEADER OF THE NEGATIVE ZONE AND OUR HOST.
QUEEN OF THE BROOD.
THE ALL-MOTHER OF THE ASGARDIANS, FREYJA.
Y-GAAAR OF THE BROTHERHOOD OF THE BADOON.
IT IS VERY GOOD, AFTER ALL THAT WE HAVE BEEN THROUGH, TO SEE YOU HERE.
I HOPE THAT THIS IS THE FIRST OF A LONG LINE OF SUCH MEETINGS--WHERE WE CAN GATHER TO DISCUSS ISSUES WHICH AFFECT US ALL.
AND, YES, WE GATHER HERE TODAY TO DISCUSS ONE PLANET WHOSE VERY EXISTENCE MAY BE A THREAT TO EACH OF OUR WELL-BEING.
IF NOT TODAY, CERTAINLY IN THE LONG TERM, ONE PLANET HAS TURNED ITSELF INTO A CAULDRON OF IRRESPONSIBILITY.
A PLANET OF MADNESS.

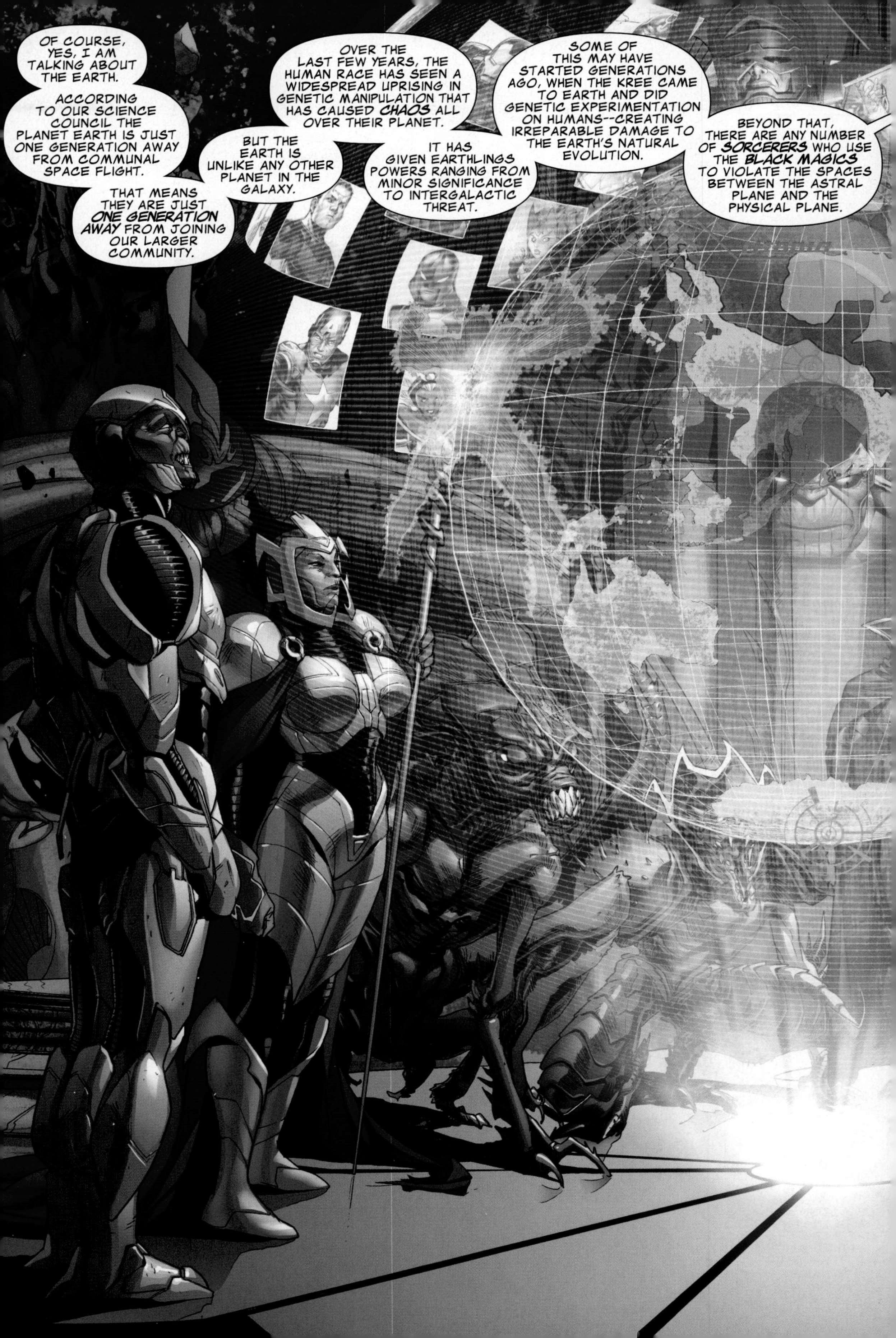
OF COURSE, YES, I AM TALKING ABOUT THE EARTH.
ACCORDING TO OUR SCIENCE COUNCIL THE PLANET EARTH IS JUST ONE GENERATION AWAY FROM COMMUNAL SPACE FLIGHT.
THAT MEANS THEY ARE JUST ONE GENERATION AWAY FROM JOINING OUR LARGER COMMUNITY.
BUT THE EARTH IS UNLIKE ANY OTHER PLANET IN THE GALAXY.
OVER THE LAST FEW YEARS, THE HUMAN RACE HAS SEEN A WIDESPREAD UPRISING IN GENETIC MANIPULATION THAT HAS CAUSED CHAOS ALL OVER THEIR PLANET.
IT HAS GIVEN EARTHLINGS POWERS RANGING FROM MINOR SIGNIFICANCE TO INTERGALACTIC THREAT.
SOME OF THIS MAY HAVE STARTED GENERATIONS AGO, WHEN THE KREE CAME TO EARTH AND DID GENETIC EXPERIMENTATION ON HUMANS--CREATING IRREPARABLE DAMAGE TO THE EARTH'S NATURAL EVOLUTION.
BEYOND THAT, THERE ARE ANY NUMBER OF SORCERERS WHO USE THE BLACK MAGICS TO VIOLATE THE SPACES BETWEEN THE ASTRAL PLANE AND THE PHYSICAL PLANE.

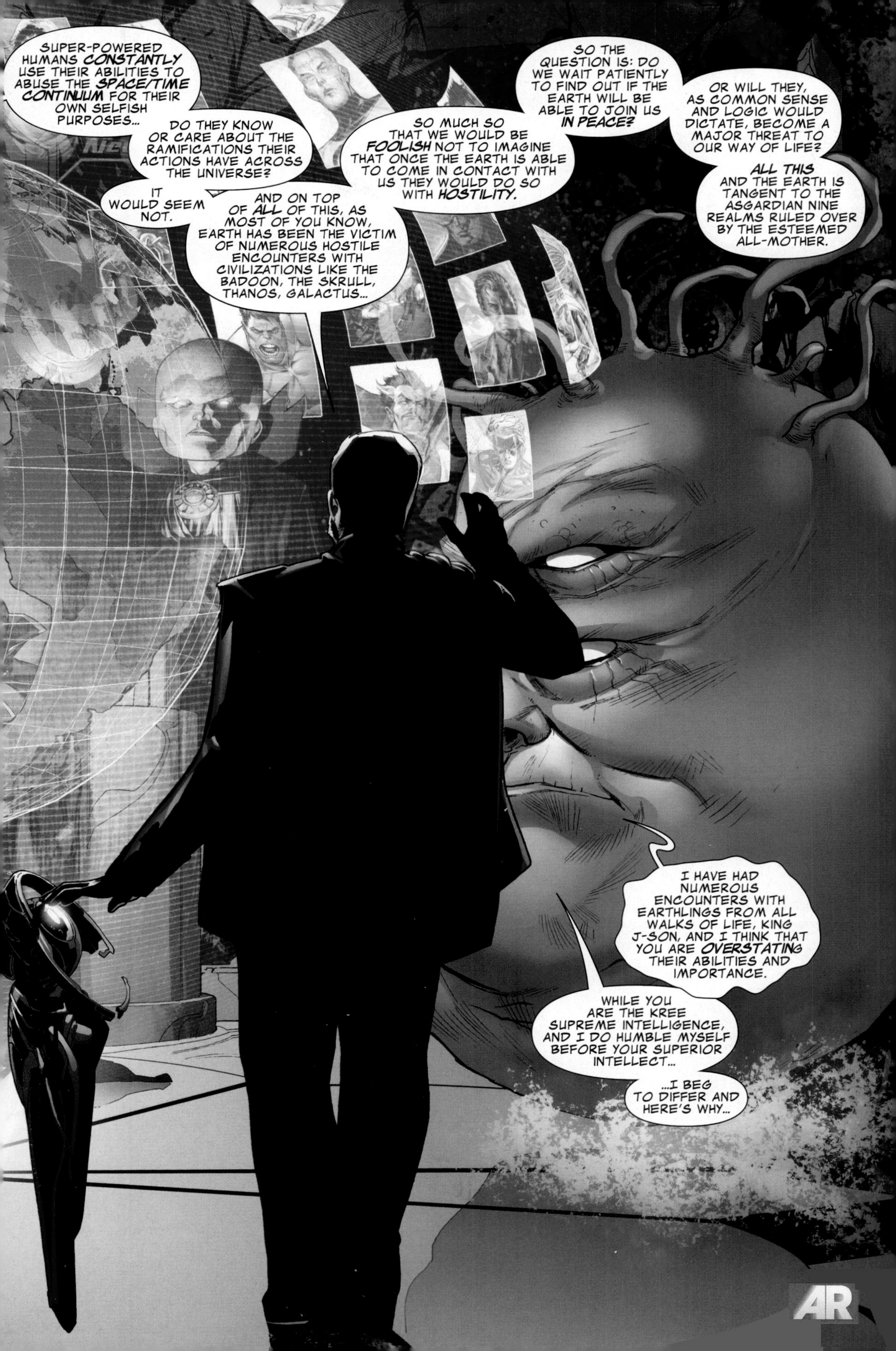
SUPER-POWERED HUMANS CONSTANTLY USE THEIR ABILITIES TO ABUSE THE SPACE/TIME CONTINUUM FOR THEIR OWN SELFISH PURPOSES...
DO THEY KNOW OR CARE ABOUT THE RAMIFICATIONS THEIR ACTIONS HAVE ACROSS THE UNIVERSE?
IT WOULD SEEM NOT.
AND ON TOP OF ALL OF THIS, AS MOST OF YOU KNOW, EARTH HAS BEEN THE VICTIM OF NUMEROUS HOSTILE ENCOUNTERS WITH CIVILIZATIONS LIKE THE BADOON, THE SKRULL, THANOS, GALACTUS...
SO MUCH SO THAT WE WOULD BE FOOLISH NOT TO IMAGINE THAT ONCE THE EARTH IS ABLE TO COME IN CONTACT WITH US THEY WOULD DO SO WITH HOSTILITY.
SO THE QUESTION IS: DO WE WAIT PATIENTLY TO FIND OUT IF THE EARTH WILL BE ABLE TO JOIN US IN PEACE?
OR WILL THEY, AS COMMON SENSE AND LOGIC WOULD DICTATE, BECOME A MAJOR THREAT TO OUR WAY OF LIFE?
ALL THIS AND THE EARTH IS TANGENT TO THE ASGARDIAN NINE REALMS RULED OVER BY THE ESTEEMED ALL-MOTHER.
I HAVE HAD NUMEROUS ENCOUNTERS WITH EARTHLINGS FROM ALL WALKS OF LIFE, KING J-SON, AND I THINK THAT YOU ARE OVERSTATING THEIR ABILITIES AND IMPORTANCE.
WHILE YOU ARE THE KREE SUPREME INTELLIGENCE, AND I DO HUMBLE MYSELF BEFORE YOUR SUPERIOR INTELLECT...
...I BEG TO DIFFER AND HERE'S WHY...
AR

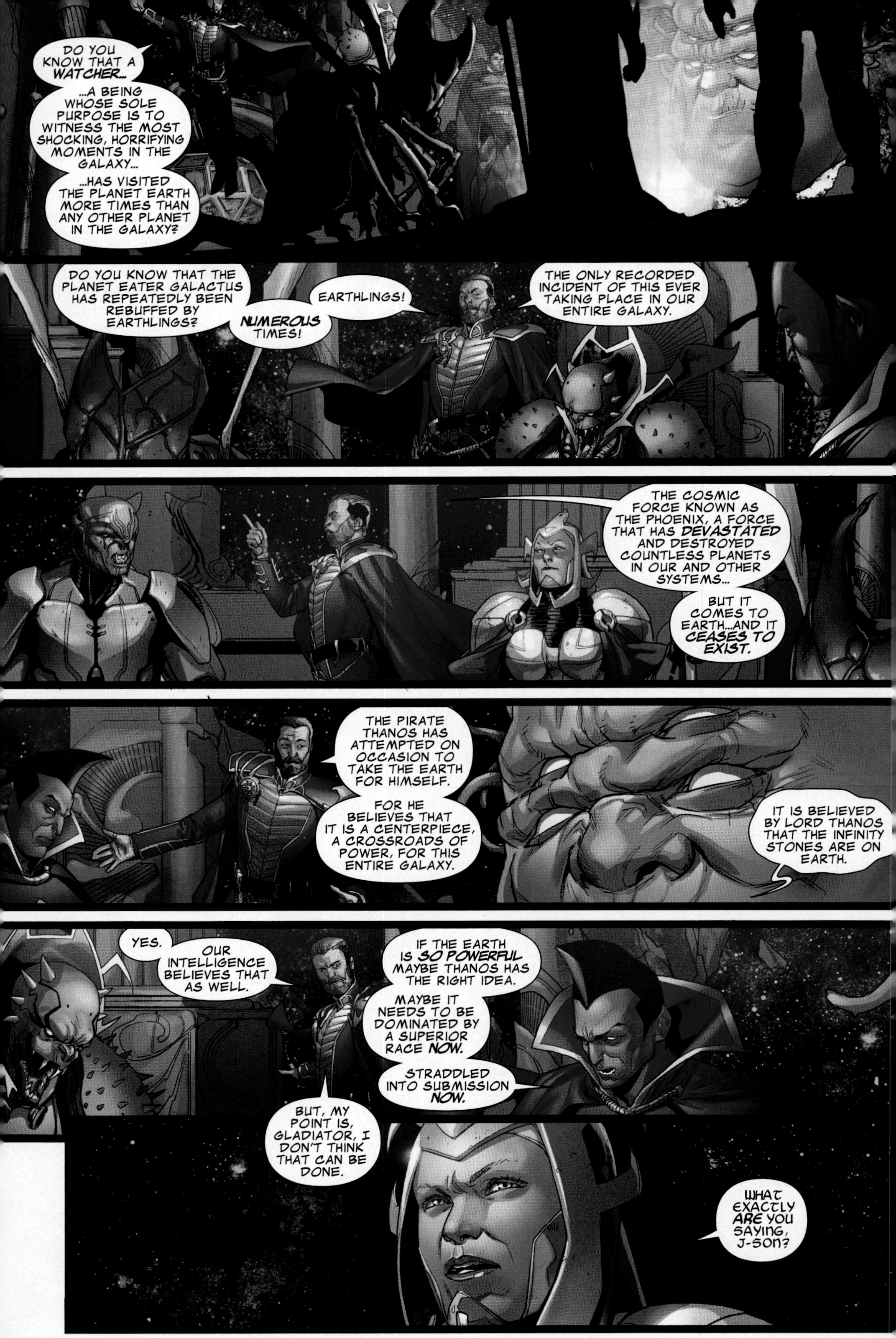
DO YOU KNOW THAT A WATCHER...
...A BEING WHOSE SOLE PURPOSE IS TO WITNESS THE MOST SHOCKING, HORRIFYING MOMENTS IN THE GALAXY...
...HAS VISITED THE PLANET EARTH MORE TIMES THAN ANY OTHER PLANET IN THE GALAXY?
DO YOU KNOW THAT THE PLANET EATER GALACTUS HAS REPEATEDLY BEEN REBUFFED BY EARTHLINGS?
EARTHLINGS!
NUMEROUS TIMES!
THE ONLY RECORDED INCIDENT OF THIS EVER TAKING PLACE IN OUR ENTIRE GALAXY.
THE COSMIC FORCE KNOWN AS THE PHOENIX, A FORCE THAT HAS DEVASTATED AND DESTROYED COUNTLESS PLANETS IN OUR AND OTHER SYSTEMS...
BUT IT COMES TO EARTH...AND IT CEASES TO EXIST.
THE PIRATE THANOS HAS ATTEMPTED ON OCCASION TO TAKE THE EARTH FOR HIMSELF.
FOR HE BELIEVES THAT IT IS A CENTERPIECE, A CROSSROADS OF POWER, FOR THIS ENTIRE GALAXY.
IT IS BELIEVED BY LORD THANOS THAT THE INFINITY STONES ARE ON EARTH.
YES.
OUR INTELLIGENCE BELIEVES THAT AS WELL.
IF THE EARTH IS SO POWERFUL MAYBE THANOS HAS THE RIGHT IDEA.
MAYBE IT NEEDS TO BE DOMINATED BY A SUPERIOR RACE NOW.
STRADDLED INTO SUBMISSION NOW.
BUT, MY POINT IS, GLADIATOR, I DON'T THINK THAT CAN BE DONE.
WHAT EXACTLY ARE YOU SAYING, J-SON?

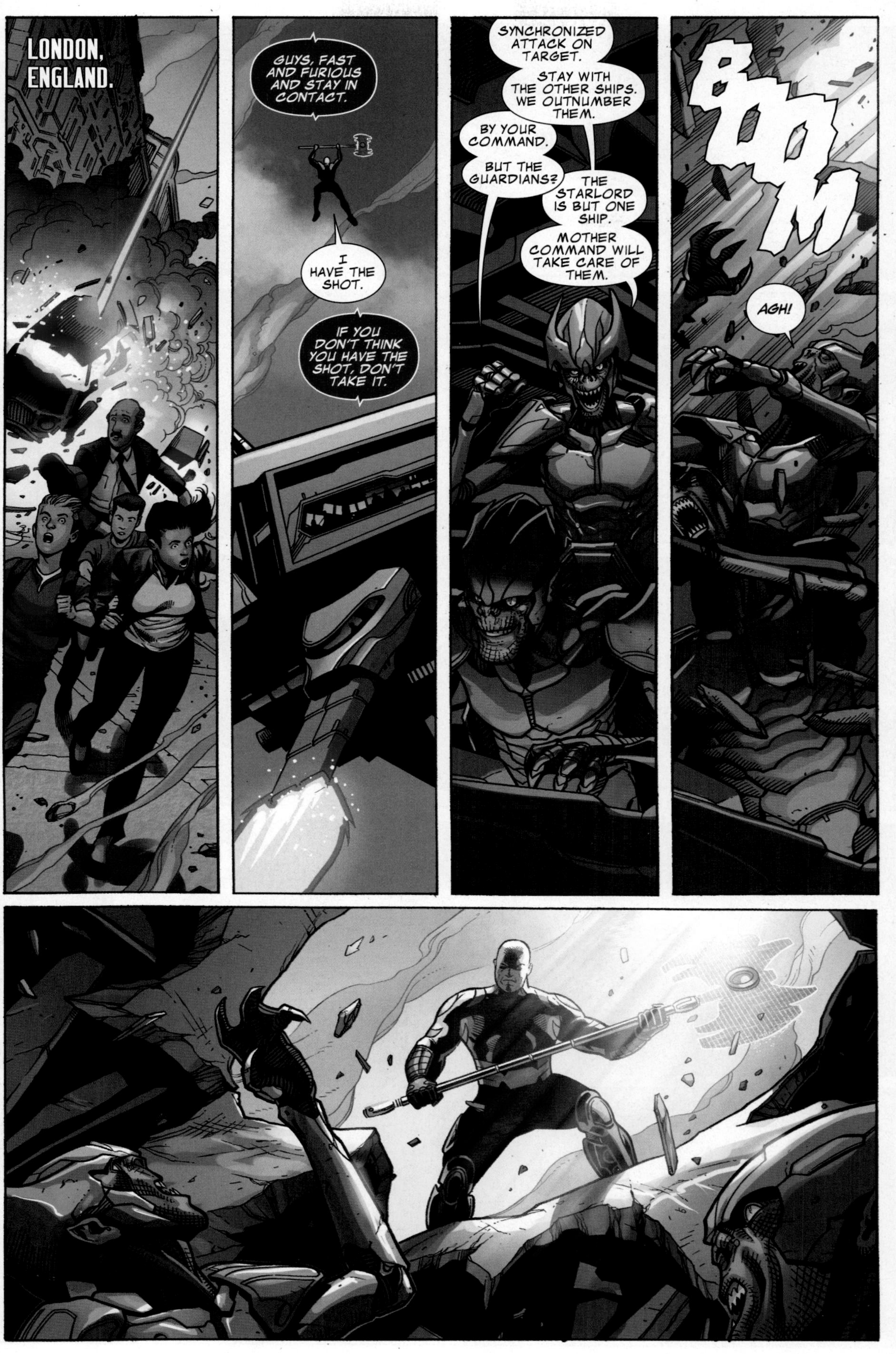
LONDON, ENGLAND.
GUYS, FAST AND FURIOUS AND STAY IN CONTACT.
I HAVE THE SHOT.
IF YOU DON'T THINK YOU HAVE THE SHOT, DON'T TAKE IT.
SYNCHRONIZED ATTACK ON TARGET.
STAY WITH THE OTHER SHIPS. WE OUTNUMBER THEM.
BY YOUR COMMAND.
BUT THE GUARDIANS?
THE STARLORD IS BUT ONE SHIP.
MOTHER COMMAND WILL TAKE CARE OF THEM.
BOOM
AGH!

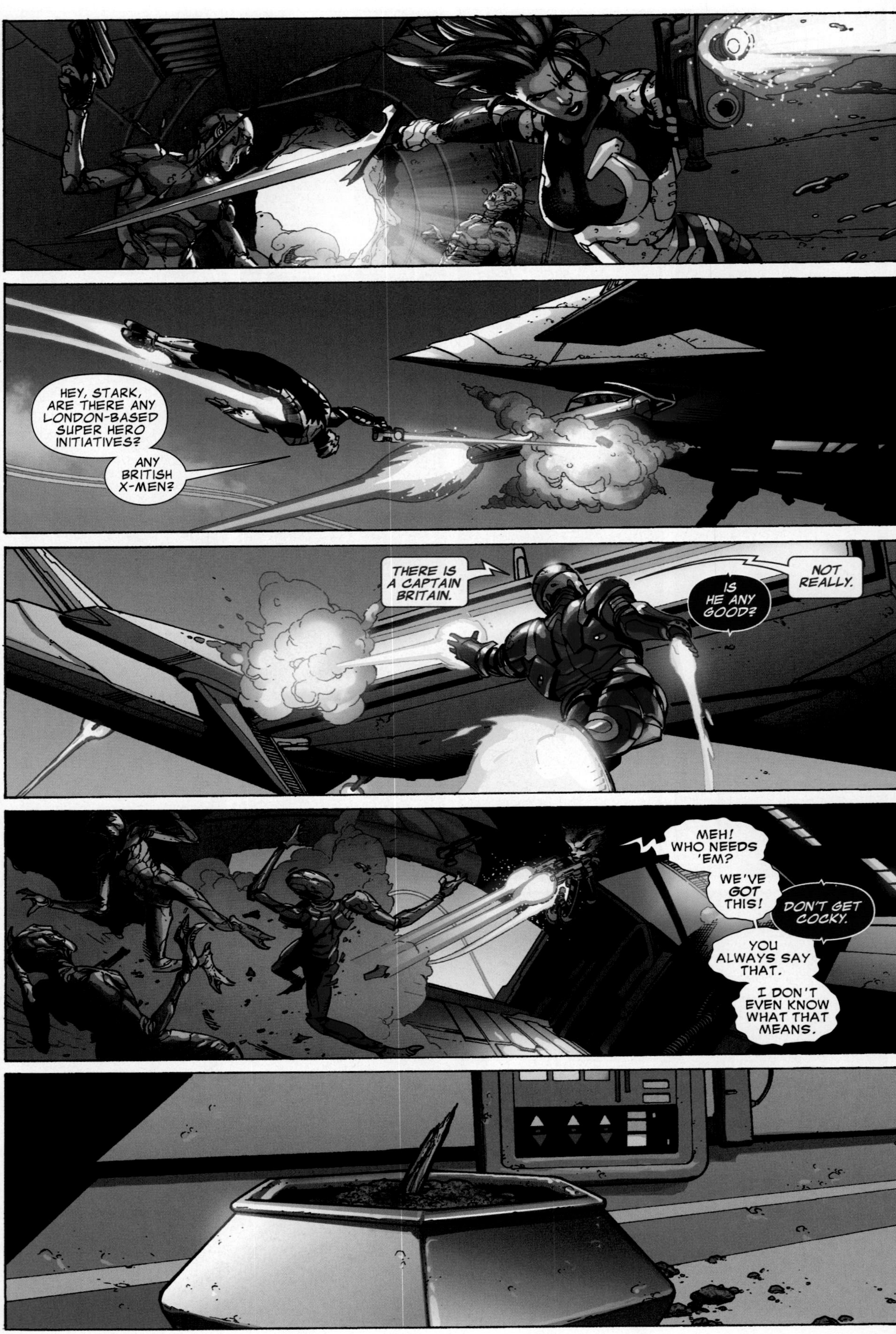

HEY, STARK, ARE THERE ANY LONDON-BASED SUPER HERO INITIATIVES?
ANY BRITISH X-MEN?
THERE IS A CAPTAIN BRITAIN.
IS HE ANY GOOD?
NOT REALLY.
MEH! WHO NEEDS 'EM?
WE'VE GOT THIS!
DON'T GET COCKY.
YOU ALWAYS SAY THAT.
I DON'T EVEN KNOW WHAT THAT MEANS.

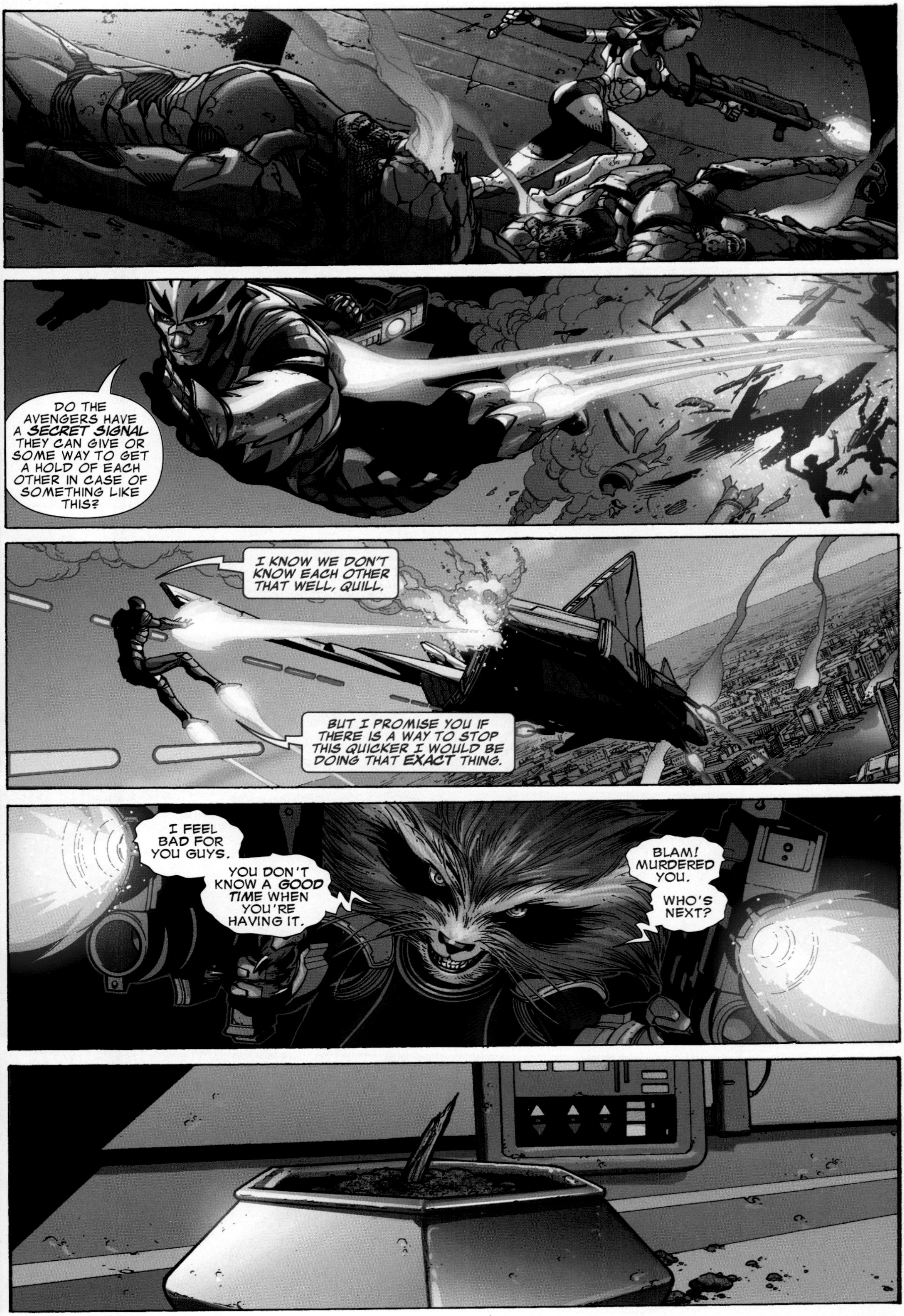
DO THE AVENGERS HAVE A SECRET SIGNAL THEY CAN GIVE OR SOME WAY TO GET A HOLD OF EACH OTHER IN CASE OF SOMETHING LIKE THIS?
I KNOW WE DON'T KNOW EACH OTHER THAT WELL, QUILL.
BUT I PROMISE YOU IF THERE IS A WAY TO STOP THIS QUICKER I WOULD BE DOING THAT EXACT THING.
I FEEL BAD FOR YOU GUYS.
YOU DON'T KNOW A GOOD TIME WHEN YOU'RE HAVING IT.
BLAM! MURDERED YOU.
WHO'S NEXT?

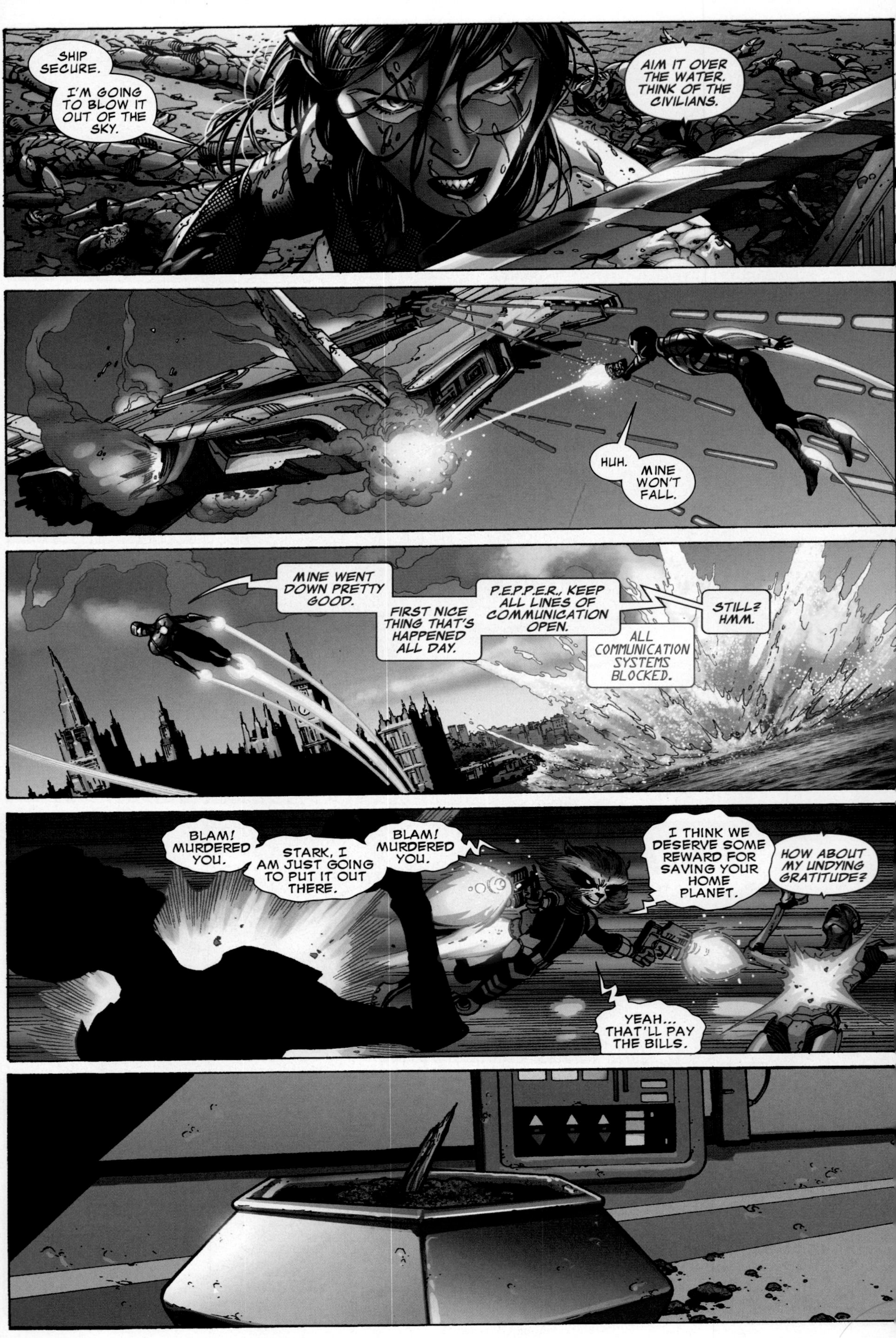
SHIP SECURE.
I'M GOING TO BLOW IT OUT OF THE SKY.
AIM IT OVER THE WATER. THINK OF THE CIVILIANS.
HUH.
MINE WON'T FALL.
MINE WENT DOWN PRETTY GOOD.
FIRST NICE THING THAT'S HAPPENED ALL DAY.
P.E.P.P.E.R., KEEP ALL LINES OF COMMUNICATION OPEN.
STILL? HMM.
ALL COMMUNICATION SYSTEMS BLOCKED.
BLAM! MURDERED YOU.
STARK, I AM JUST GOING TO PUT IT OUT THERE.
BLAM! MURDERED YOU.
I THINK WE DESERVE SOME REWARD FOR SAVING YOUR HOME PLANET.
HOW ABOUT MY UNDYING GRATITUDE?
YEAH... THAT'LL PAY THE BILLS.

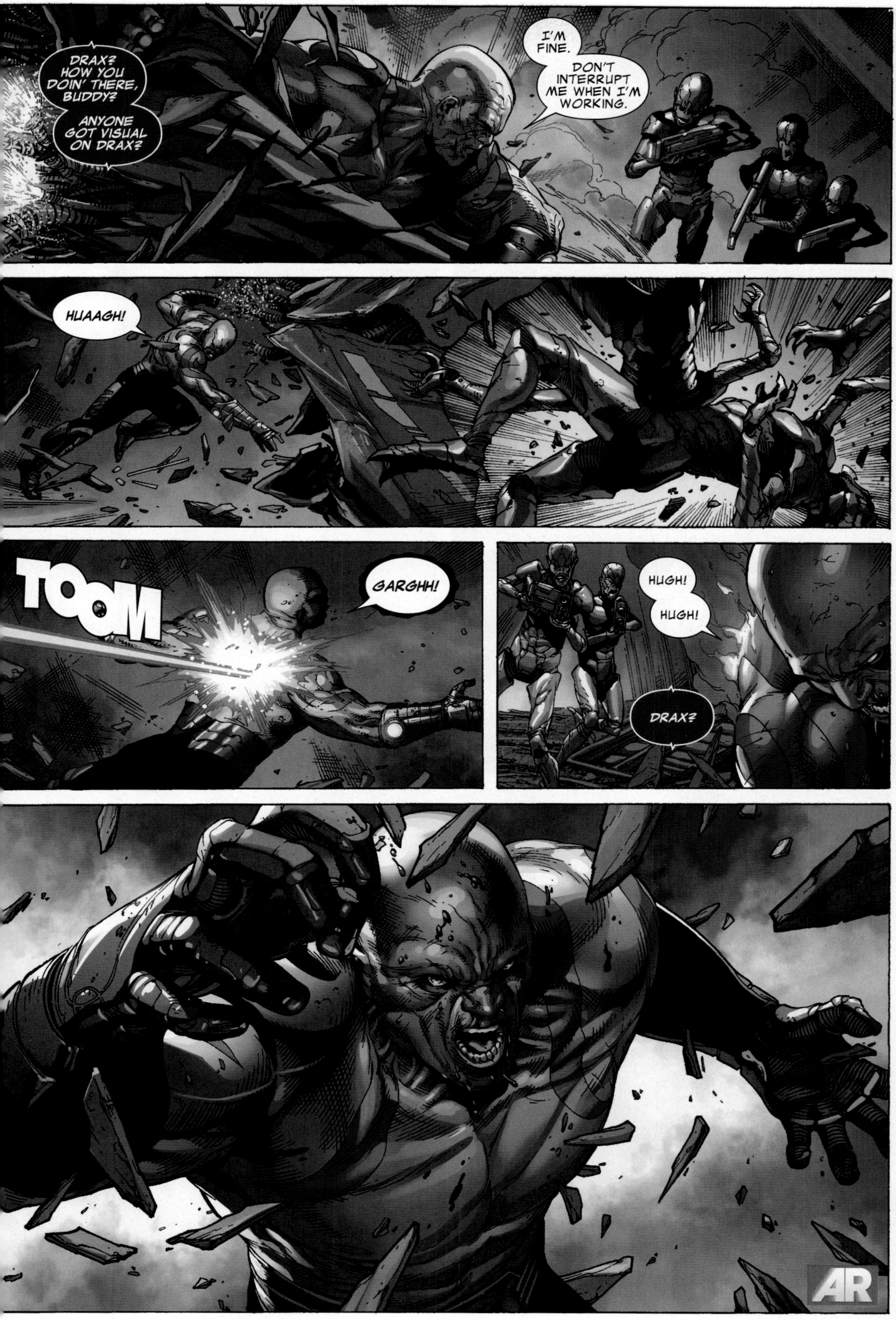
DRAX? HOW YOU DOIN' THERE, BUDDY?
ANYONE GOT VISUAL ON DRAX?
I'M FINE.
DON'T INTERRUPT ME WHEN I'M WORKING.
HUAAGH!
TOOM
GARGHH!
HUGH!
HUGH!
DRAX?
AR

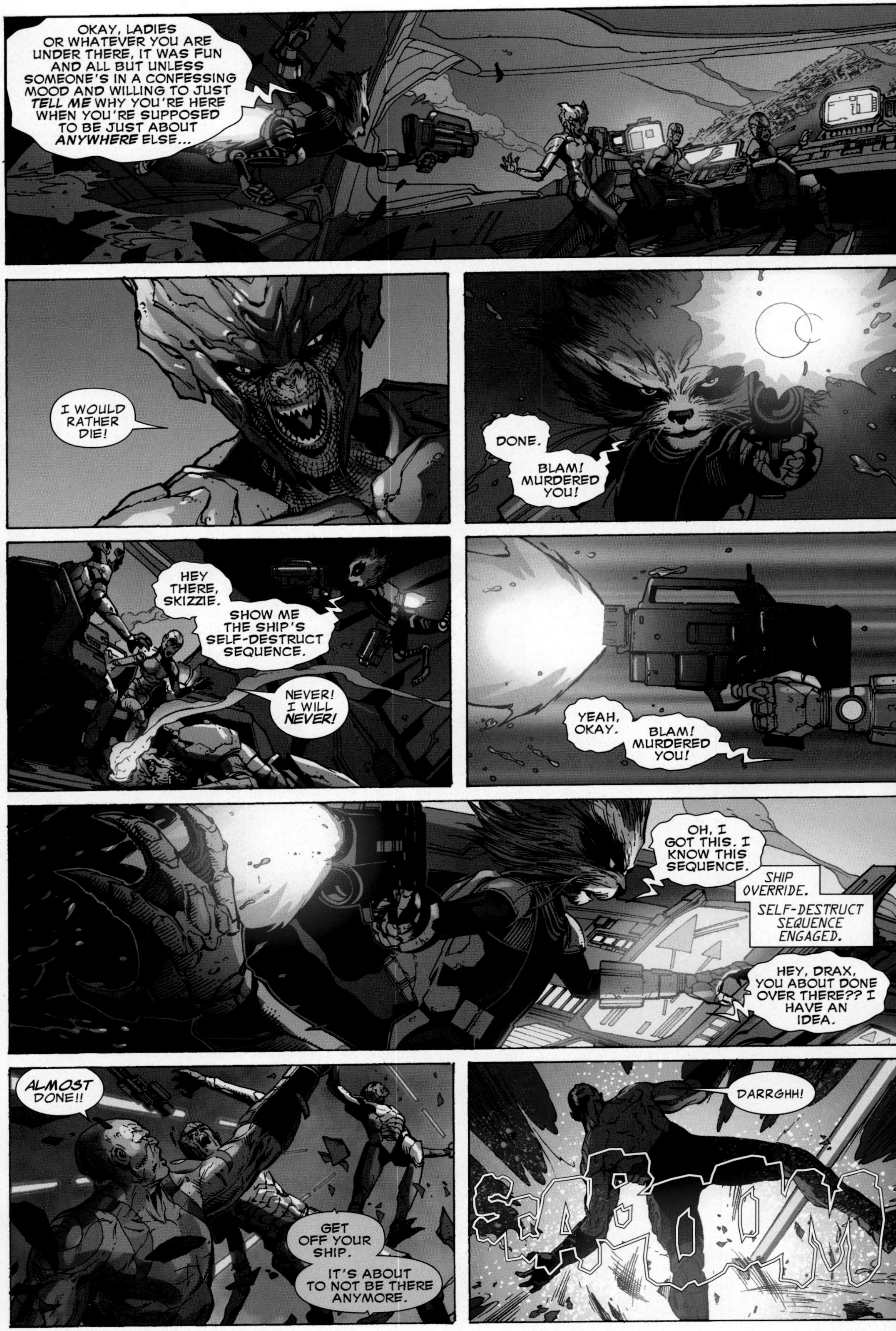
OKAY, LADIES OR WHATEVER YOU ARE UNDER THERE, IT WAS FUN AND ALL BUT UNLESS SOMEONE'S IN A CONFESSING MOOD AND WILLING TO JUST TELL ME WHY YOU'RE HERE WHEN YOU'RE SUPPOSED TO BE JUST ABOUT ANYWHERE ELSE...
I WOULD RATHER DIE!
DONE.
BLAM! MURDERED YOU!
HEY THERE, SKIZZIE.
SHOW ME THE SHIP'S SELF-DESTRUCT SEQUENCE.
NEVER! I WILL NEVER!
YEAH, OKAY.
BLAM! MURDERED YOU!
OH, I GOT THIS. I KNOW THIS SEQUENCE.
SHIP OVERRIDE.
SELF-DESTRUCT SEQUENCE ENGAGED.
HEY, DRAX, YOU ABOUT DONE OVER THERE?? I HAVE AN IDEA.
ALMOST DONE!!
GET OFF YOUR SHIP.
IT'S ABOUT TO NOT BE THERE ANYMORE.
DARRGHH!
SABOOM

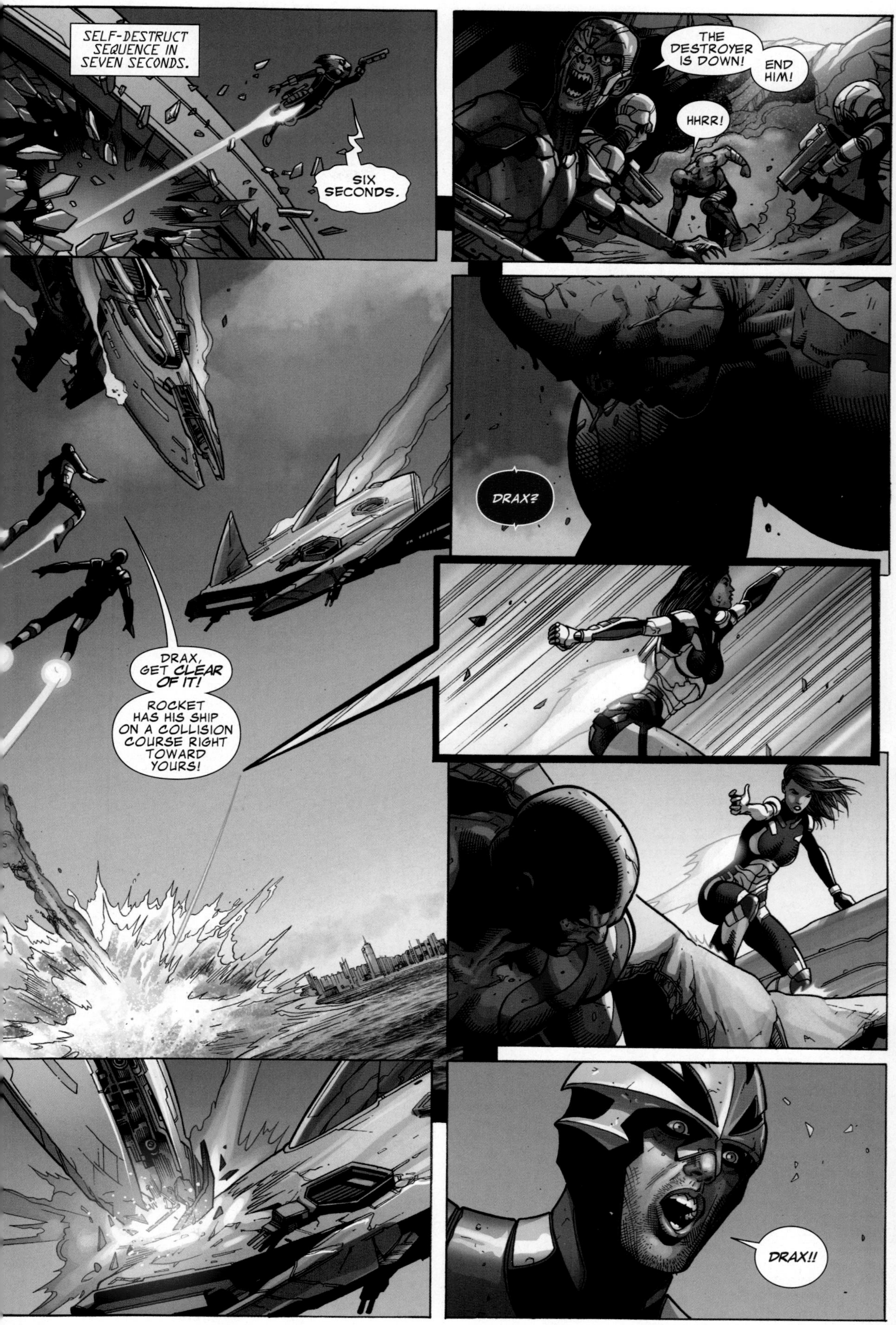
SELF-DESTRUCT SEQUENCE IN SEVEN SECONDS.
SIX SECONDS.
THE DESTROYER IS DOWN!
END HIM!
HHRR!
DRAX, GET CLEAR OF IT!
ROCKET HAS HIS SHIP ON A COLLISION COURSE RIGHT TOWARD YOURS!
DRAX?
DRAX!!

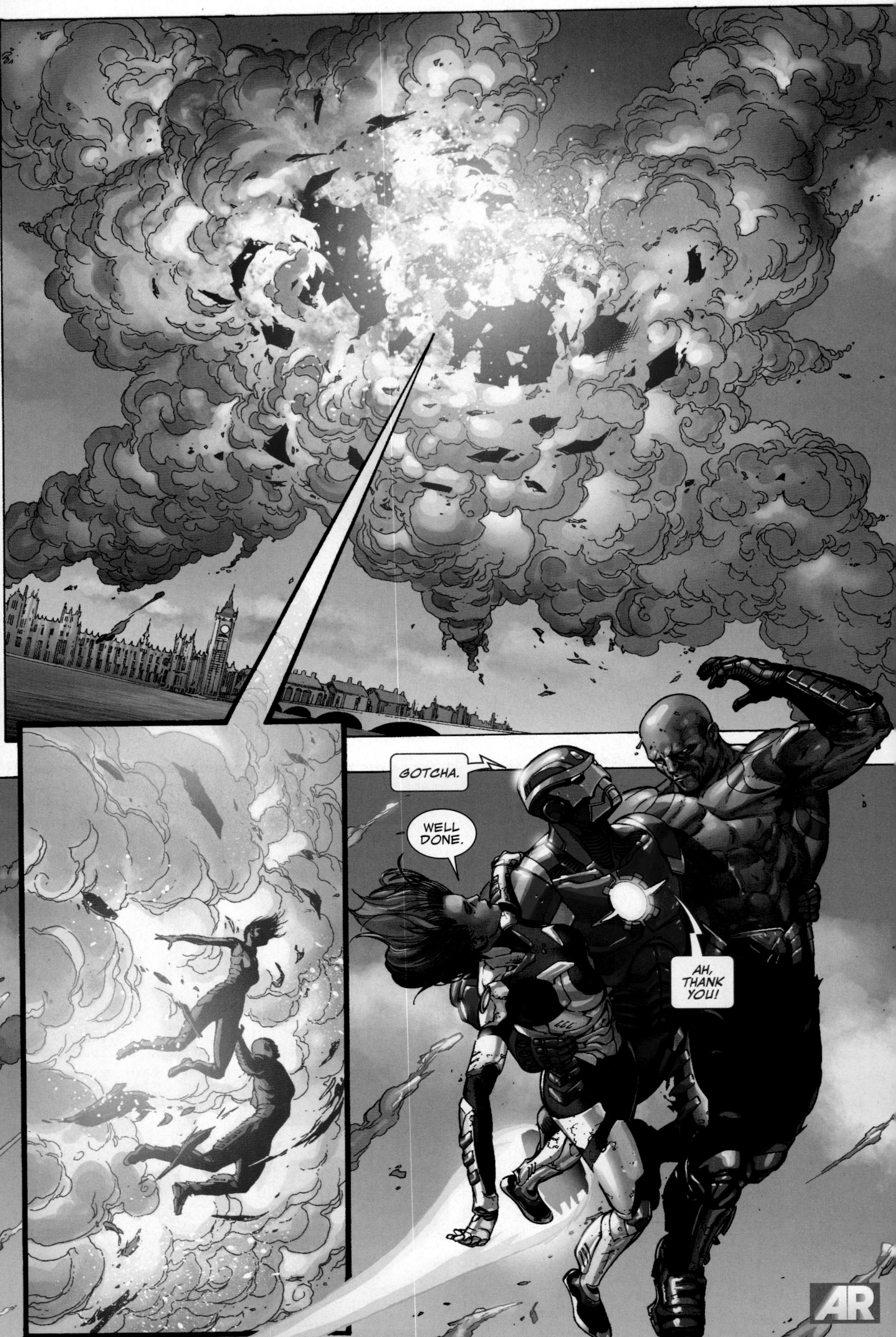
GOTCHA.
WELL DONE.
AH, THANK YOU!
AR

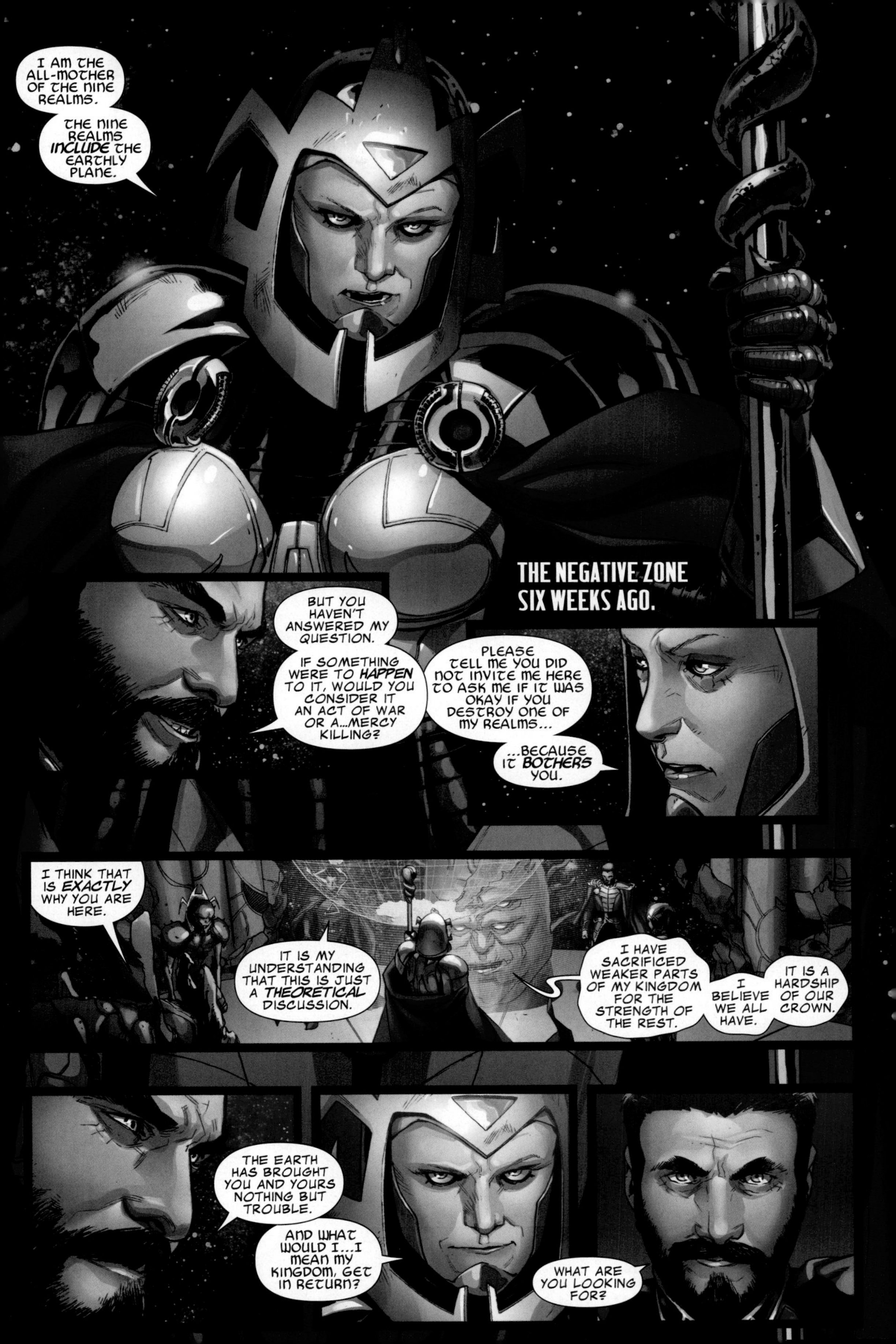
I AM THE ALL-MOTHER OF THE NINE REALMS.
THE NINE REALMS INCLUDE THE EARTHLY PLANE.
THE NEGATIVE ZONE SIX WEEKS AGO.
BUT YOU HAVEN'T ANSWERED MY QUESTION.
IF SOMETHING WERE TO HAPPEN TO IT, WOULD YOU CONSIDER IT AN ACT OF WAR OR A...MERCY KILLING?
PLEASE TELL ME YOU DID NOT INVITE ME HERE TO ASK ME IF IT WAS OKAY IF YOU DESTROY ONE OF MY REALMS...
...BECAUSE IT BOTHERS YOU.
I THINK THAT IS EXACTLY WHY YOU ARE HERE.
IT IS MY UNDERSTANDING THAT THIS IS JUST A THEORETICAL DISCUSSION.
I HAVE SACRIFICED WEAKER PARTS OF MY KINGDOM FOR THE STRENGTH OF THE REST.
I BELIEVE WE ALL HAVE.
IT IS A HARDSHIP OF OUR CROWN.
THE EARTH HAS BROUGHT YOU AND YOURS NOTHING BUT TROUBLE.
AND WHAT WOULD I...I MEAN MY KINGDOM, GET IN RETURN?
WHAT ARE YOU LOOKING FOR?

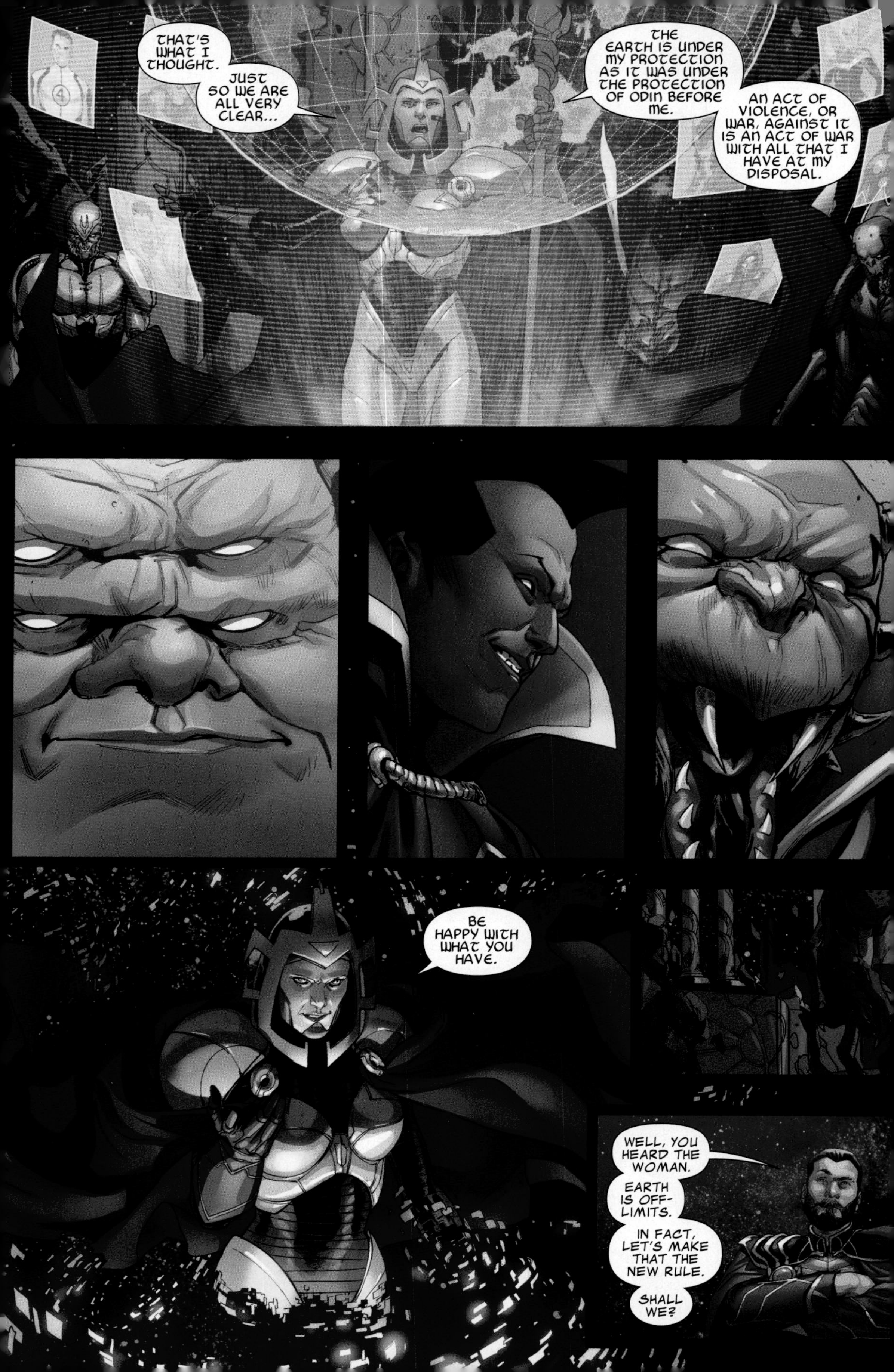
THAT'S WHAT I THOUGHT.
JUST SO WE ARE ALL VERY CLEAR...
THE EARTH IS UNDER MY PROTECTION AS IT WAS UNDER THE PROTECTION OF ODIN BEFORE ME.
AN ACT OF VIOLENCE, OR WAR, AGAINST IT IS AN ACT OF WAR WITH ALL THAT I HAVE AT MY DISPOSAL.
BE HAPPY WITH WHAT YOU HAVE.
WELL, YOU HEARD THE WOMAN.
EARTH IS OFF-LIMITS.
IN FACT, LET'S MAKE THAT THE NEW RULE.
SHALL WE?

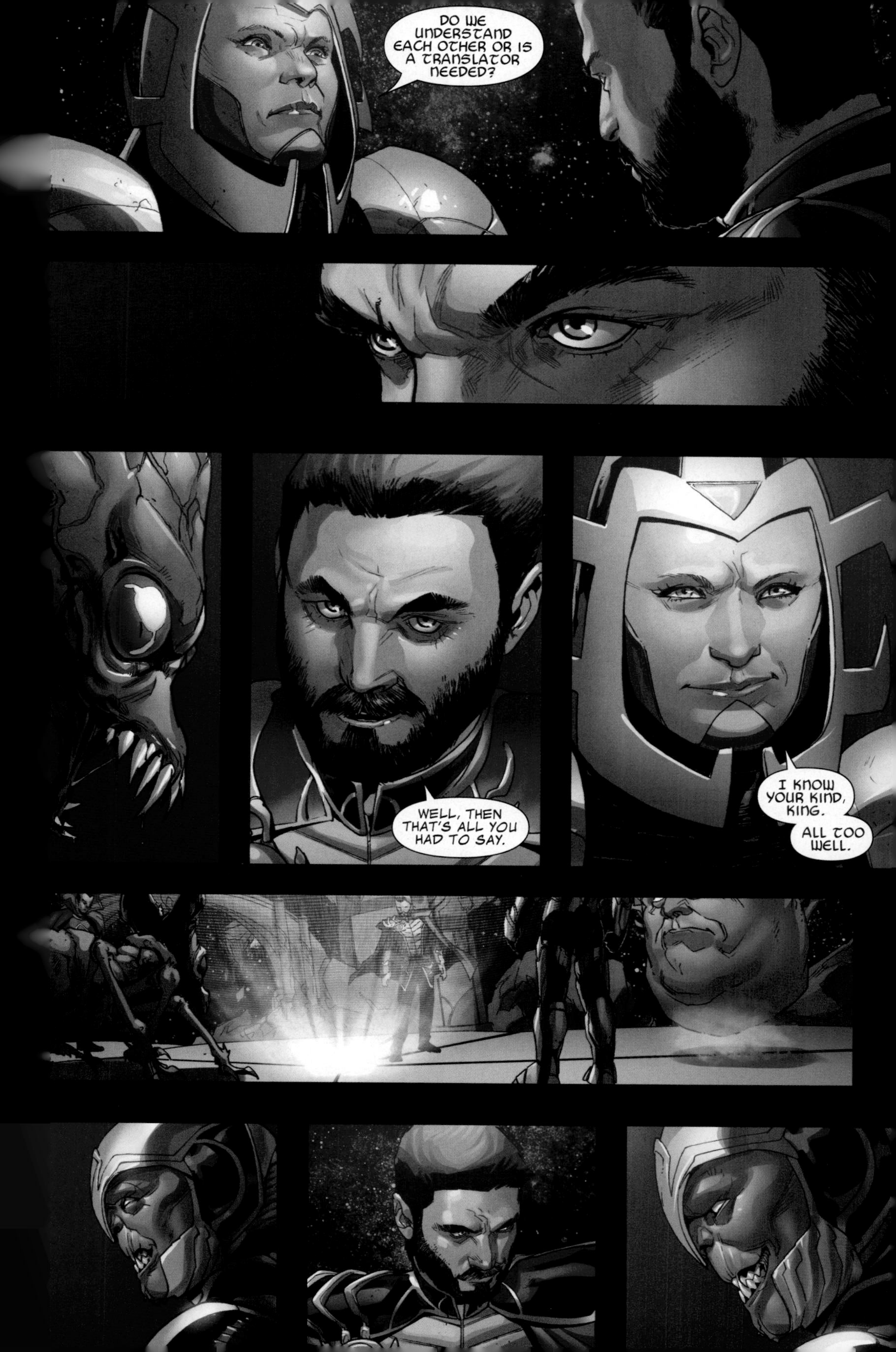
DO WE UNDERSTAND EACH OTHER OR IS A TRANSLATOR NEEDED?
WELL, THEN THAT'S ALL YOU HAD TO SAY.
I KNOW YOUR KIND, KING.
ALL TOO WELL.

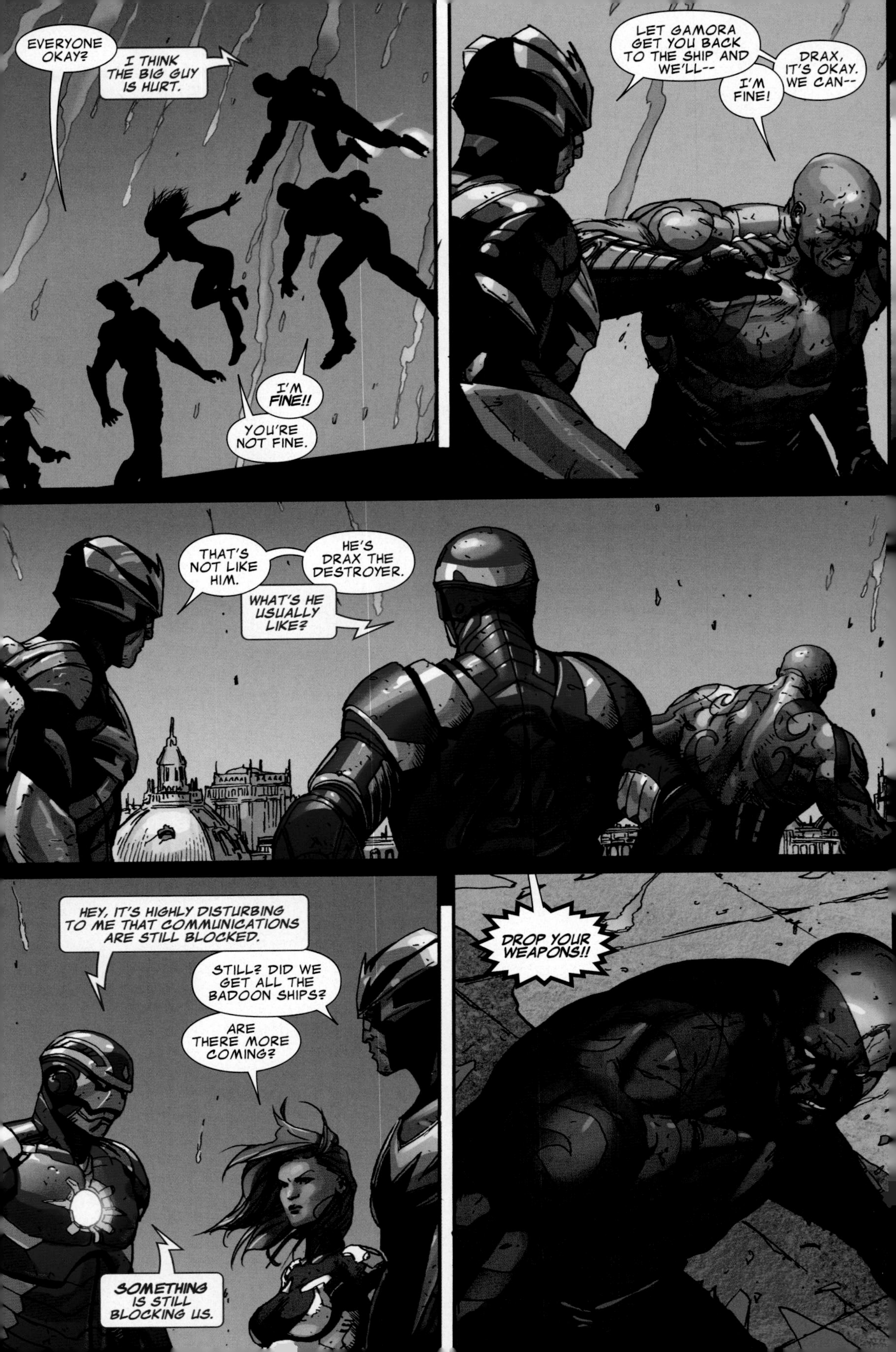
EVERYONE OKAY?
I THINK THE BIG GUY IS HURT.
I'M FINE!!
YOU'RE NOT FINE.
LET GAMORA GET YOU BACK TO THE SHIP AND WE'LL--
I'M FINE!
DRAX, IT'S OKAY. WE CAN--
THAT'S NOT LIKE HIM.
HE'S DRAX THE DESTROYER.
WHAT'S HE USUALLY LIKE?
HEY, IT'S HIGHLY DISTURBING TO ME THAT COMMUNICATIONS ARE STILL BLOCKED.
STILL? DID WE GET ALL THE BADOON SHIPS?
ARE THERE MORE COMING?
SOMETHING IS STILL BLOCKING US.
DROP YOUR WEAPONS!!

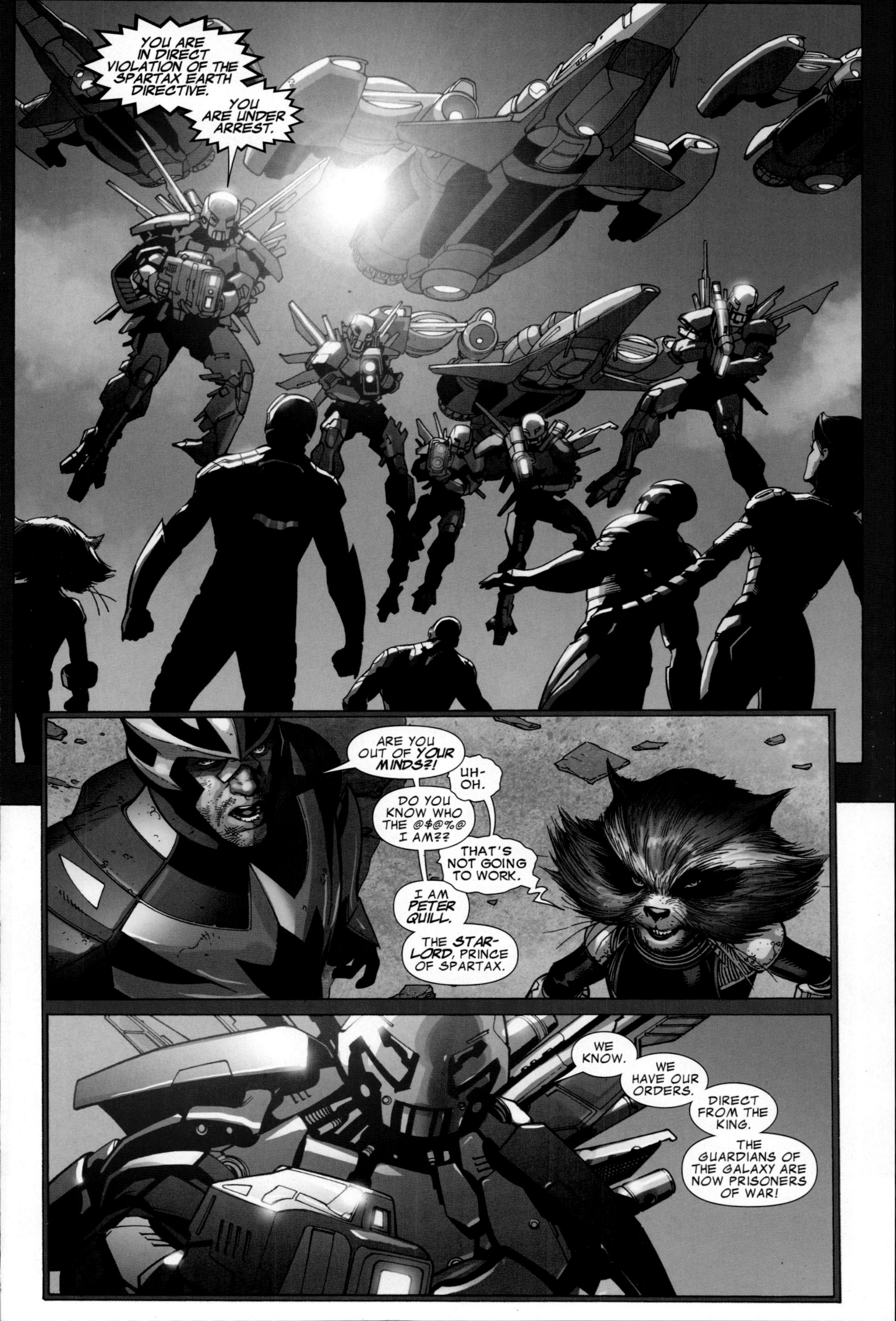
YOU ARE IN DIRECT VIOLATION OF THE SPARTAX EARTH DIRECTIVE.
YOU ARE UNDER ARREST.
ARE YOU OUT OF YOUR MINDS?!
UH-OH.
DO YOU KNOW WHO THE @$@%@ I AM??
THAT'S NOT GOING TO WORK.
I AM PETER QUILL.
THE STAR-LORD, PRINCE OF SPARTAX.
WE KNOW.
WE HAVE OUR ORDERS.
DIRECT FROM THE KING.
THE GUARDIANS OF THE GALAXY ARE NOW PRISONERS OF WAR!

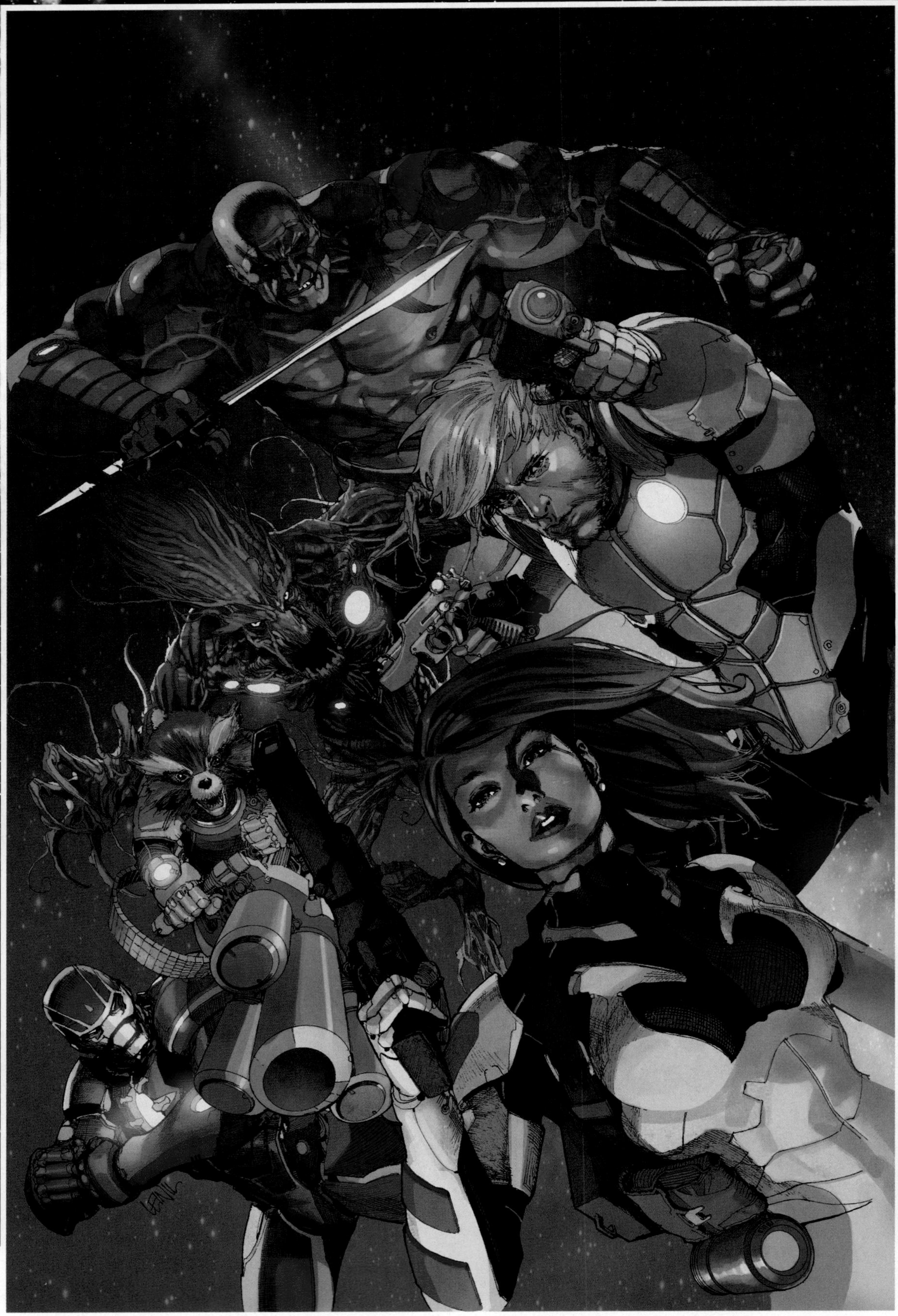

#3 VARIANT BY LEINIL YU & SUNNY GHO

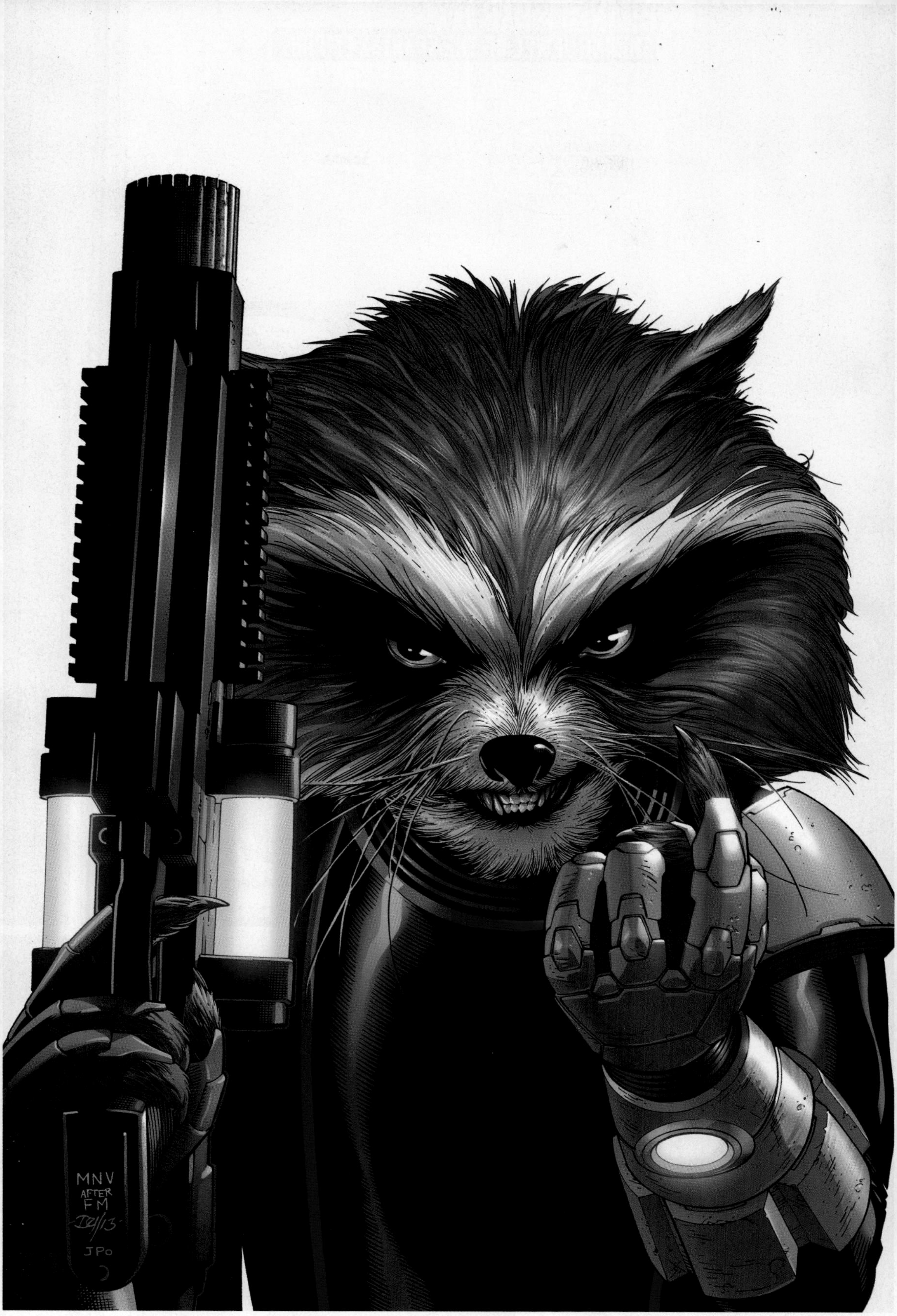
MNV
AFTER
FM
JPo

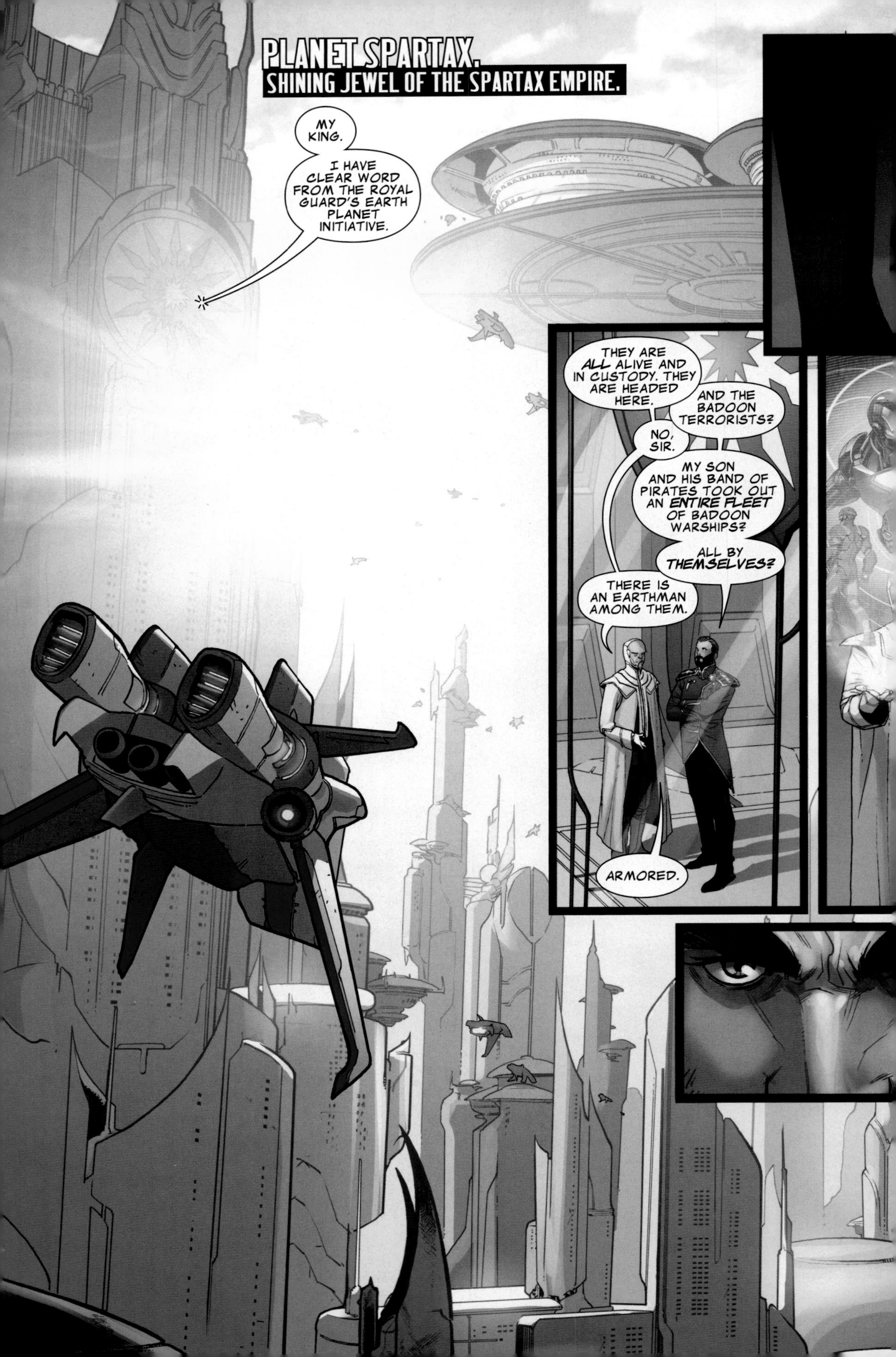
PLANET SPARTAX.
SHINING JEWEL OF THE SPARTAX EMPIRE.
MY KING.
I HAVE CLEAR WORD FROM THE ROYAL GUARD'S EARTH PLANET INITIATIVE.
THEY ARE ALL ALIVE AND IN CUSTODY. THEY ARE HEADED HERE.
AND THE BADOON TERRORISTS?
NO, SIR.
MY SON AND HIS BAND OF PIRATES TOOK OUT AN ENTIRE FLEET OF BADOON WARSHIPS?
ALL BY THEMSELVES?
THERE IS AN EARTHMAN AMONG THEM.
ARMORED.

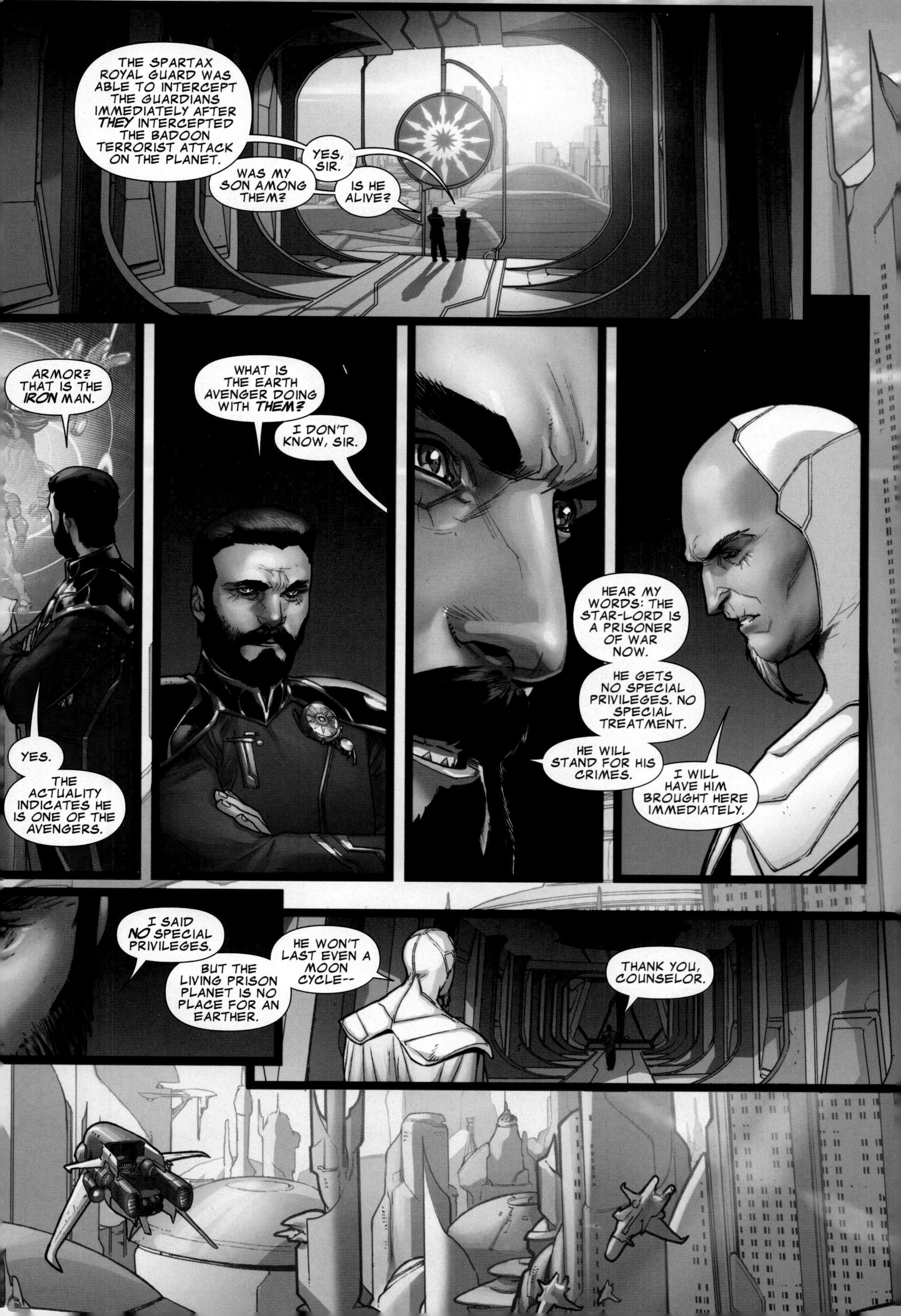
THE SPARTAX ROYAL GUARD WAS ABLE TO INTERCEPT THE GUARDIANS IMMEDIATELY AFTER THEY INTERCEPTED THE BADOON TERRORIST ATTACK ON THE PLANET.
WAS MY SON AMONG THEM?
YES, SIR.
IS HE ALIVE?
ARMOR? THAT IS THE IRON MAN.
YES.
THE ACTUALITY INDICATES HE IS ONE OF THE AVENGERS.
WHAT IS THE EARTH AVENGER DOING WITH THEM?
I DON'T KNOW, SIR.
HEAR MY WORDS: THE STAR-LORD IS A PRISONER OF WAR NOW.
HE GETS NO SPECIAL PRIVILEGES. NO SPECIAL TREATMENT.
HE WILL STAND FOR HIS CRIMES.
I WILL HAVE HIM BROUGHT HERE IMMEDIATELY.
I SAID NO SPECIAL PRIVILEGES.
BUT THE LIVING PRISON PLANET IS NO PLACE FOR AN EARTHER.
HE WON'T LAST EVEN A MOON CYCLE--
THANK YOU, COUNSELOR.

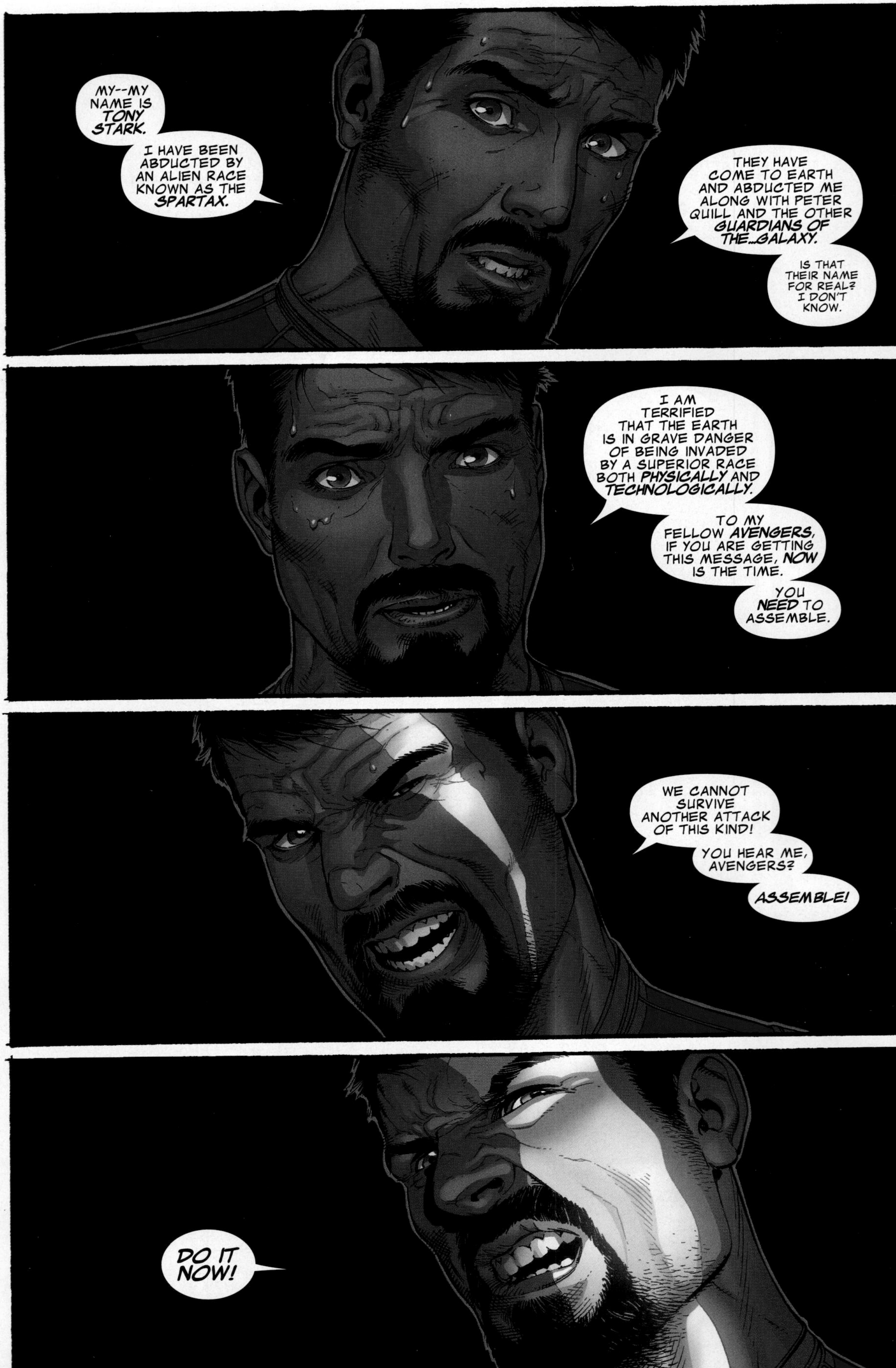

MY--MY NAME IS *TONY STARK.*
I HAVE BEEN ABDUCTED BY AN ALIEN RACE KNOWN AS THE *SPARTAX.*
THEY HAVE COME TO EARTH AND ABDUCTED ME ALONG WITH PETER QUILL AND THE OTHER *GUARDIANS OF THE...GALAXY.*
IS THAT THEIR NAME FOR REAL? I DON'T KNOW.
I AM TERRIFIED THAT THE EARTH IS IN GRAVE DANGER OF BEING INVADED BY A SUPERIOR RACE BOTH *PHYSICALLY* AND *TECHNOLOGICALLY.*
TO MY FELLOW *AVENGERS,* IF YOU ARE GETTING THIS MESSAGE, *NOW* IS THE TIME.
YOU *NEED* TO ASSEMBLE.
WE CANNOT SURVIVE ANOTHER ATTACK OF THIS KIND!
YOU HEAR ME, AVENGERS?
ASSEMBLE!
DO IT NOW!

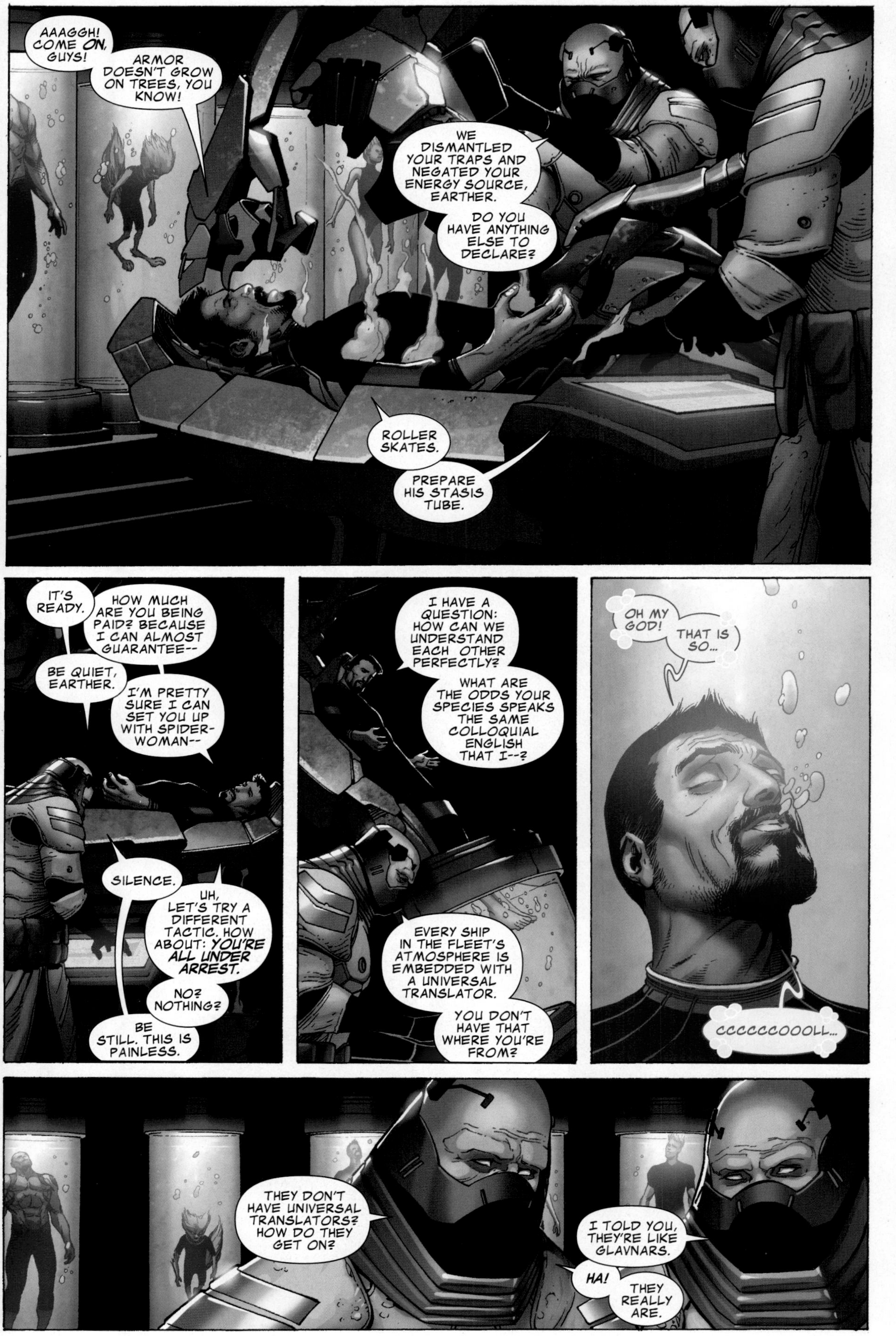
AAAGGH! COME *ON*, GUYS!
ARMOR DOESN'T GROW ON TREES, YOU KNOW!
WE DISMANTLED YOUR TRAPS AND NEGATED YOUR ENERGY SOURCE, EARTHER.
DO YOU HAVE ANYTHING ELSE TO DECLARE?
ROLLER SKATES.
PREPARE HIS STASIS TUBE.
IT'S READY.
HOW MUCH ARE YOU BEING PAID? BECAUSE I CAN ALMOST GUARANTEE--
BE QUIET, EARTHER.
I'M PRETTY SURE I CAN SET YOU UP WITH SPIDER-WOMAN--
SILENCE.
UH, LET'S TRY A DIFFERENT TACTIC. HOW ABOUT: ***YOU'RE ALL UNDER ARREST.***
NO? NOTHING?
BE STILL. THIS IS PAINLESS.
I HAVE A QUESTION: HOW CAN WE UNDERSTAND EACH OTHER PERFECTLY?
WHAT ARE THE ODDS YOUR SPECIES SPEAKS THE SAME COLLOQUIAL ENGLISH THAT I--?
EVERY SHIP IN THE FLEET'S ATMOSPHERE IS EMBEDDED WITH A UNIVERSAL TRANSLATOR.
YOU DON'T HAVE THAT WHERE YOU'RE FROM?
OH MY GOD!
THAT IS SO...
CCCCCCOOOLL...
THEY DON'T HAVE UNIVERSAL TRANSLATORS? HOW DO THEY GET ON?
I TOLD YOU, THEY'RE LIKE GLAVNARS.
HA!
THEY REALLY ARE.

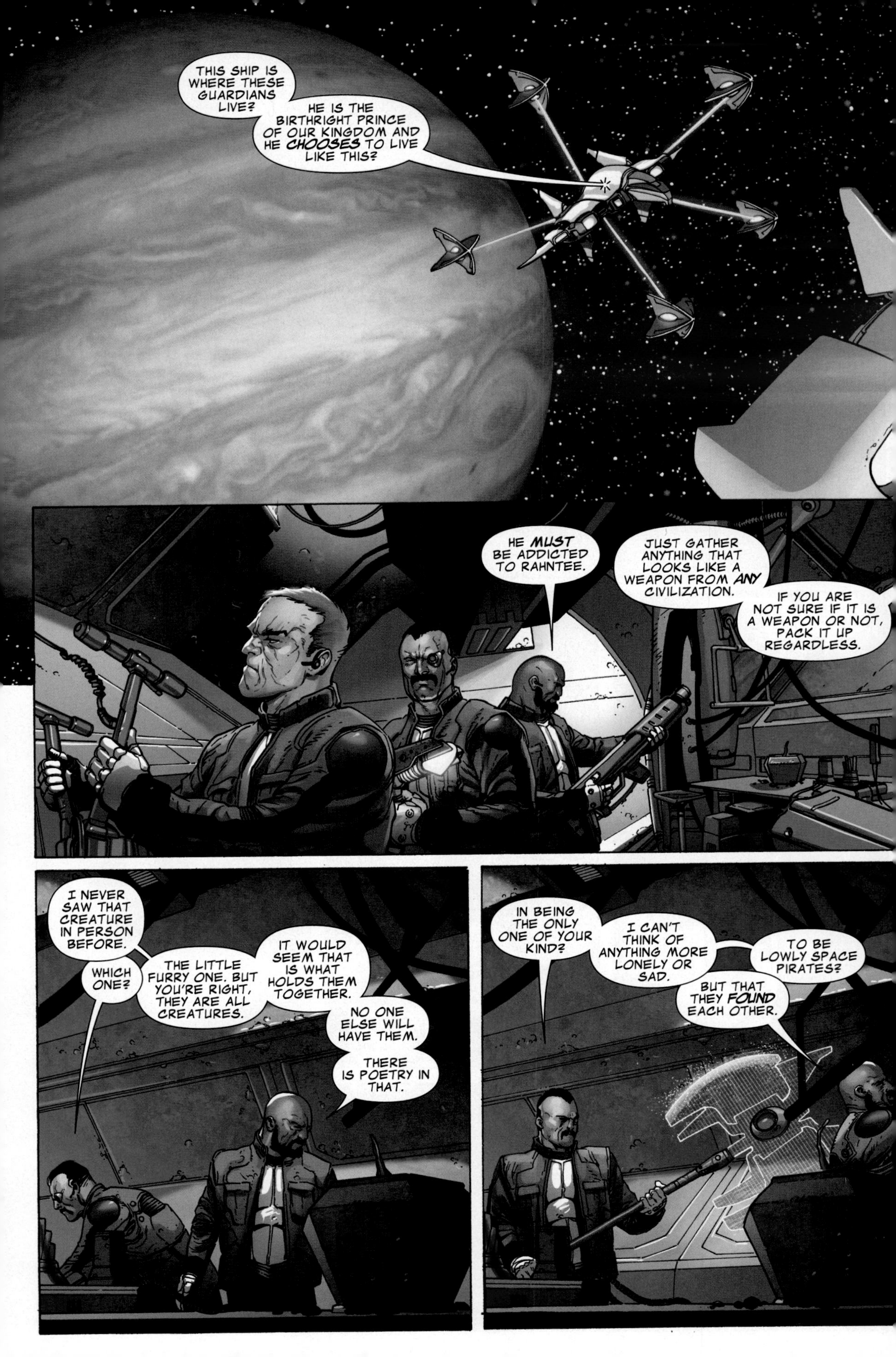

THIS SHIP IS WHERE THESE GUARDIANS LIVE?
HE IS THE BIRTHRIGHT PRINCE OF OUR KINGDOM AND HE *CHOOSES* TO LIVE LIKE THIS?
HE *MUST* BE ADDICTED TO RAHNTEE.
JUST GATHER ANYTHING THAT LOOKS LIKE A WEAPON FROM *ANY* CIVILIZATION.
IF YOU ARE NOT SURE IF IT IS A WEAPON OR NOT, PACK IT UP REGARDLESS.
I NEVER SAW THAT CREATURE IN PERSON BEFORE.
WHICH ONE?
THE LITTLE FURRY ONE. BUT YOU'RE RIGHT, THEY ARE ALL CREATURES.
IT WOULD SEEM THAT IS WHAT HOLDS THEM TOGETHER.
NO ONE ELSE WILL HAVE THEM.
THERE IS POETRY IN THAT.
IN BEING THE ONLY ONE OF YOUR KIND?
I CAN'T THINK OF ANYTHING MORE LONELY OR SAD.
TO BE LOWLY SPACE PIRATES?
BUT THAT THEY *FOUND* EACH OTHER.

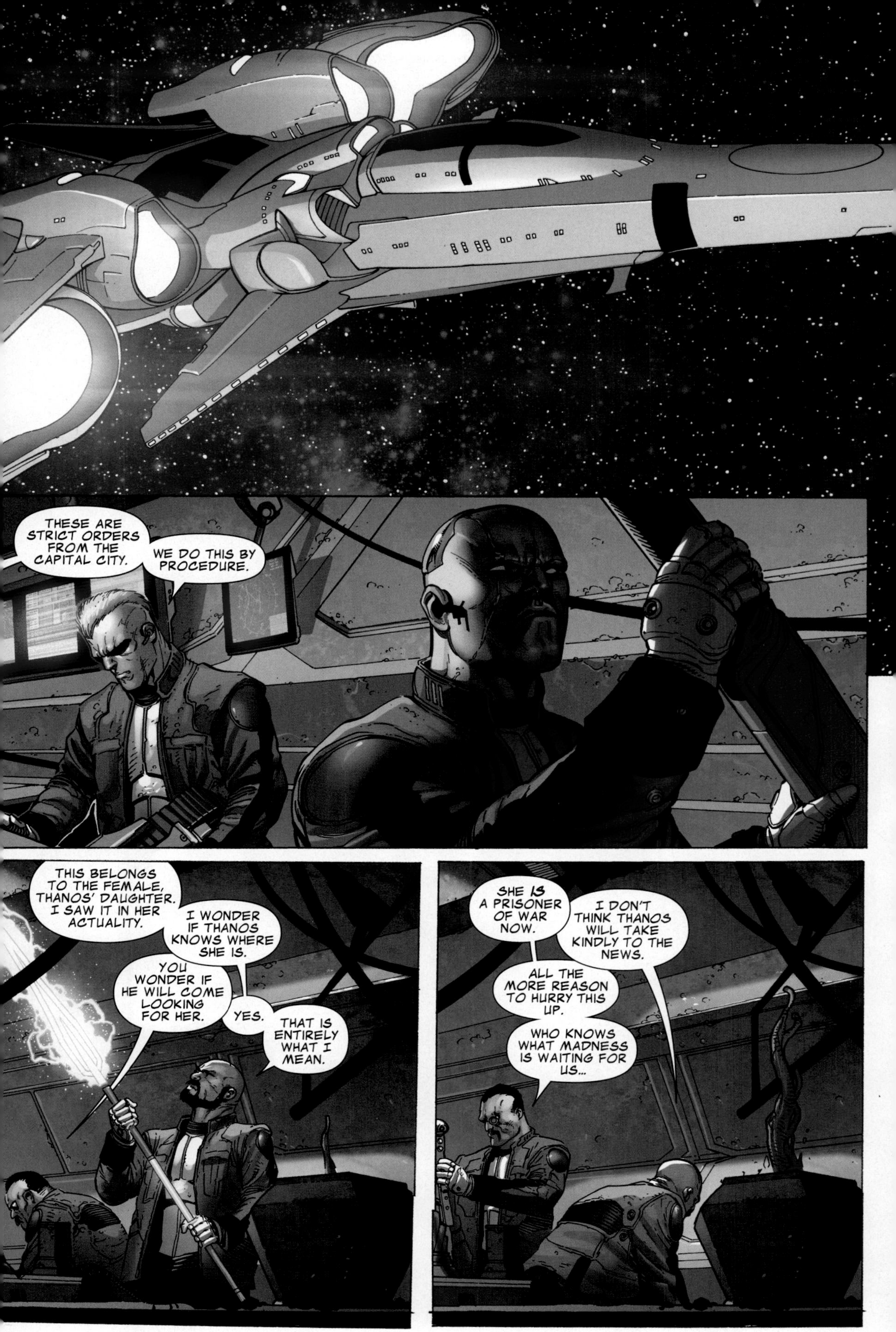

THESE ARE STRICT ORDERS FROM THE CAPITAL CITY.
WE DO THIS BY PROCEDURE.
THIS BELONGS TO THE FEMALE, THANOS' DAUGHTER. I SAW IT IN HER ACTUALITY.
I WONDER IF THANOS KNOWS WHERE SHE IS.
YOU WONDER IF HE WILL COME LOOKING FOR HER.
YES.
THAT IS ENTIRELY WHAT I MEAN.
SHE IS A PRISONER OF WAR NOW.
I DON'T THINK THANOS WILL TAKE KINDLY TO THE NEWS.
ALL THE MORE REASON TO HURRY THIS UP.
WHO KNOWS WHAT MADNESS IS WAITING FOR US...

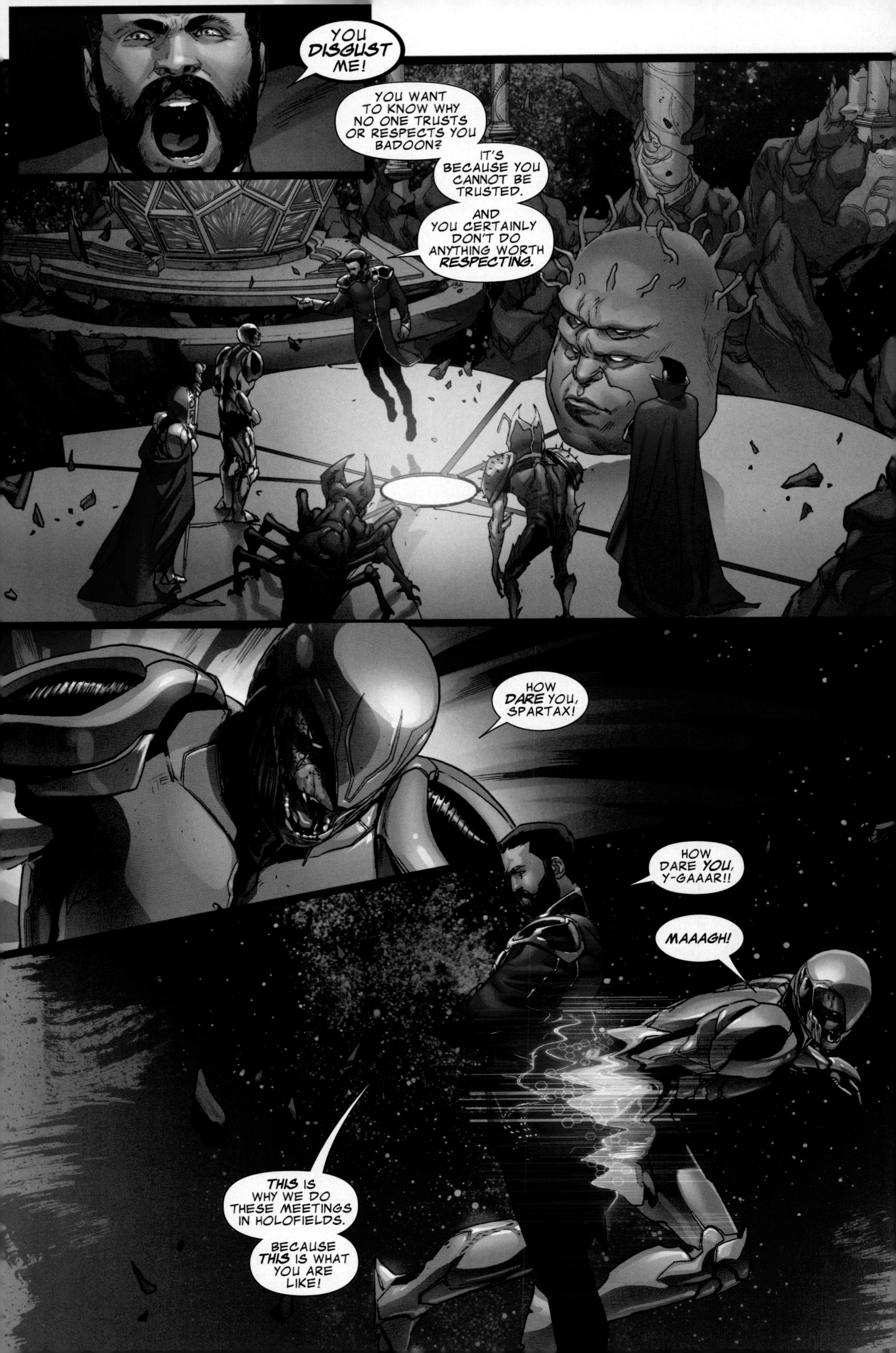
YOU DISGUST ME!
YOU WANT TO KNOW WHY NO ONE TRUSTS OR RESPECTS YOU BADOON?
IT'S BECAUSE YOU CANNOT BE TRUSTED.
AND YOU CERTAINLY DON'T DO ANYTHING WORTH RESPECTING.
HOW DARE YOU, SPARTAX!
HOW DARE YOU, Y-GAAAR!!
MAAAGH!
THIS IS WHY WE DO THESE MEETINGS IN HOLOFIELDS.
BECAUSE THIS IS WHAT YOU ARE LIKE!

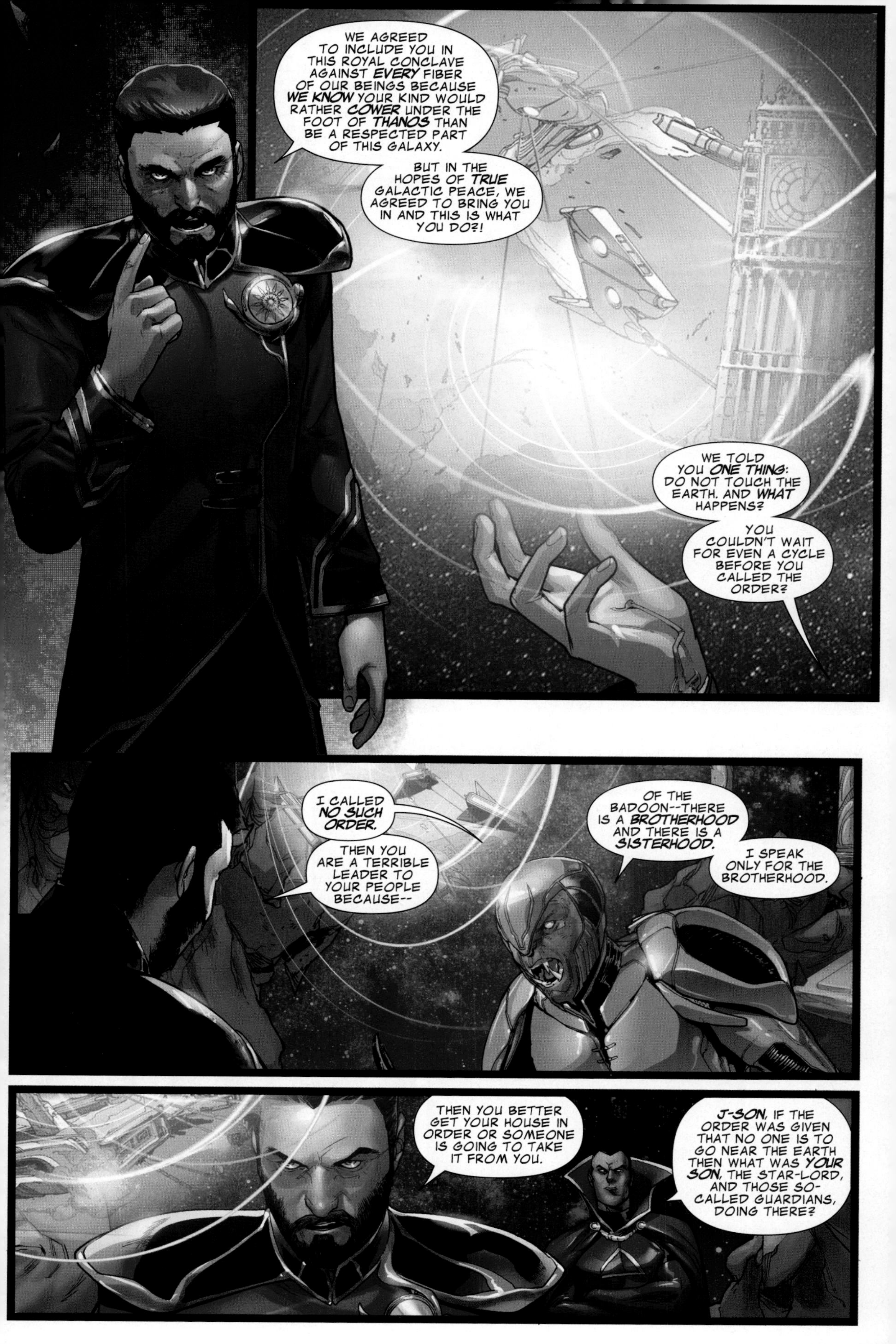
WE AGREED TO INCLUDE YOU IN THIS ROYAL CONCLAVE AGAINST EVERY FIBER OF OUR BEINGS BECAUSE WE KNOW YOUR KIND WOULD RATHER COWER UNDER THE FOOT OF THANOS THAN BE A RESPECTED PART OF THIS GALAXY.
BUT IN THE HOPES OF TRUE GALACTIC PEACE, WE AGREED TO BRING YOU IN AND THIS IS WHAT YOU DO?!
WE TOLD YOU ONE THING: DO NOT TOUCH THE EARTH. AND WHAT HAPPENS?
YOU COULDN'T WAIT FOR EVEN A CYCLE BEFORE YOU CALLED THE ORDER?
I CALLED NO SUCH ORDER.
THEN YOU ARE A TERRIBLE LEADER TO YOUR PEOPLE BECAUSE--
OF THE BADOON--THERE IS A BROTHERHOOD AND THERE IS A SISTERHOOD.
I SPEAK ONLY FOR THE BROTHERHOOD.
THEN YOU BETTER GET YOUR HOUSE IN ORDER OR SOMEONE IS GOING TO TAKE IT FROM YOU.
J-SON, IF THE ORDER WAS GIVEN THAT NO ONE IS TO GO NEAR THE EARTH THEN WHAT WAS YOUR SON, THE STAR-LORD, AND THOSE SO-CALLED GUARDIANS, DOING THERE?

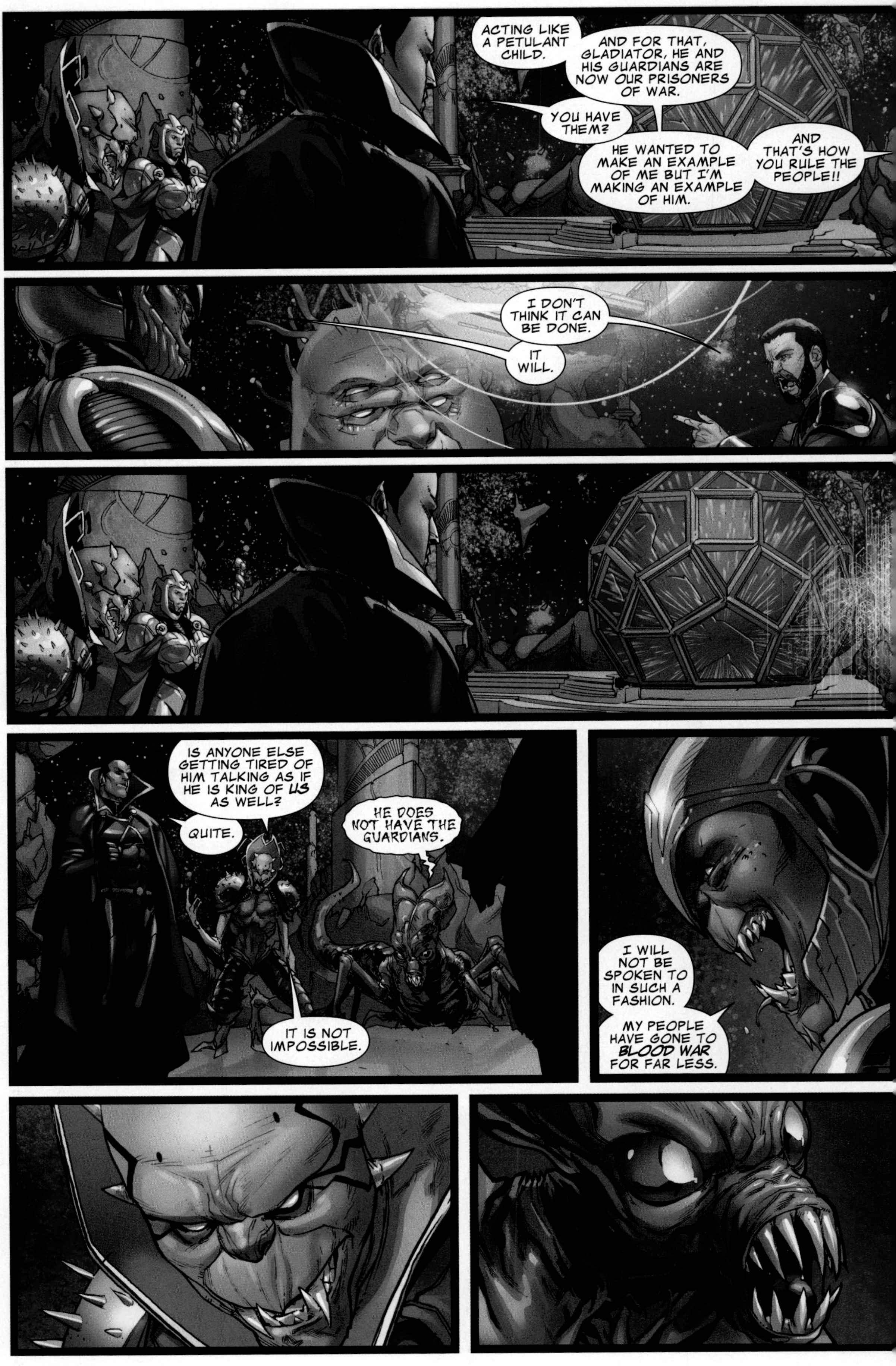
ACTING LIKE A PETULANT CHILD.
AND FOR THAT, GLADIATOR, HE AND HIS GUARDIANS ARE NOW OUR PRISONERS OF WAR.
YOU HAVE THEM?
HE WANTED TO MAKE AN EXAMPLE OF ME BUT I'M MAKING AN EXAMPLE OF HIM.
AND THAT'S HOW YOU RULE THE PEOPLE!!
I DON'T THINK IT CAN BE DONE.
IT WILL.
IS ANYONE ELSE GETTING TIRED OF HIM TALKING AS IF HE IS KING OF *US* AS WELL?
QUITE.
HE DOES NOT HAVE THE GUARDIANS.
IT IS NOT IMPOSSIBLE.
I WILL NOT BE SPOKEN TO IN SUCH A FASHION.
MY PEOPLE HAVE GONE TO ***BLOOD WAR*** FOR FAR LESS.

MAYBE WE NEED TO BROKER AN EXCHANGE BETWEEN THE BROTHERHOOD AND SISTERHOOD OF THE BADOON?

IF YOU WOULD LIKE TO DO THAT, SUPREME INTELLIGENCE, GO RIGHT AHEAD...

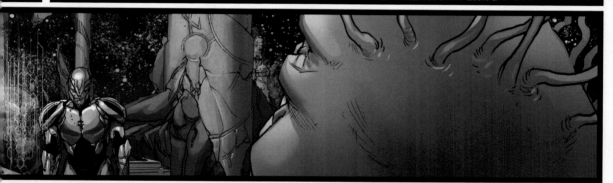

I WILL TAKE THAT AS A PROMISE.

AND THE NEXT TIME WE MEET, THAT PROMISE WILL BE KEPT.

PROVE YOURSELF, Y-GAAAR.

AND PROVE J-SON WRONG...

...AND YOU WILL HAVE ALL OUR RESPECT.

I BELIEVE KING J-SON IS PLAYING A MORE COMPLICATED GAME THAN WE FIRST REALIZED.

I AM ALMOST CERTAIN OF IT.

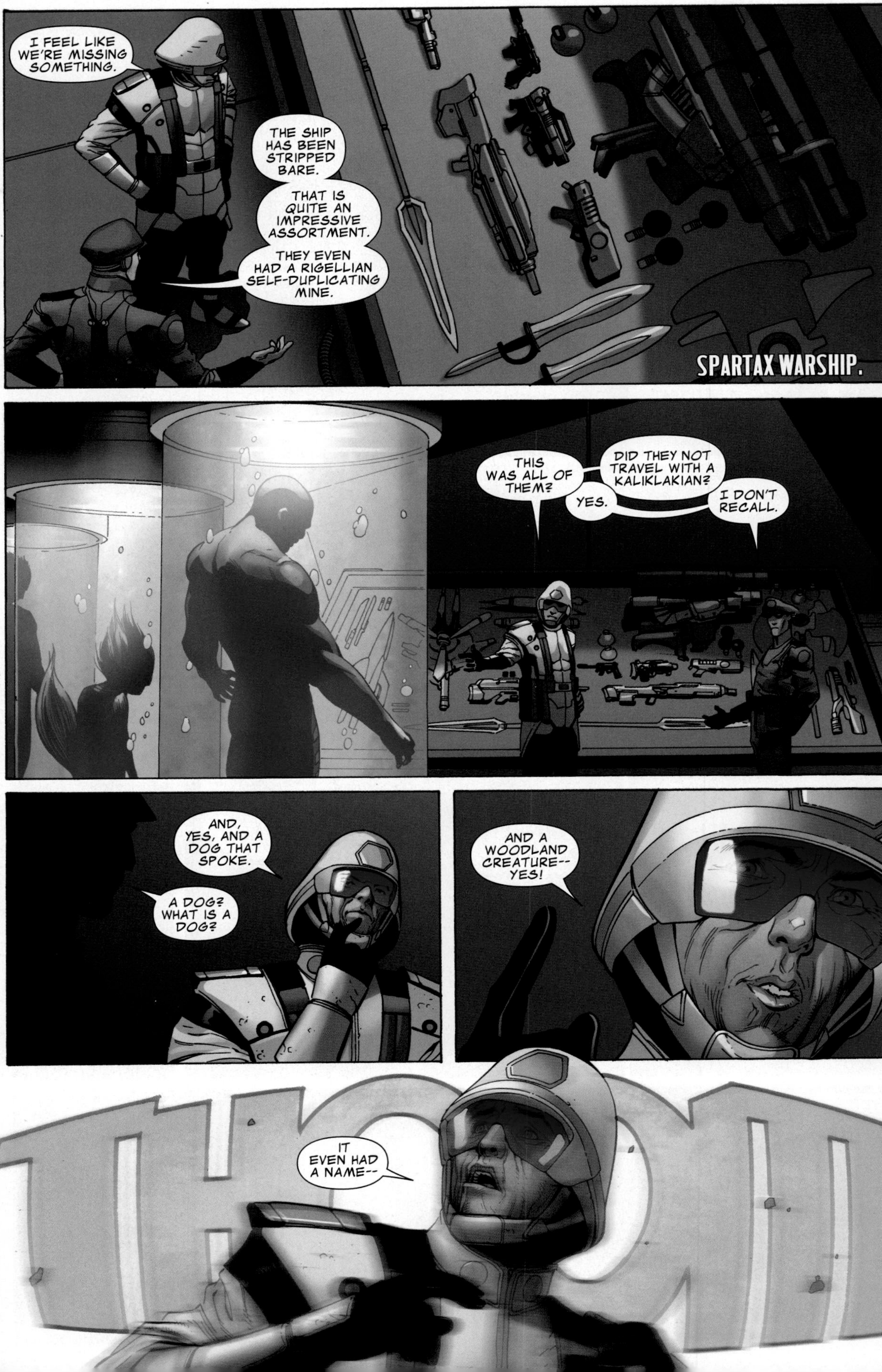
I FEEL LIKE WE'RE MISSING SOMETHING.
THE SHIP HAS BEEN STRIPPED BARE.
THAT IS QUITE AN IMPRESSIVE ASSORTMENT.
THEY EVEN HAD A RIGELLIAN SELF-DUPLICATING MINE.
SPARTAX WARSHIP.
THIS WAS ALL OF THEM?
DID THEY NOT TRAVEL WITH A KALIKLAKIAN?
YES.
I DON'T RECALL.
AND, YES, AND A DOG THAT SPOKE.
A DOG? WHAT IS A DOG?
AND A WOODLAND CREATURE-- YES!
IT EVEN HAD A NAME--

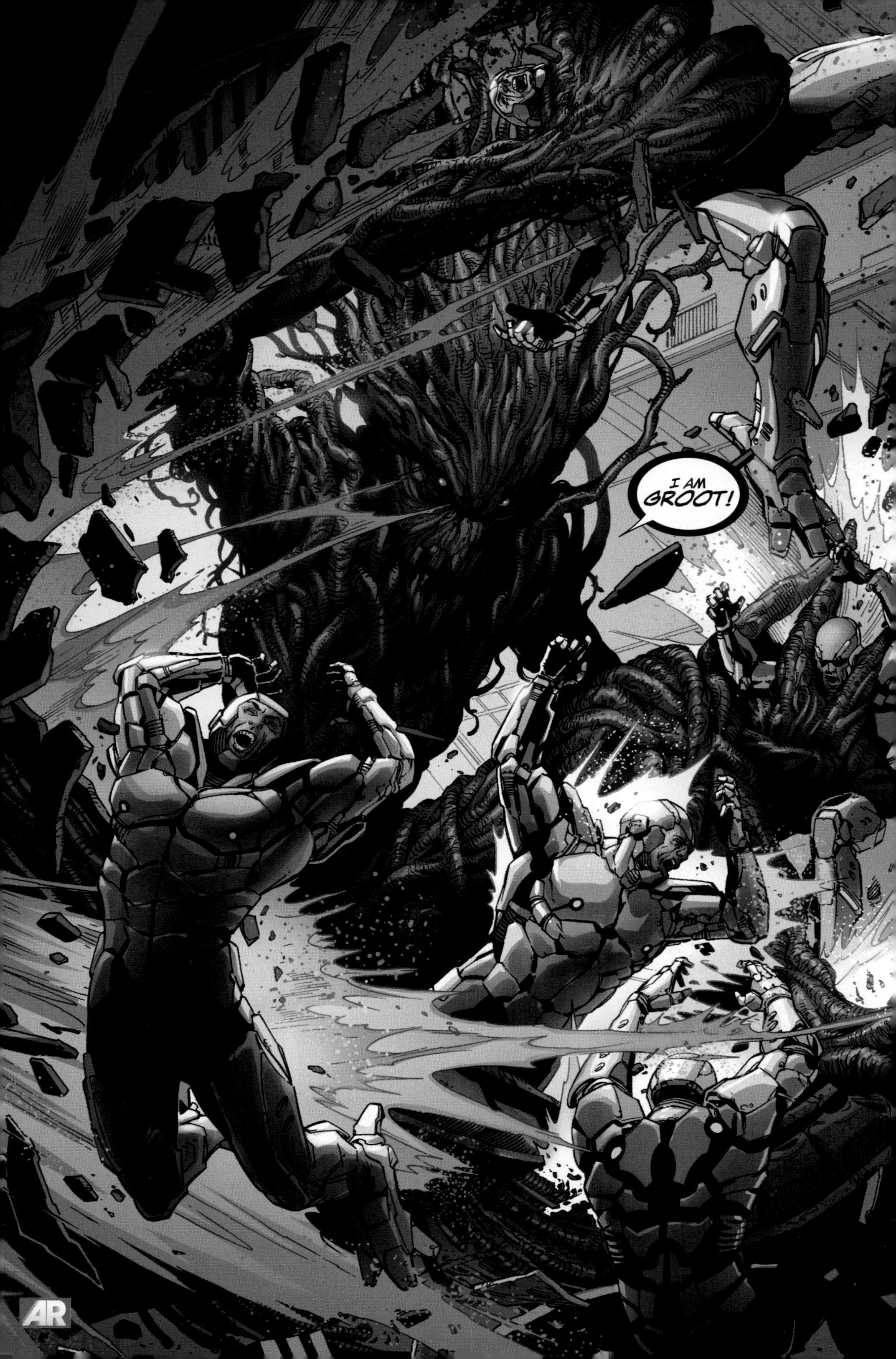
I AM GROOT!

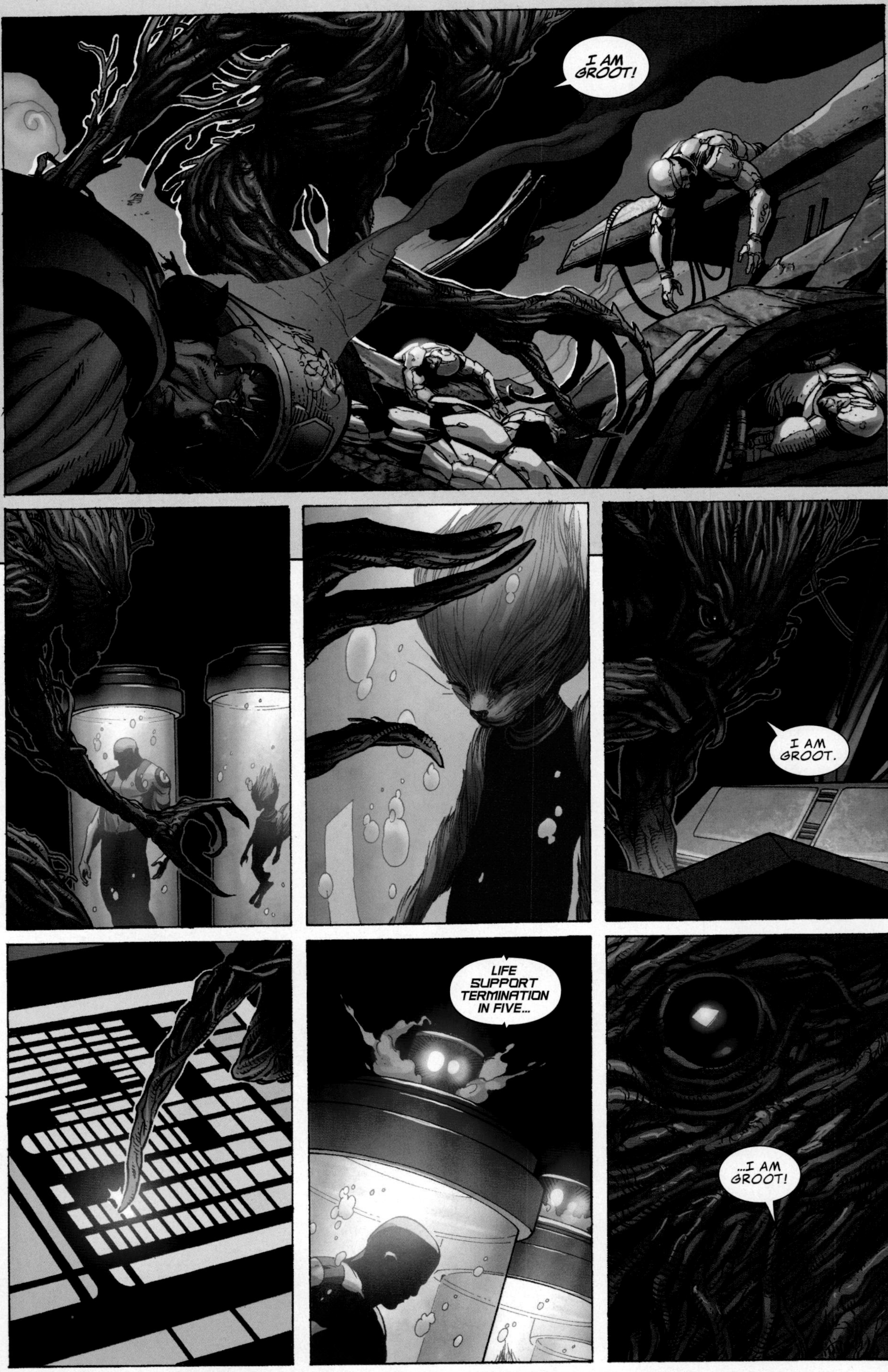
I AM GROOT!
I AM GROOT.
LIFE SUPPORT TERMINATION IN FIVE...
...I AM GROOT!

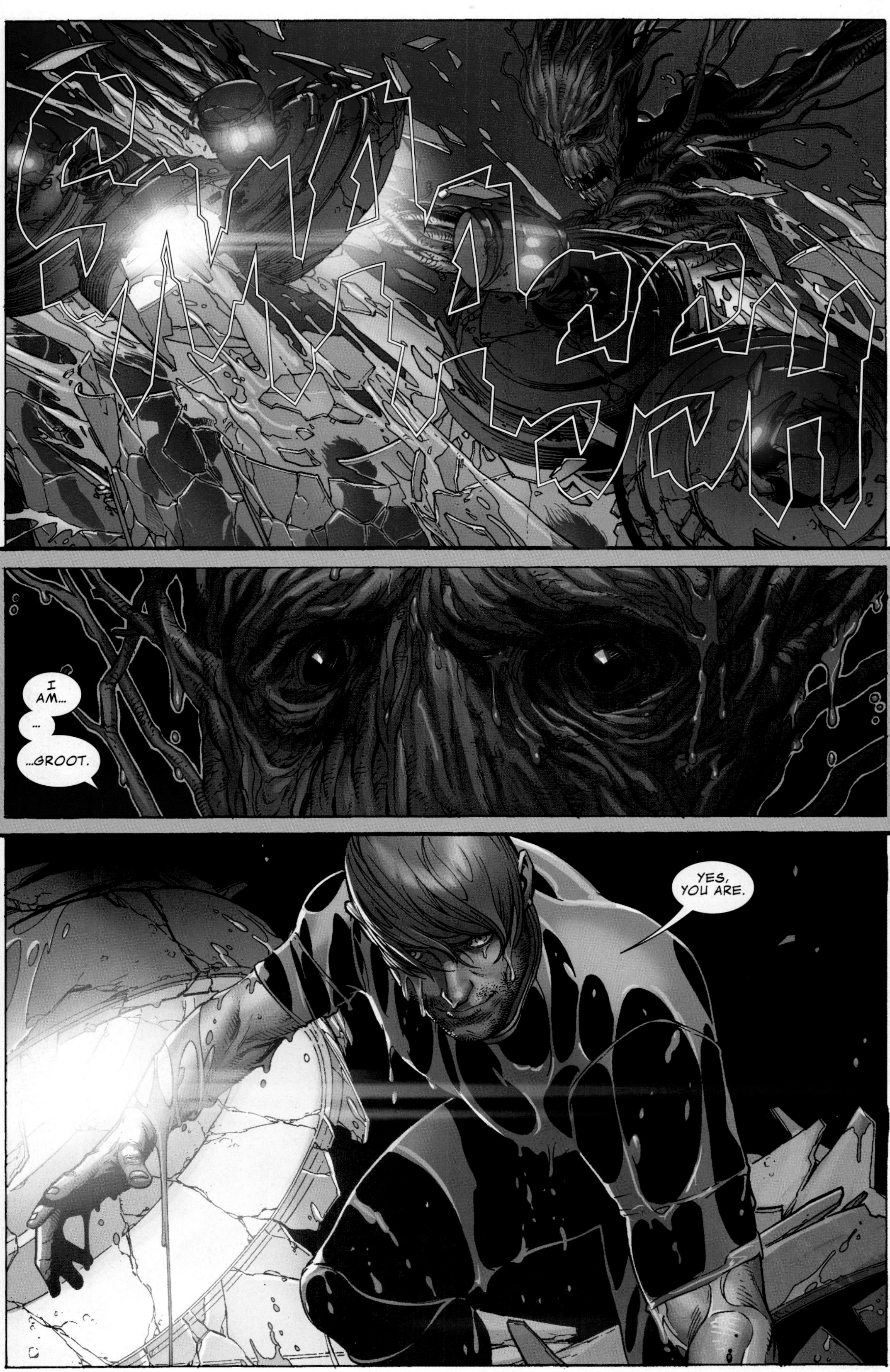
I AM...
...
...GROOT.
YES, YOU ARE.

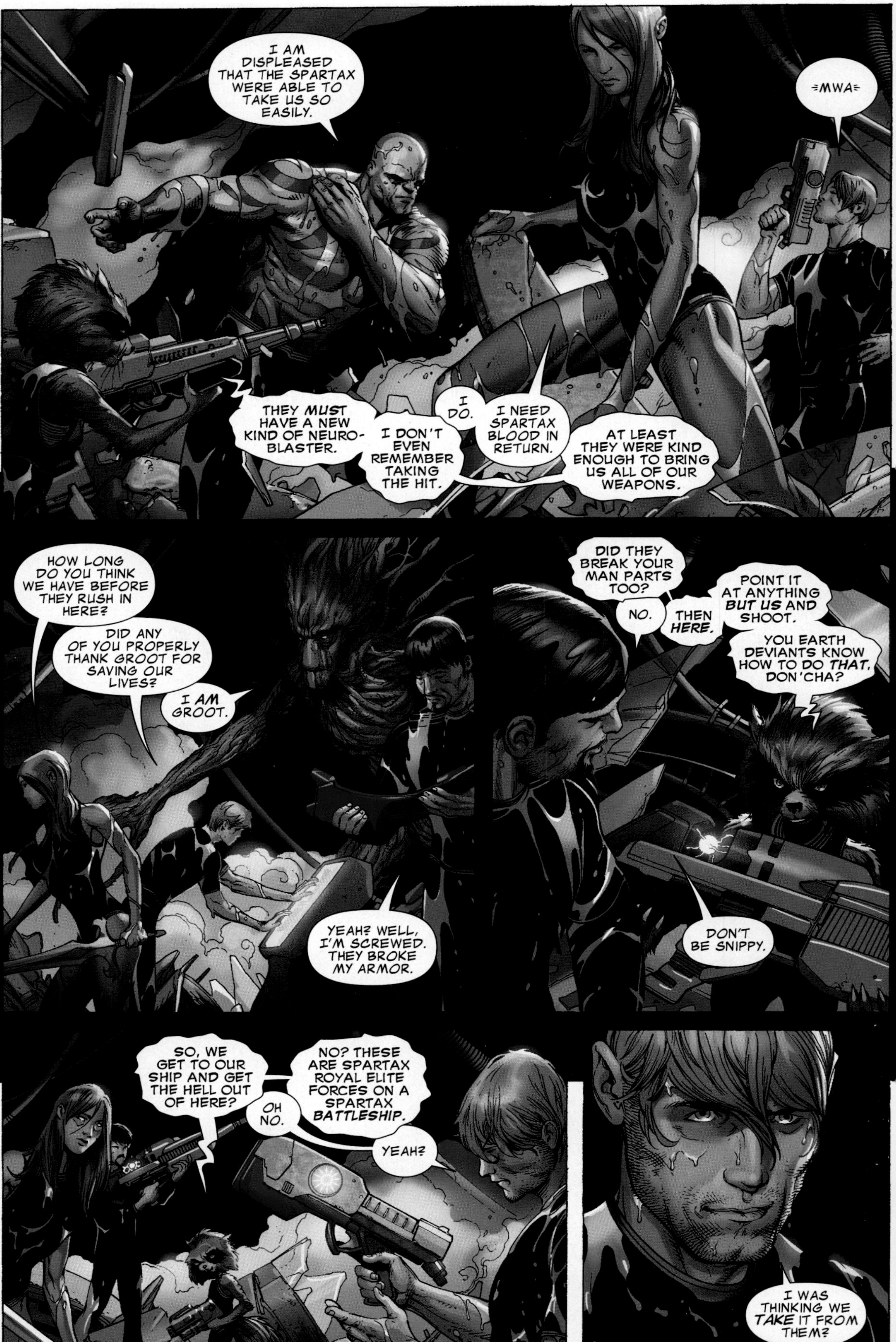
I AM DISPLEASED THAT THE SPARTAX WERE ABLE TO TAKE US SO EASILY.
=MWA=
THEY MUST HAVE A NEW KIND OF NEURO-BLASTER.
I DON'T EVEN REMEMBER TAKING THE HIT.
I DO.
I NEED SPARTAX BLOOD IN RETURN.
AT LEAST THEY WERE KIND ENOUGH TO BRING US ALL OF OUR WEAPONS.
HOW LONG DO YOU THINK WE HAVE BEFORE THEY RUSH IN HERE?
DID ANY OF YOU PROPERLY THANK GROOT FOR SAVING OUR LIVES?
I AM GROOT.
YEAH? WELL, I'M SCREWED. THEY BROKE MY ARMOR.
DID THEY BREAK YOUR MAN PARTS TOO?
NO.
THEN HERE.
POINT IT AT ANYTHING BUT US AND SHOOT.
YOU EARTH DEVIANTS KNOW HOW TO DO THAT, DON'CHA?
DON'T BE SNIPPY.
SO, WE GET TO OUR SHIP AND GET THE HELL OUT OF HERE?
OH NO.
NO? THESE ARE SPARTAX ROYAL ELITE FORCES ON A SPARTAX BATTLESHIP.
YEAH?
I WAS THINKING WE TAKE IT FROM THEM?

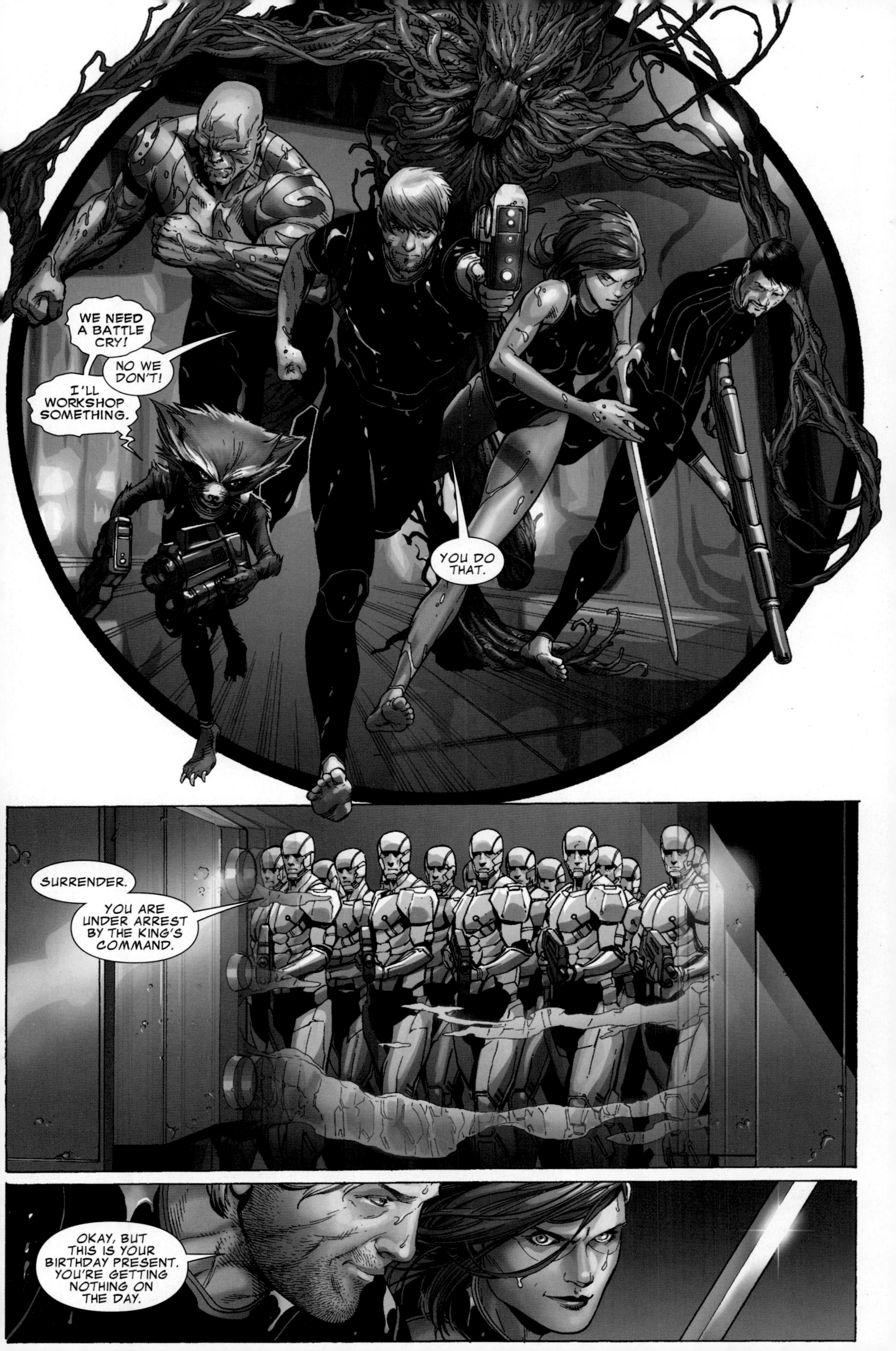
WE NEED A BATTLE CRY!
NO WE DON'T!
I'LL WORKSHOP SOMETHING.
YOU DO THAT.
SURRENDER.
YOU ARE UNDER ARREST BY THE KING'S COMMAND.
OKAY, BUT THIS IS YOUR BIRTHDAY PRESENT. YOU'RE GETTING NOTHING ON THE DAY.

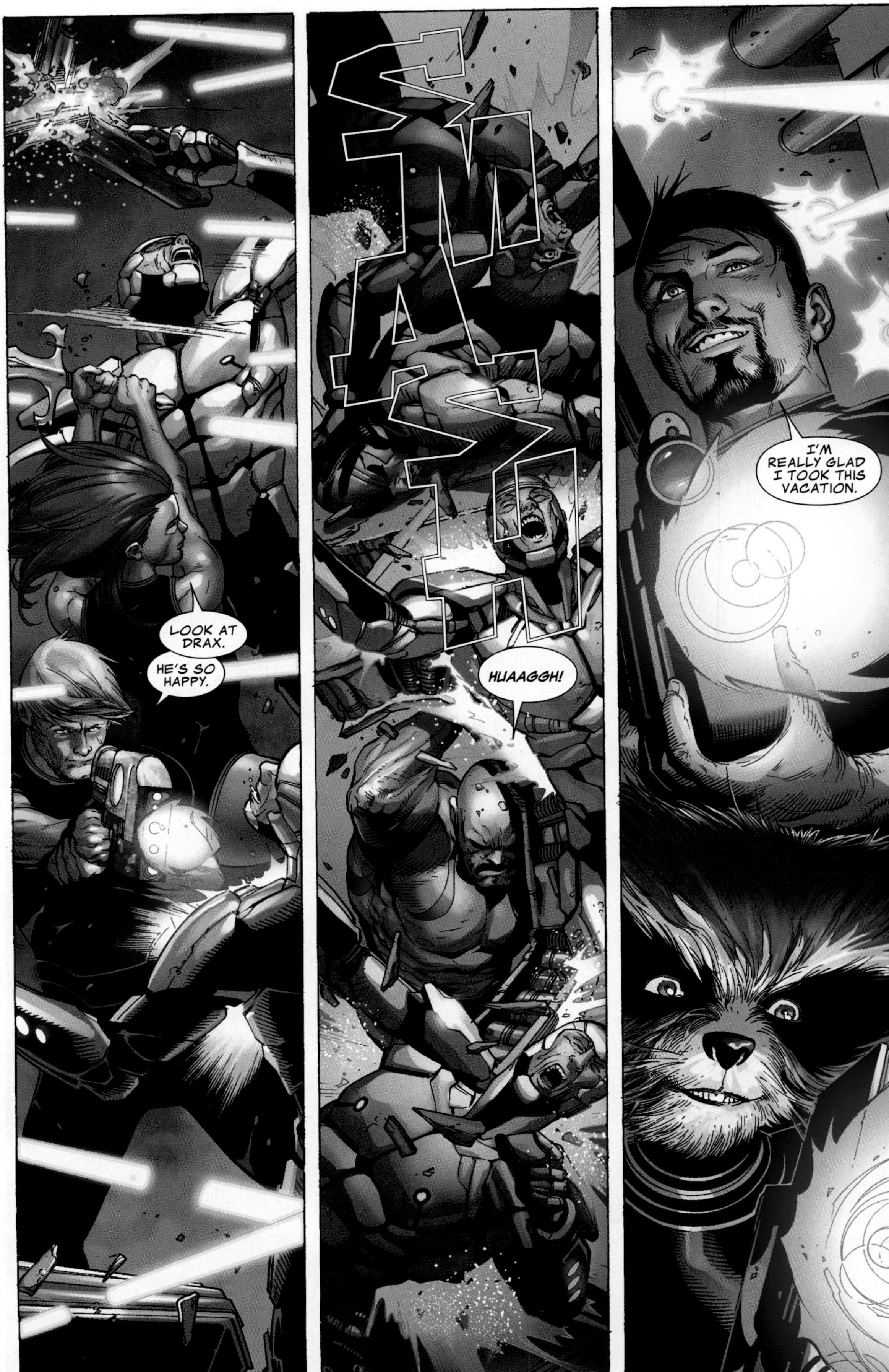
LOOK AT DRAX.
HE'S SO HAPPY.
SMASH
HUAAGGH!
I'M REALLY GLAD I TOOK THIS VACATION.

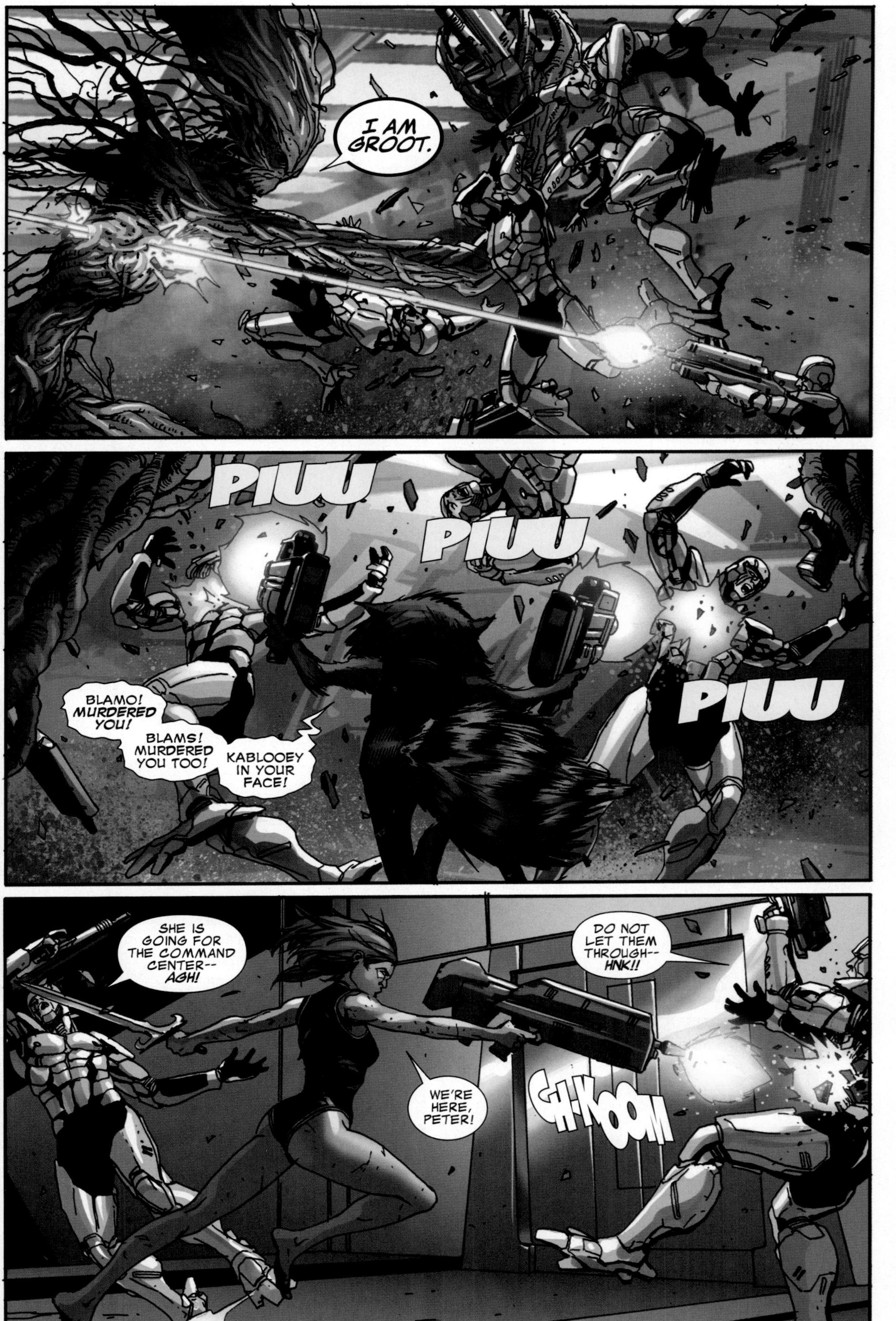
I AM GROOT.
PIUU
PIUU
BLAMO! MURDERED YOU!
BLAMS! MURDERED YOU TOO!
KABLOOEY IN YOUR FACE!
PIUU
SHE IS GOING FOR THE COMMAND CENTER-- AGH!
DO NOT LET THEM THROUGH-- HNK!!
WE'RE HERE, PETER!
CH-KOOM

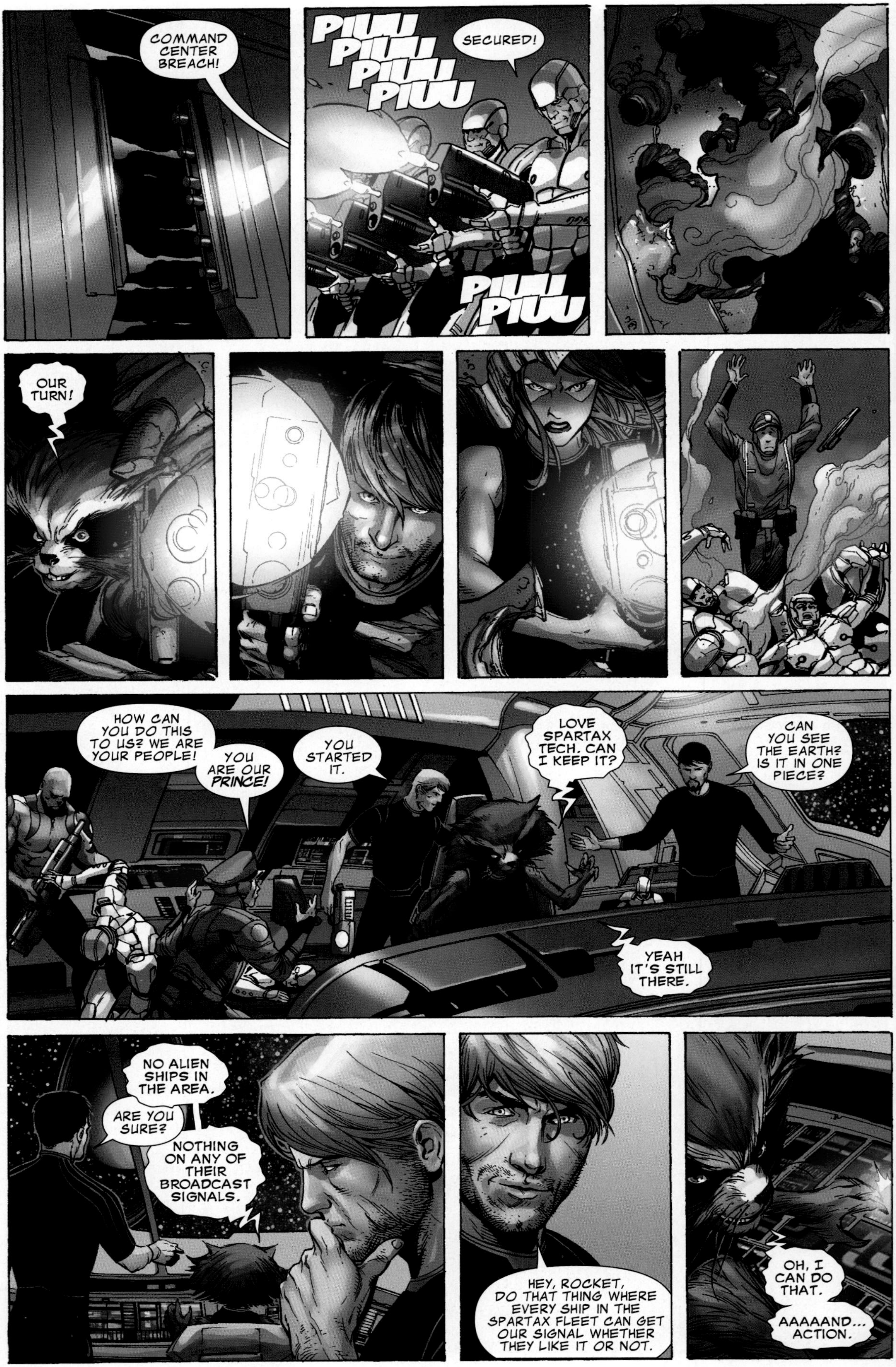
COMMAND CENTER BREACH!
PIUU PIUU PIUU PIUU
SECURED!
PIUU PIUU
OUR TURN!
HOW CAN YOU DO THIS TO US? WE ARE YOUR PEOPLE!
YOU ARE OUR PRINCE!
YOU STARTED IT.
LOVE SPARTAX TECH. CAN I KEEP IT?
CAN YOU SEE THE EARTH? IS IT IN ONE PIECE?
YEAH IT'S STILL THERE.
NO ALIEN SHIPS IN THE AREA.
ARE YOU SURE?
NOTHING ON ANY OF THEIR BROADCAST SIGNALS.
HEY, ROCKET, DO THAT THING WHERE EVERY SHIP IN THE SPARTAX FLEET CAN GET OUR SIGNAL WHETHER THEY LIKE IT OR NOT.
OH, I CAN DO THAT.
AAAAAND... ACTION.

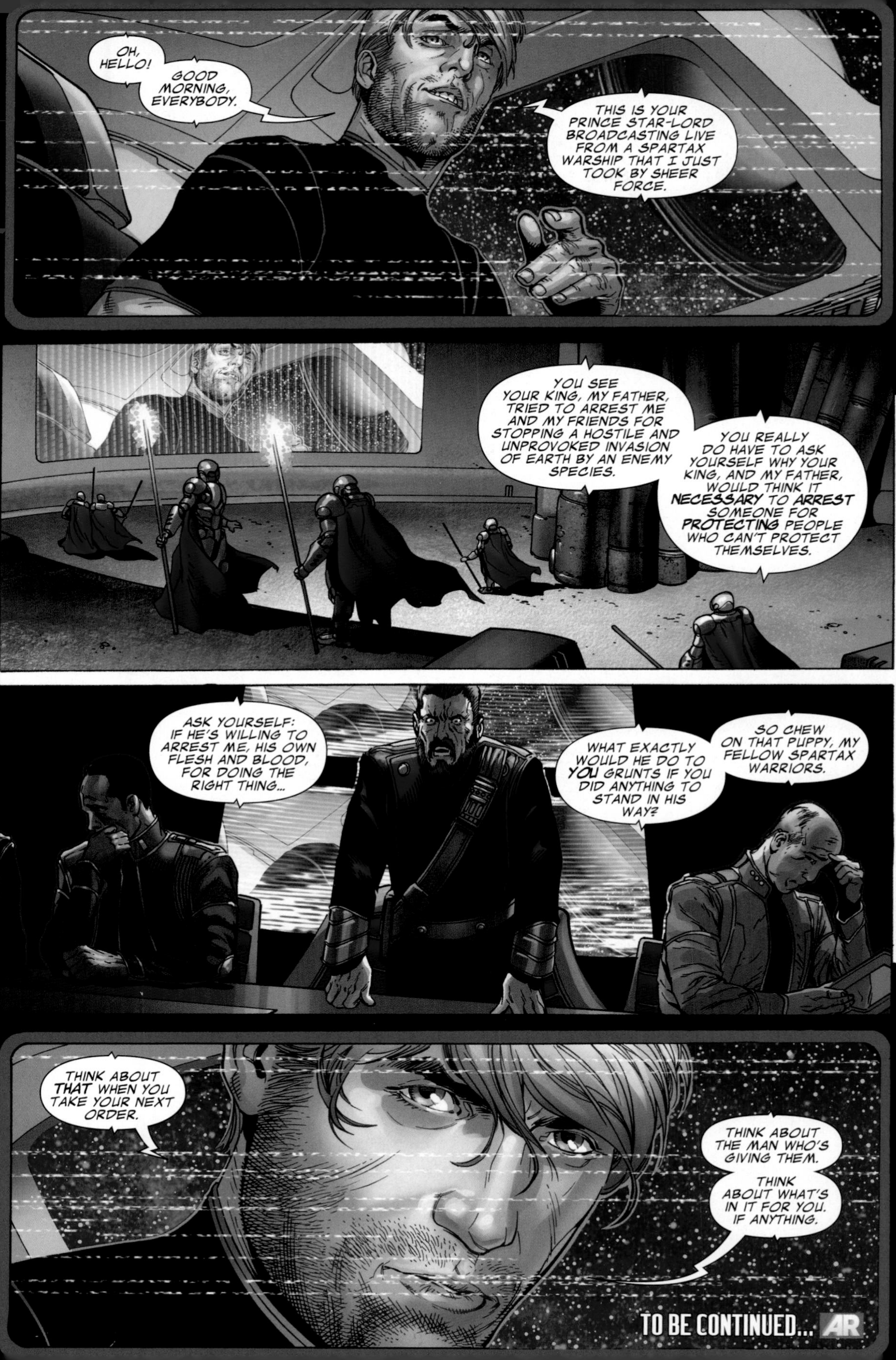
OH, HELLO!
GOOD MORNING, EVERYBODY.
THIS IS YOUR PRINCE STAR-LORD BROADCASTING LIVE FROM A SPARTAX WARSHIP THAT I JUST TOOK BY SHEER FORCE.
YOU SEE YOUR KING, MY FATHER, TRIED TO ARREST ME AND MY FRIENDS FOR STOPPING A HOSTILE AND UNPROVOKED INVASION OF EARTH BY AN ENEMY SPECIES.
YOU REALLY DO HAVE TO ASK YOURSELF WHY YOUR KING, AND MY FATHER, WOULD THINK IT NECESSARY TO ARREST SOMEONE FOR PROTECTING PEOPLE WHO CAN'T PROTECT THEMSELVES.
ASK YOURSELF: IF HE'S WILLING TO ARREST ME, HIS OWN FLESH AND BLOOD, FOR DOING THE RIGHT THING...
WHAT EXACTLY WOULD HE DO TO YOU GRUNTS IF YOU DID ANYTHING TO STAND IN HIS WAY?
SO CHEW ON THAT PUPPY, MY FELLOW SPARTAX WARRIORS.
THINK ABOUT THAT WHEN YOU TAKE YOUR NEXT ORDER.
THINK ABOUT THE MAN WHO'S GIVING THEM.
THINK ABOUT WHAT'S IN IT FOR YOU. IF ANYTHING.
TO BE CONTINUED...

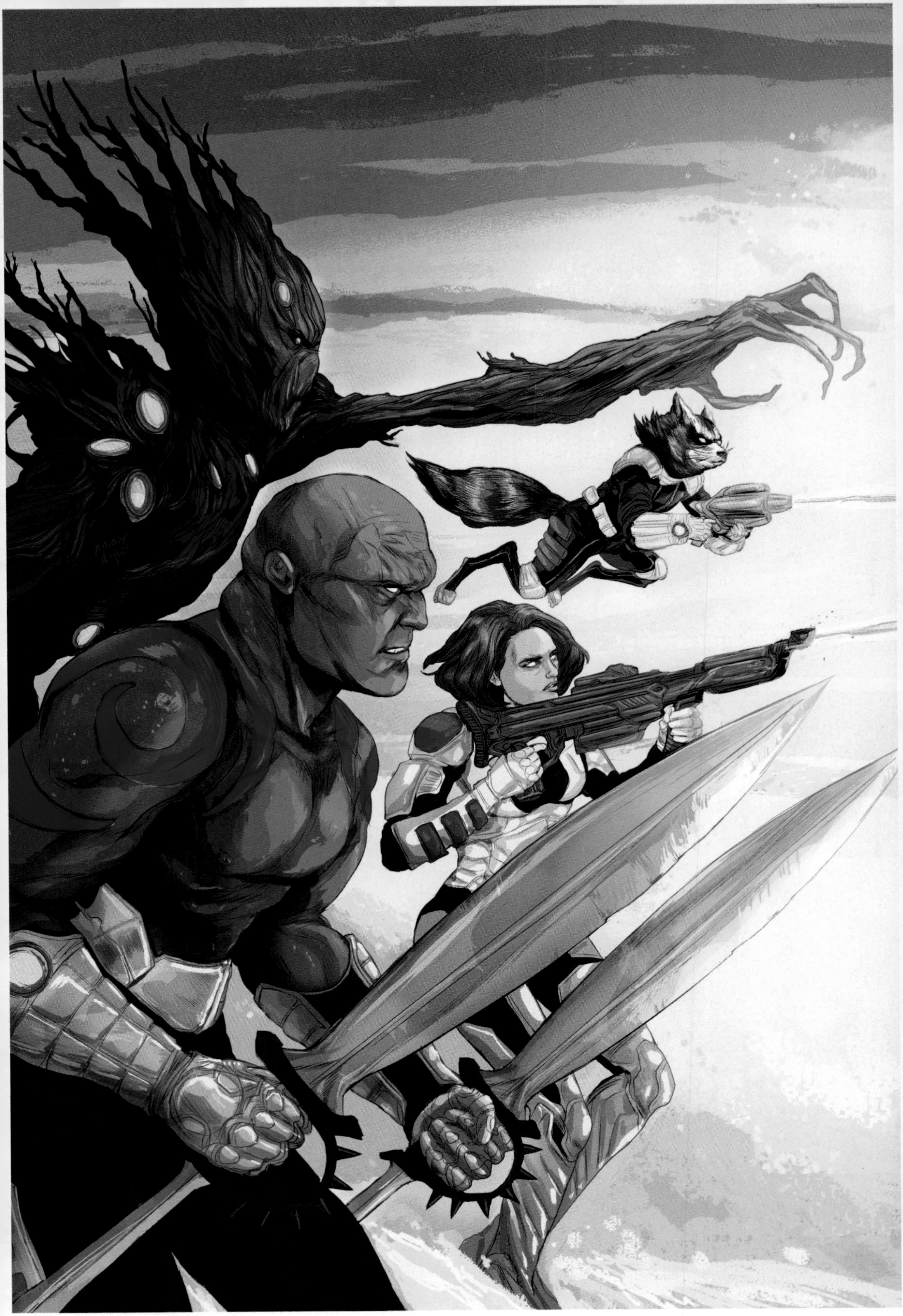

GUARDIANS OF THE GALAXY: TOMORROW'S AVENGERS #1

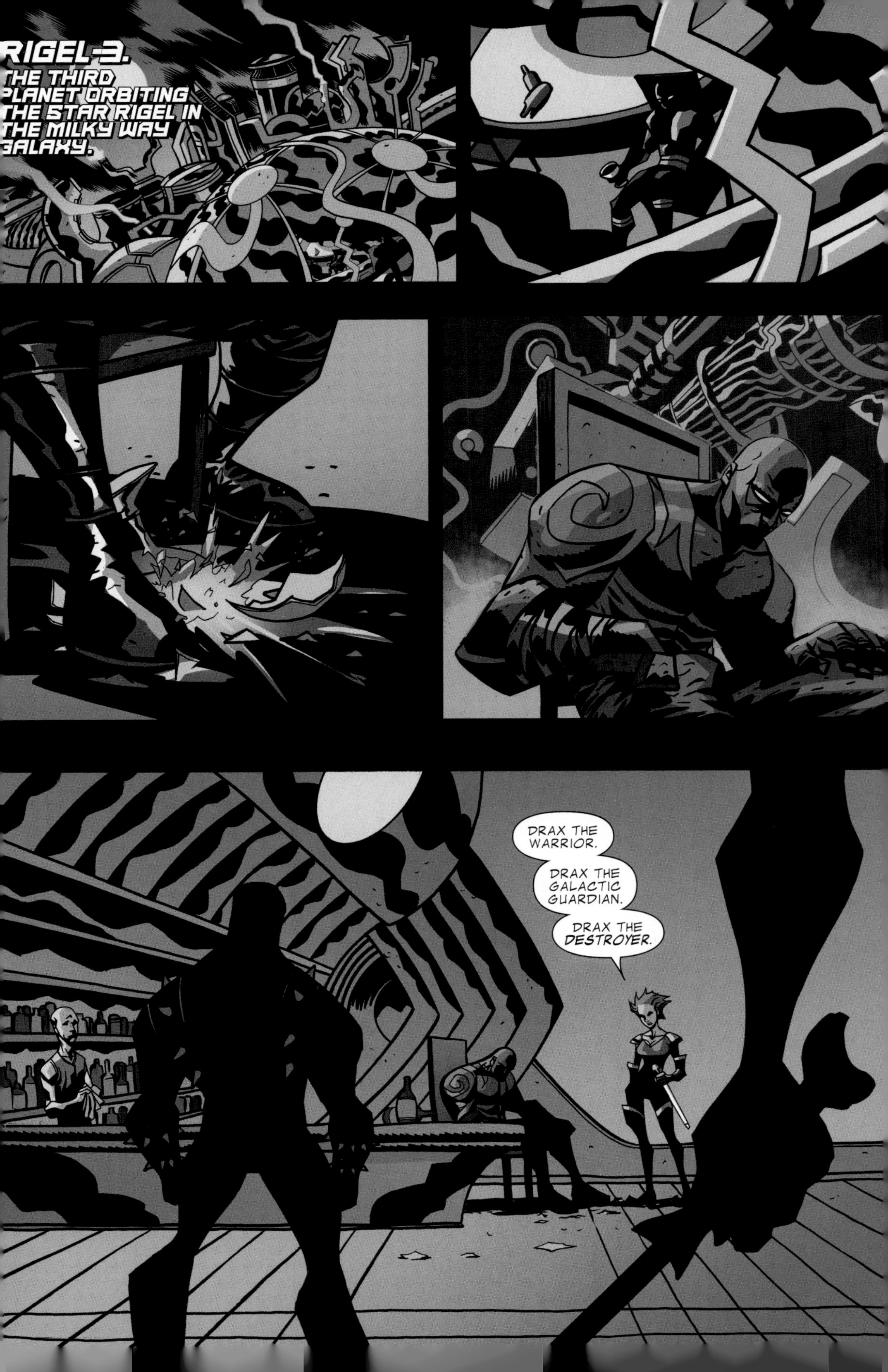
RIGEL-3.
THE THIRD PLANET ORBITING THE STAR RIGEL IN THE MILKY WAY GALAXY.
DRAX THE WARRIOR.
DRAX THE GALACTIC GUARDIAN.
DRAX THE DESTROYER.

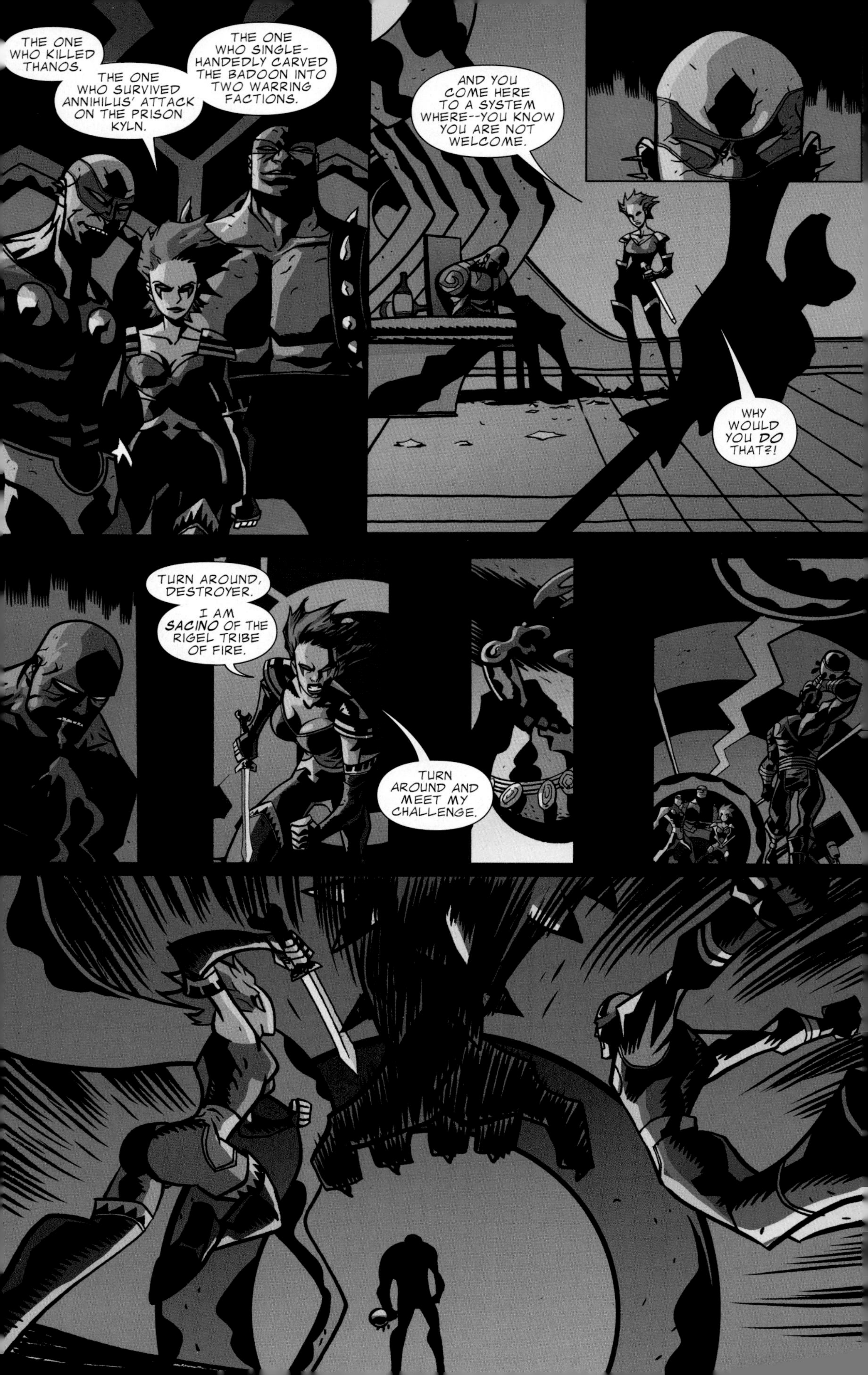
THE ONE WHO KILLED THANOS.
THE ONE WHO SURVIVED ANNIHILUS' ATTACK ON THE PRISON KYLN.
THE ONE WHO SINGLE-HANDEDLY CARVED THE BADOON INTO TWO WARRING FACTIONS.
AND YOU COME HERE TO A SYSTEM WHERE--YOU KNOW YOU ARE NOT WELCOME.
WHY WOULD YOU DO THAT?!
TURN AROUND, DESTROYER.
I AM SACINO OF THE RIGEL TRIBE OF FIRE.
TURN AROUND AND MEET MY CHALLENGE.

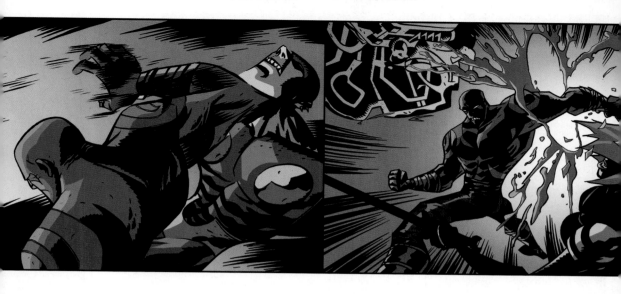

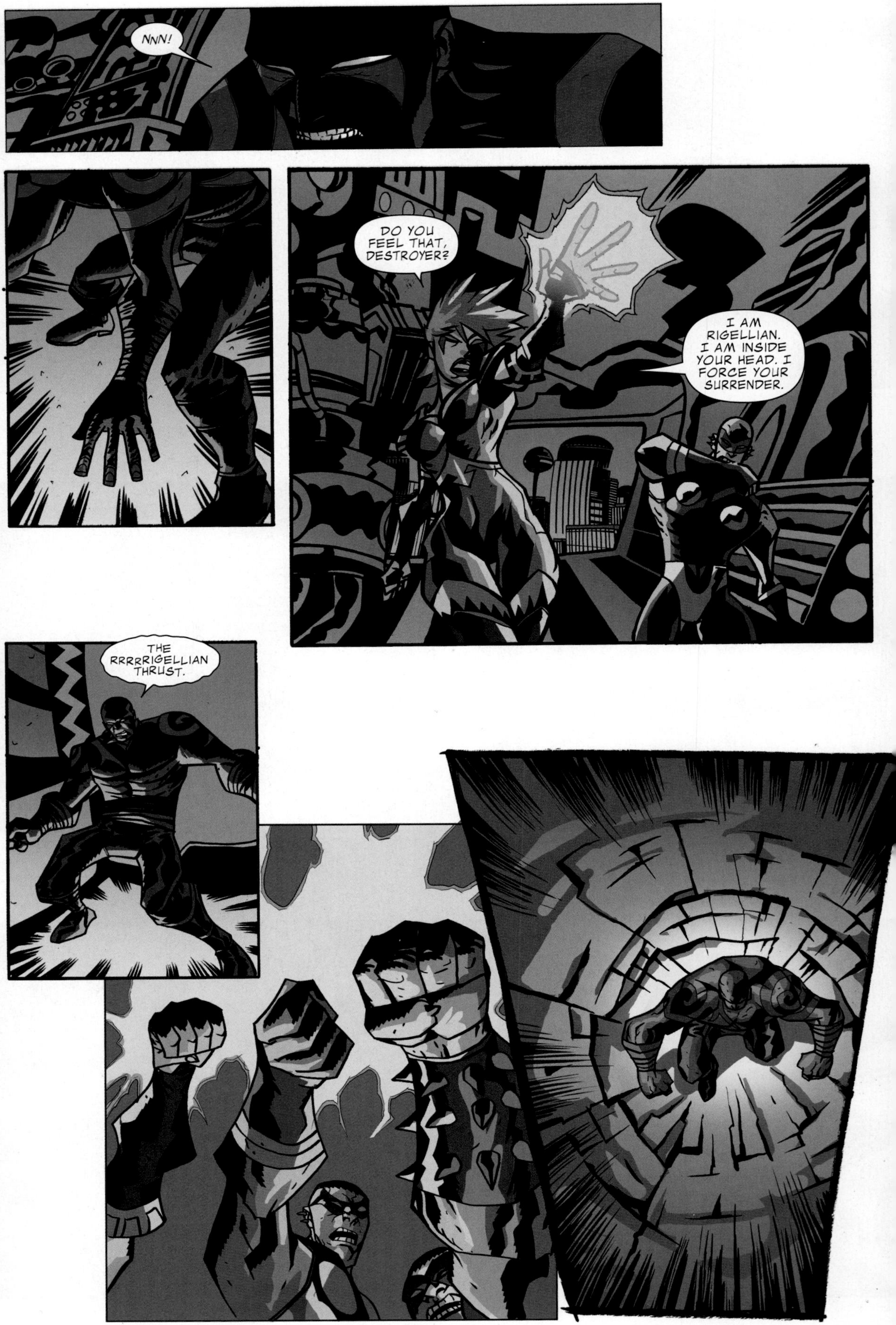
NNN!
DO YOU FEEL THAT, DESTROYER?
I AM RIGELLIAN. I AM INSIDE YOUR HEAD. I FORCE YOUR SURRENDER.
THE RRRRRIGELLIAN THRUST.

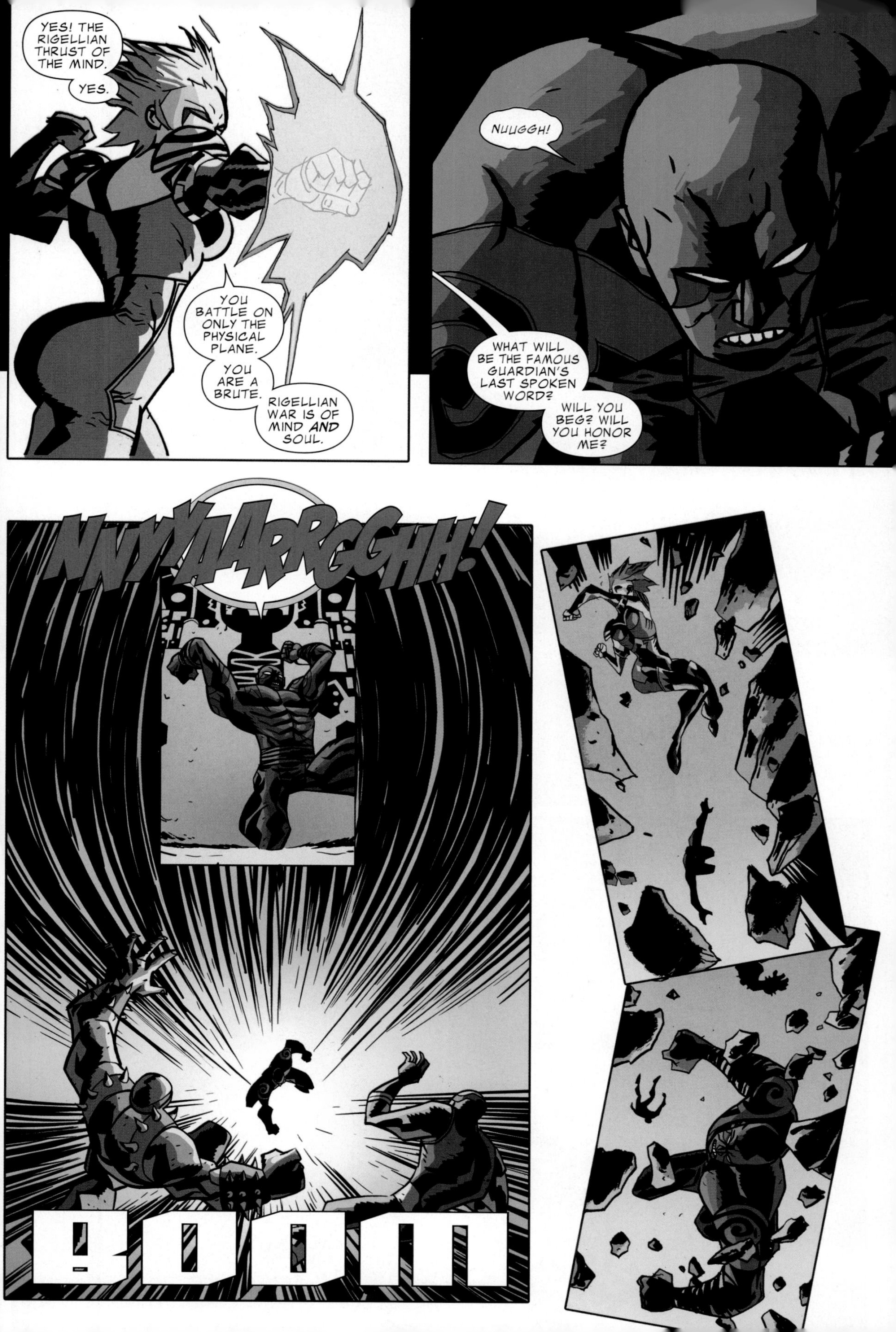
YES! THE RIGELLIAN THRUST OF THE MIND.
YES.
YOU BATTLE ON ONLY THE PHYSICAL PLANE.
YOU ARE A BRUTE.
RIGELLIAN WAR IS OF MIND AND SOUL.
NUUGGH!
WHAT WILL BE THE FAMOUS GUARDIAN'S LAST SPOKEN WORD?
WILL YOU BEG? WILL YOU HONOR ME?
NNYYAARRGGHH!
BOOM

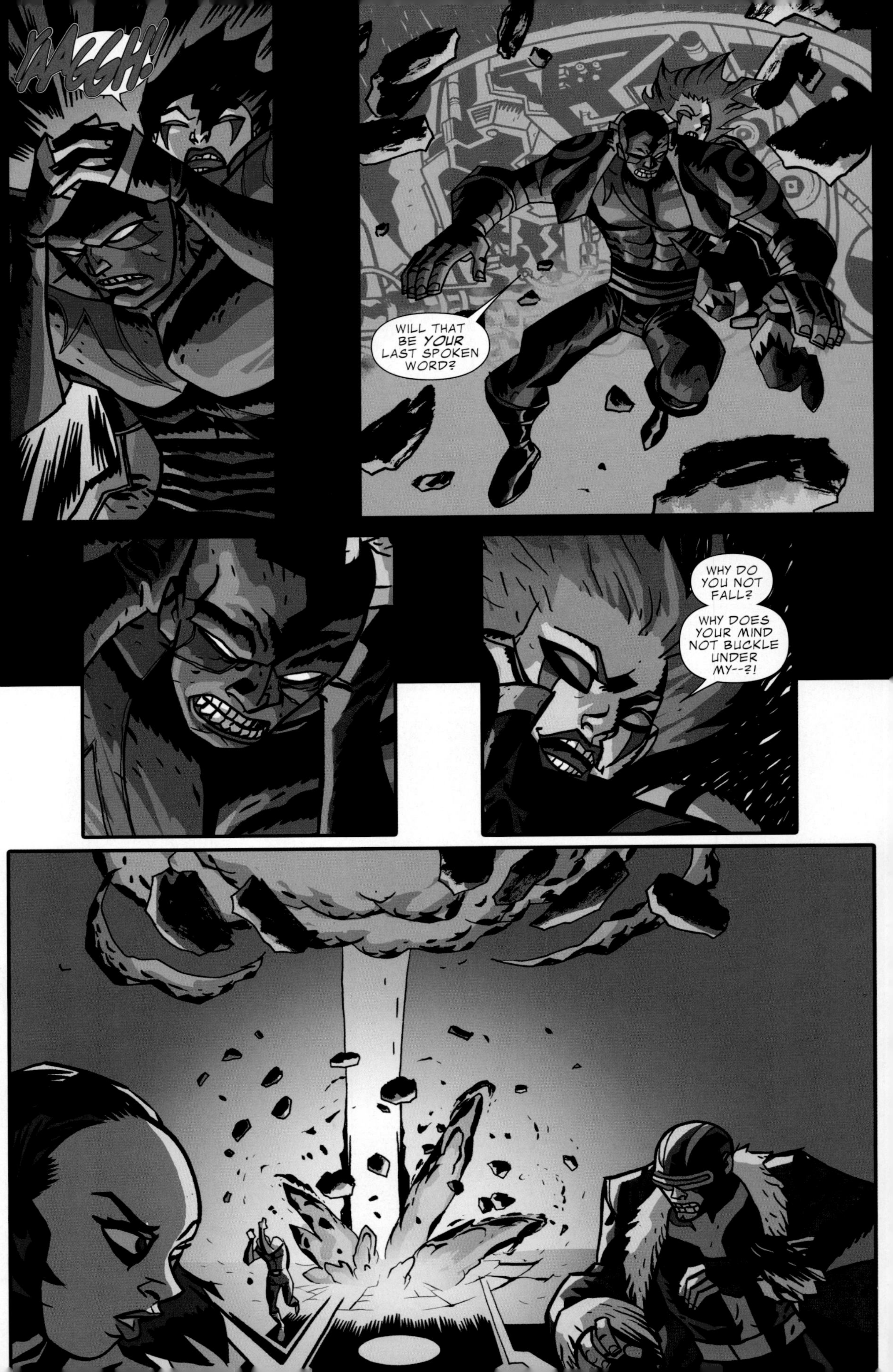
YAAGGH!
WILL THAT BE YOUR LAST SPOKEN WORD?
WHY DO YOU NOT FALL?
WHY DOES YOUR MIND NOT BUCKLE UNDER MY--?!

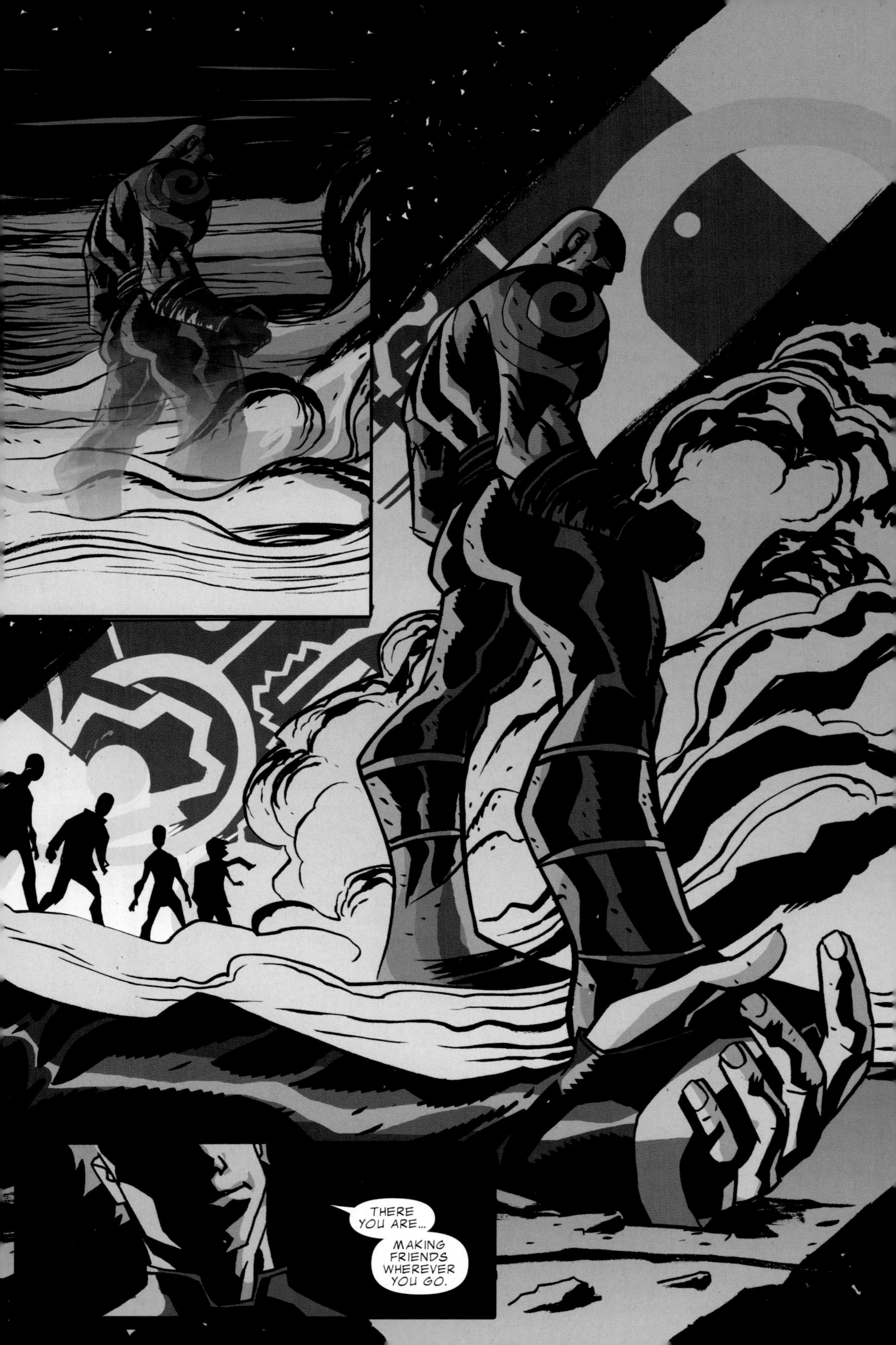
THERE YOU ARE...
MAKING FRIENDS WHEREVER YOU GO.

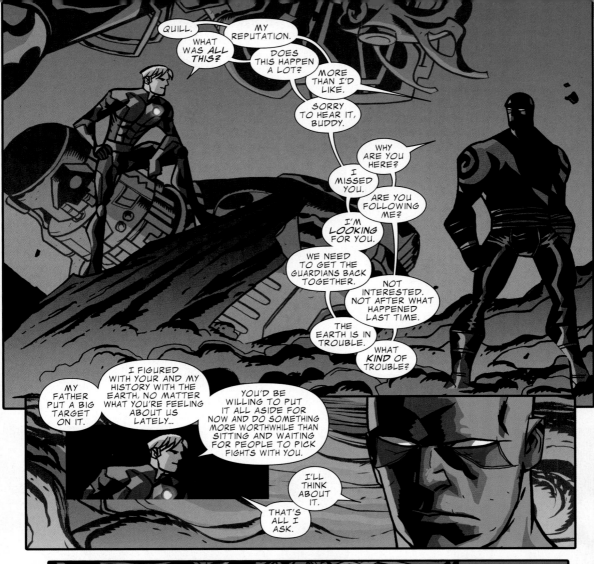

QUILL. WHAT WAS *ALL* THIS?

MY REPUTATION.

DOES THIS HAPPEN A LOT?

MORE THAN I'D LIKE.

SORRY TO HEAR IT, BUDDY.

WHY ARE YOU HERE?

I MISSED YOU.

ARE YOU FOLLOWING ME?

I'M *LOOKING* FOR YOU.

WE NEED TO GET THE GUARDIANS BACK TOGETHER.

NOT INTERESTED. NOT AFTER WHAT HAPPENED LAST TIME.

THE EARTH IS IN TROUBLE.

WHAT *KIND* OF TROUBLE?

MY FATHER PUT A BIG TARGET ON IT.

I FIGURED WITH YOUR AND MY HISTORY WITH THE EARTH, NO MATTER WHAT YOU'RE FEELING ABOUT US LATELY...

YOU'D BE WILLING TO PUT IT ALL ASIDE FOR NOW AND DO SOMETHING MORE WORTHWHILE THAN SITTING AND WAITING FOR PEOPLE TO PICK FIGHTS WITH YOU.

I'LL THINK ABOUT IT.

THAT'S ALL I ASK.

ARE YOU DONE THINKING ABOUT IT?

IS IT WORTH-WHILE?

IT IS TO US. AND THE EARTH.

GIVE ME SOMETHING WORTHWHILE TO DO, QUILL.

JUST PROMISE ME IT'LL BE WORTH-WHILE.

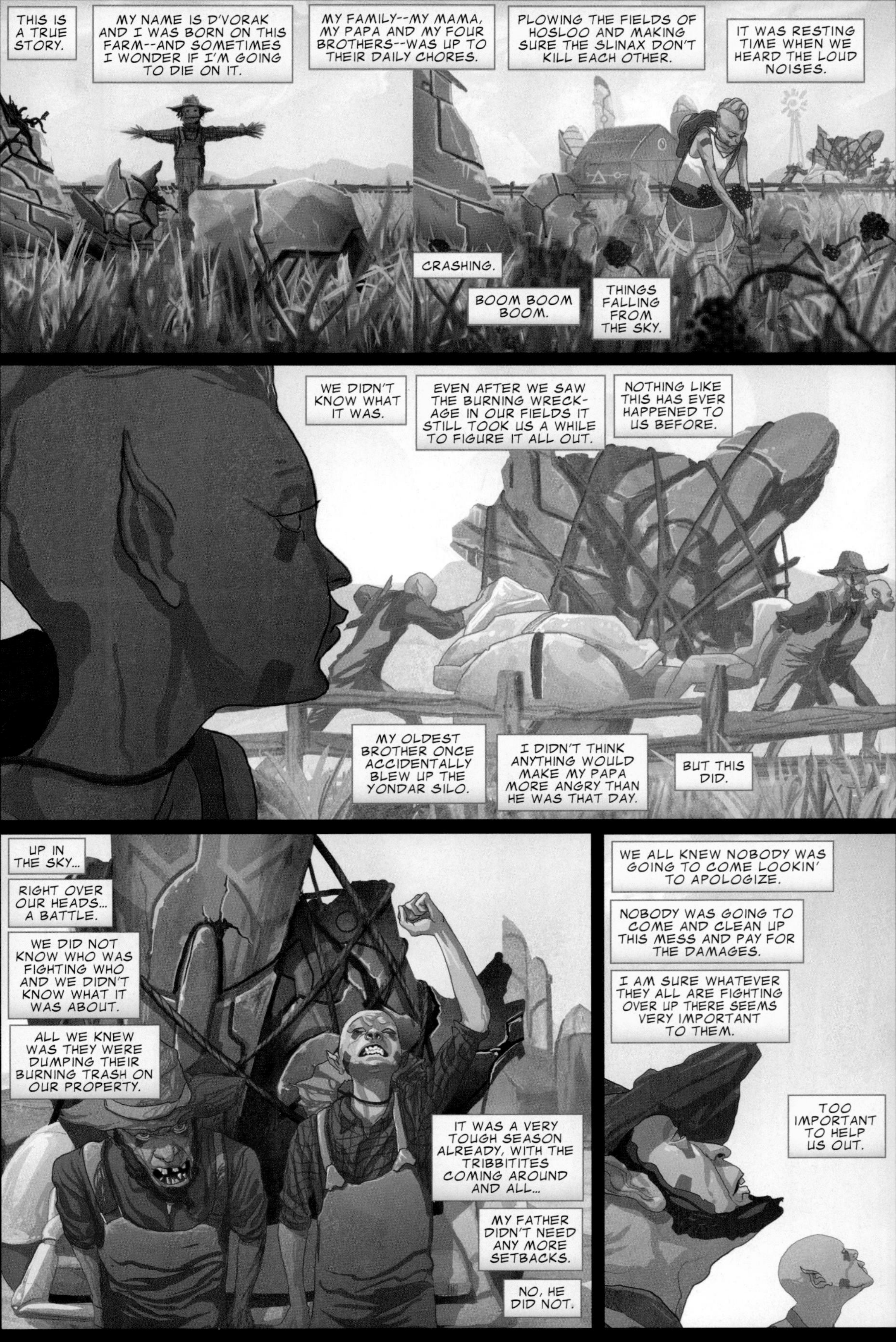
THIS IS A TRUE STORY.
MY NAME IS D'VORAK AND I WAS BORN ON THIS FARM--AND SOMETIMES I WONDER IF I'M GOING TO DIE ON IT.
MY FAMILY--MY MAMA, MY PAPA AND MY FOUR BROTHERS--WAS UP TO THEIR DAILY CHORES.
PLOWING THE FIELDS OF HOSLOO AND MAKING SURE THE SLINAX DON'T KILL EACH OTHER.
IT WAS RESTING TIME WHEN WE HEARD THE LOUD NOISES.
CRASHING.
BOOM BOOM BOOM.
THINGS FALLING FROM THE SKY.
WE DIDN'T KNOW WHAT IT WAS.
EVEN AFTER WE SAW THE BURNING WRECK-AGE IN OUR FIELDS IT STILL TOOK US A WHILE TO FIGURE IT ALL OUT.
NOTHING LIKE THIS HAS EVER HAPPENED TO US BEFORE.
MY OLDEST BROTHER ONCE ACCIDENTALLY BLEW UP THE YONDAR SILO.
I DIDN'T THINK ANYTHING WOULD MAKE MY PAPA MORE ANGRY THAN HE WAS THAT DAY.
BUT THIS DID.
UP IN THE SKY...
RIGHT OVER OUR HEADS... A BATTLE.
WE DID NOT KNOW WHO WAS FIGHTING WHO AND WE DIDN'T KNOW WHAT IT WAS ABOUT.
ALL WE KNEW WAS THEY WERE DUMPING THEIR BURNING TRASH ON OUR PROPERTY.
IT WAS A VERY TOUGH SEASON ALREADY, WITH THE TRIBBITITES COMING AROUND AND ALL...
MY FATHER DIDN'T NEED ANY MORE SETBACKS.
NO, HE DID NOT.
WE ALL KNEW NOBODY WAS GOING TO COME LOOKIN' TO APOLOGIZE.
NOBODY WAS GOING TO COME AND CLEAN UP THIS MESS AND PAY FOR THE DAMAGES.
I AM SURE WHATEVER THEY ALL ARE FIGHTING OVER UP THERE SEEMS VERY IMPORTANT TO THEM.
TOO IMPORTANT TO HELP US OUT.

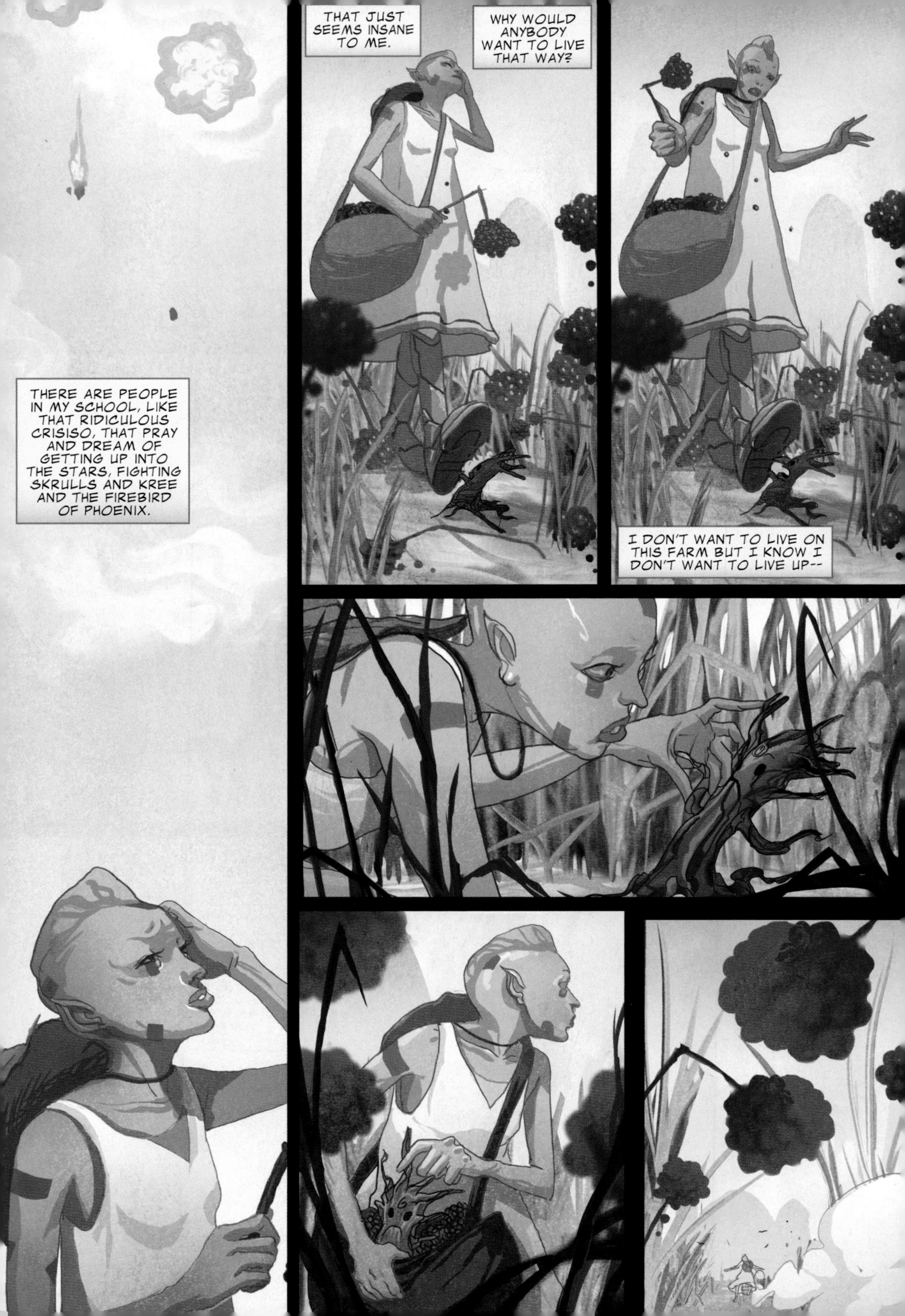
THERE ARE PEOPLE IN MY SCHOOL, LIKE THAT RIDICULOUS CRISISO, THAT PRAY AND DREAM OF GETTING UP INTO THE STARS, FIGHTING SKRULLS AND KREE AND THE FIREBIRD OF PHOENIX.
THAT JUST SEEMS INSANE TO ME.
WHY WOULD ANYBODY WANT TO LIVE THAT WAY?
I DON'T WANT TO LIVE ON THIS FARM BUT I KNOW I DON'T WANT TO LIVE UP--

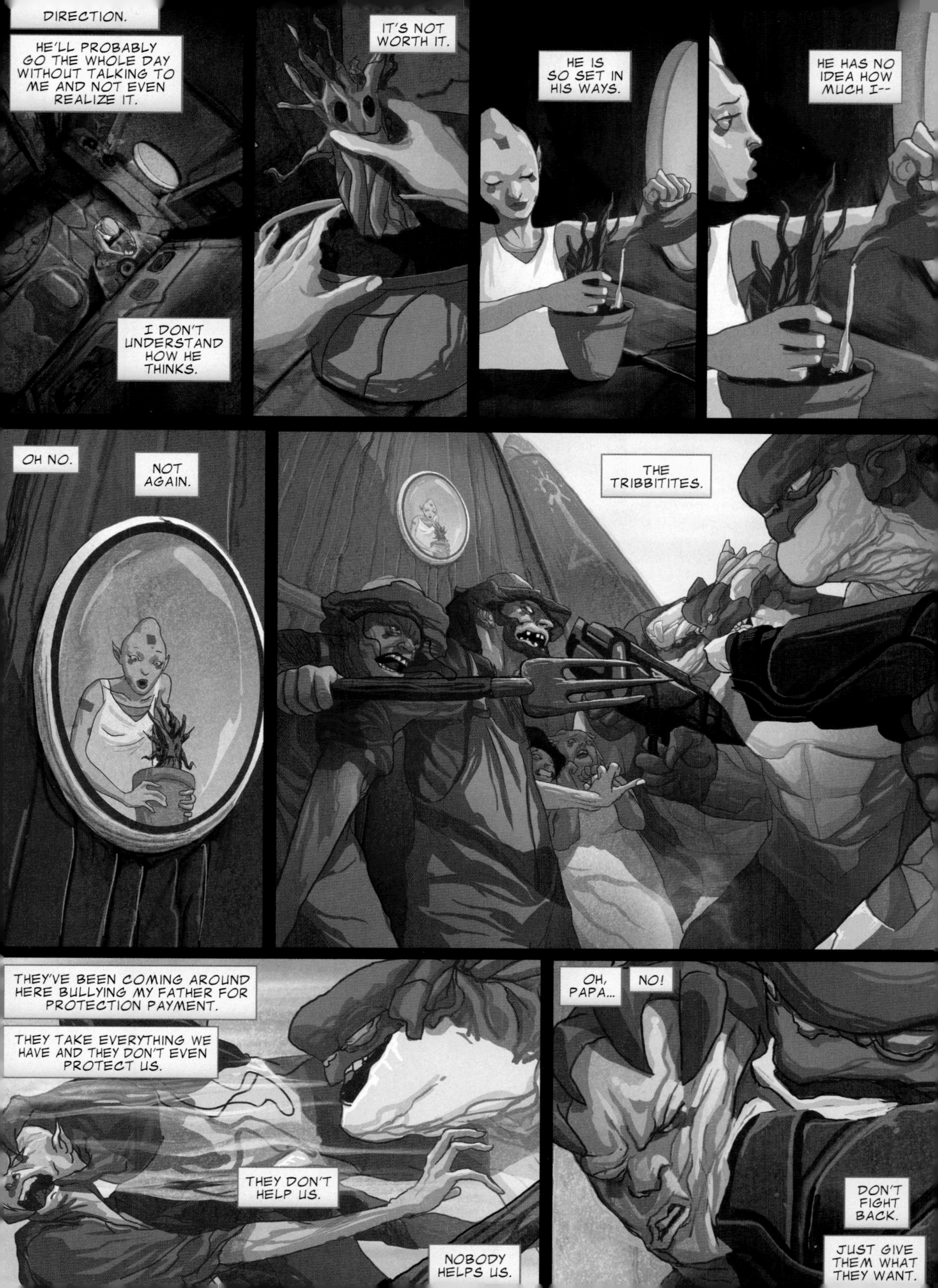
DIRECTION.
HE'LL PROBABLY GO THE WHOLE DAY WITHOUT TALKING TO ME AND NOT EVEN REALIZE IT.
I DON'T UNDERSTAND HOW HE THINKS.
IT'S NOT WORTH IT.
HE IS SO SET IN HIS WAYS.
HE HAS NO IDEA HOW MUCH I--
OH NO.
NOT AGAIN.
THE TRIBBITITES.
THEY'VE BEEN COMING AROUND HERE BULLYING MY FATHER FOR PROTECTION PAYMENT.
THEY TAKE EVERYTHING WE HAVE AND THEY DON'T EVEN PROTECT US.
THEY DON'T HELP US.
NOBODY HELPS US.
OH, PAPA...
NO!
DON'T FIGHT BACK.
JUST GIVE THEM WHAT THEY WANT.

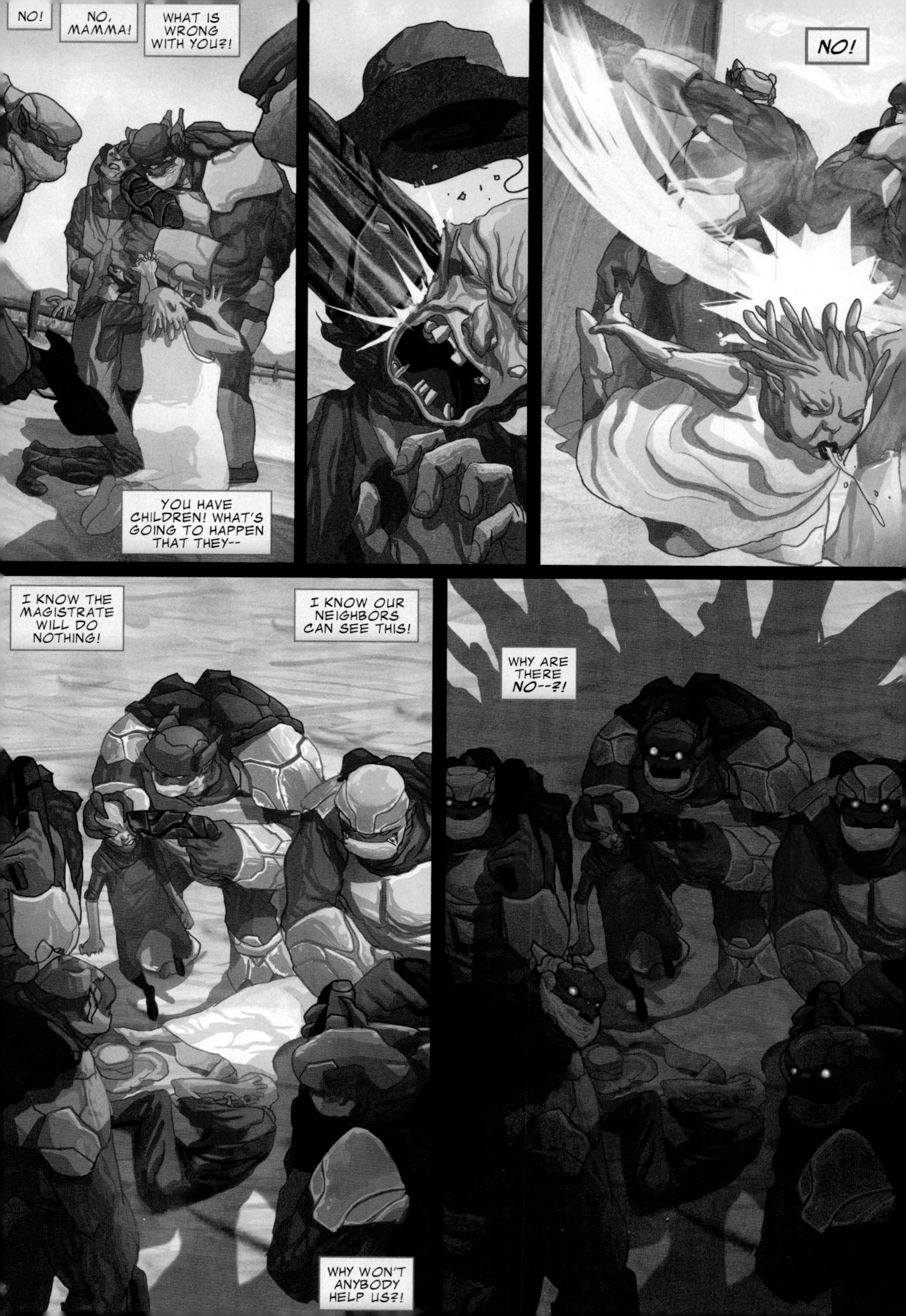

NO!
NO, MAMMA!
WHAT IS WRONG WITH YOU?!
YOU HAVE CHILDREN! WHAT'S GOING TO HAPPEN THAT THEY--
NO!
I KNOW THE MAGISTRATE WILL DO NOTHING!
I KNOW OUR NEIGHBORS CAN SEE THIS!
WHY WON'T ANYBODY HELP US?!
WHY ARE THERE NO--?!

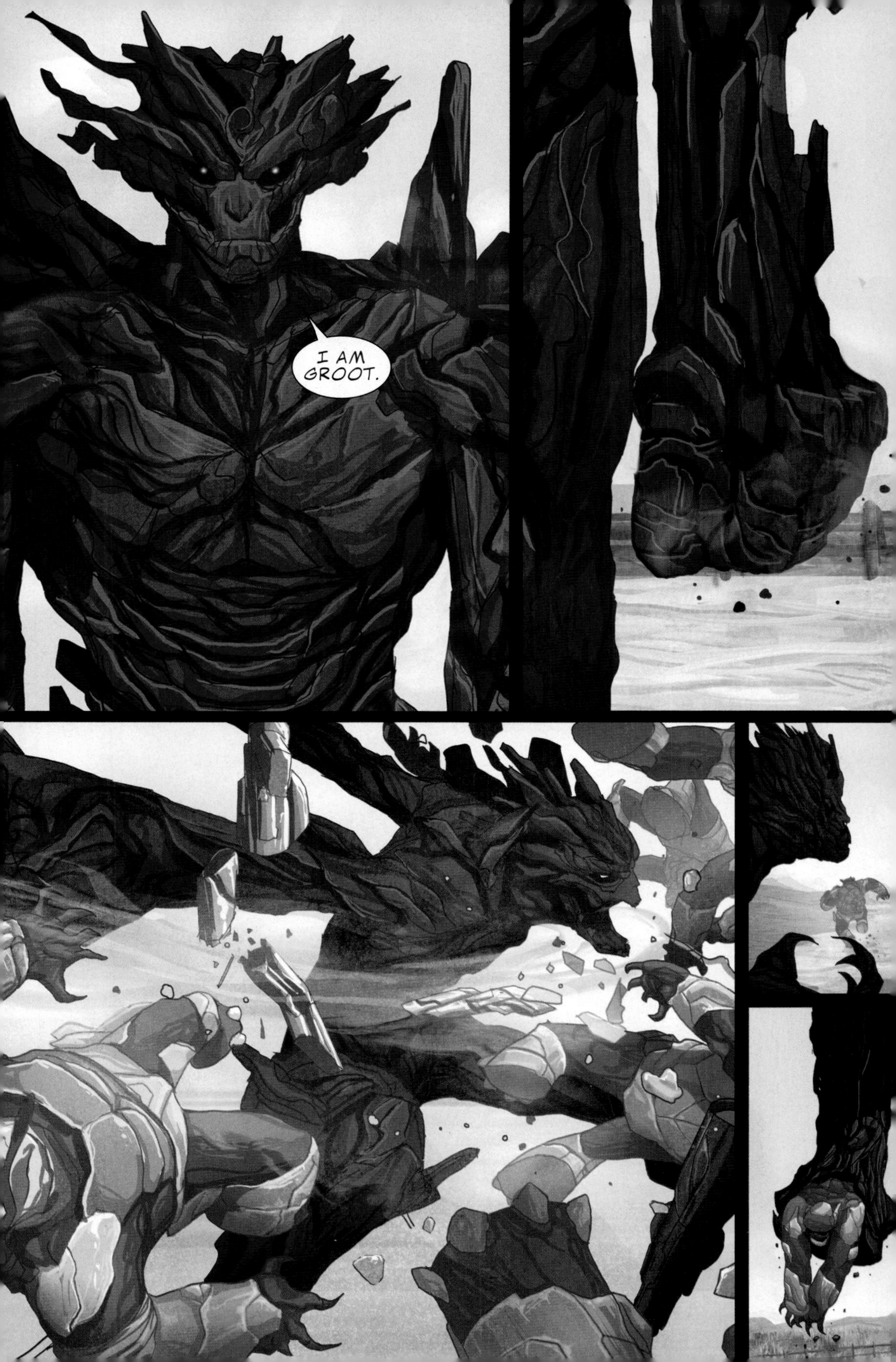
I AM GROOT.

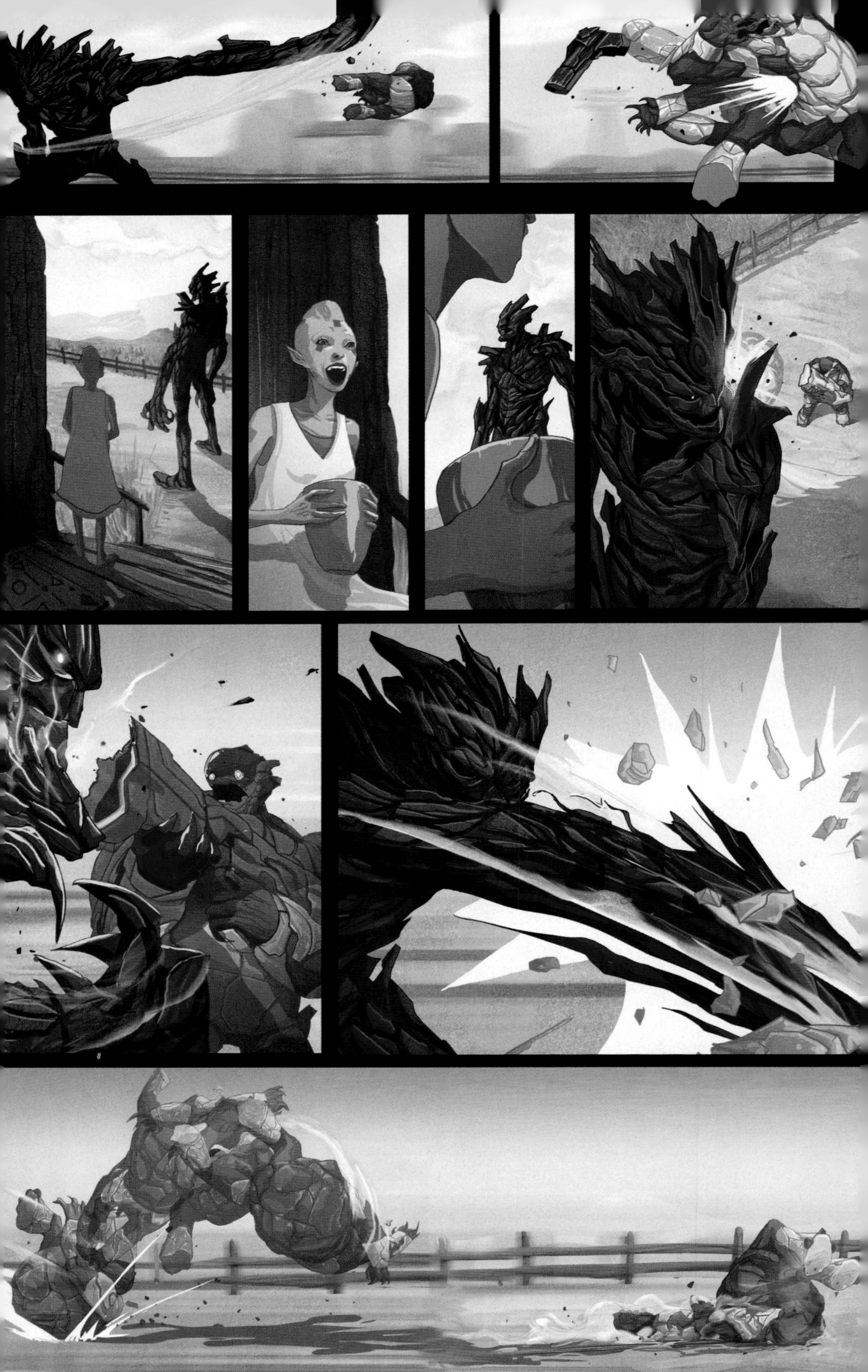

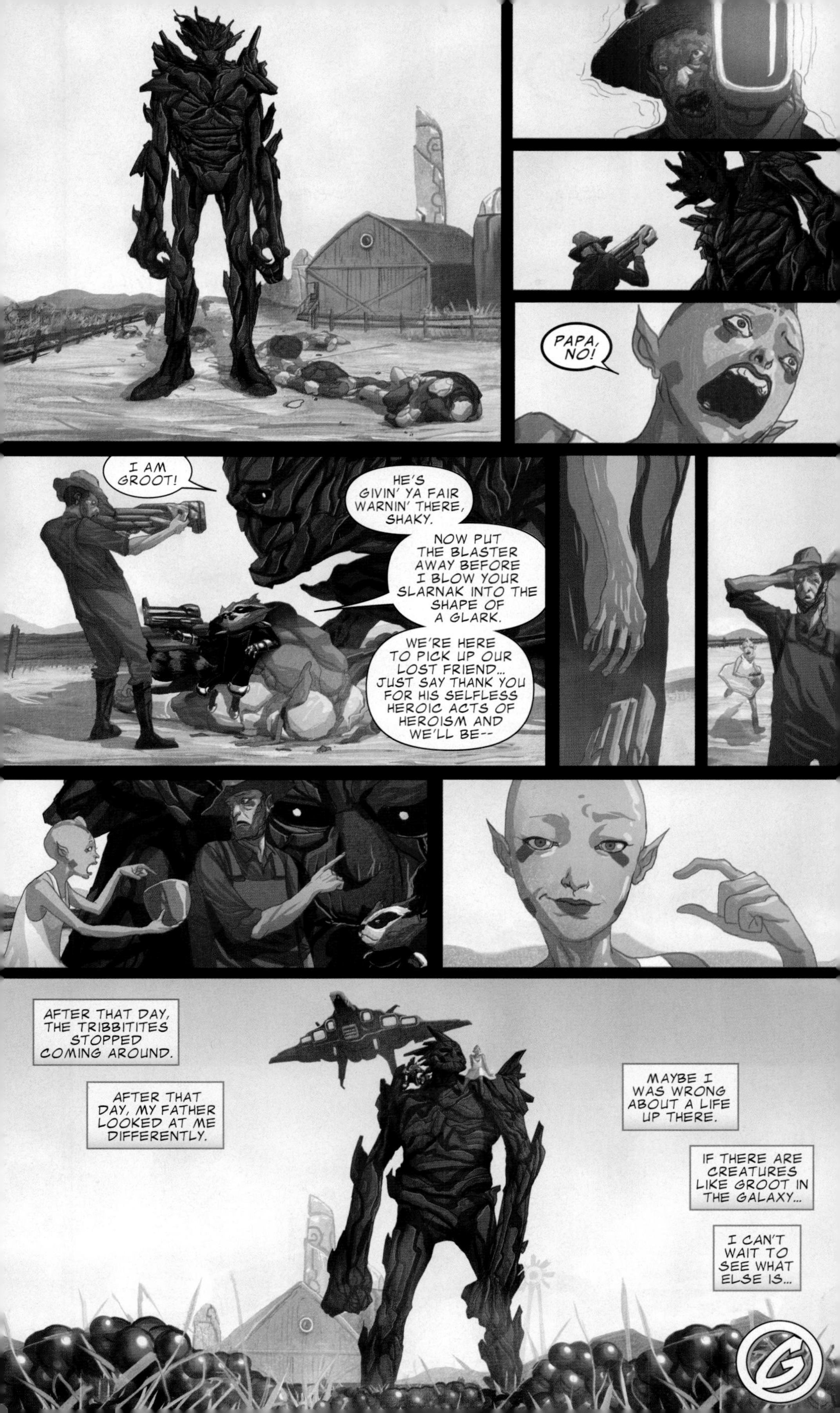
PAPA, NO!
I AM GROOT!
HE'S GIVIN' YA FAIR WARNIN' THERE, SHAKY.
NOW PUT THE BLASTER AWAY BEFORE I BLOW YOUR SLARNAK INTO THE SHAPE OF A GLARK.
WE'RE HERE TO PICK UP OUR LOST FRIEND... JUST SAY THANK YOU FOR HIS SELFLESS HEROIC ACTS OF HEROISM AND WE'LL BE--
AFTER THAT DAY, THE TRIBBITITES STOPPED COMING AROUND.
AFTER THAT DAY, MY FATHER LOOKED AT ME DIFFERENTLY.
MAYBE I WAS WRONG ABOUT A LIFE UP THERE.
IF THERE ARE CREATURES LIKE GROOT IN THE GALAXY...
I CAN'T WAIT TO SEE WHAT ELSE IS...

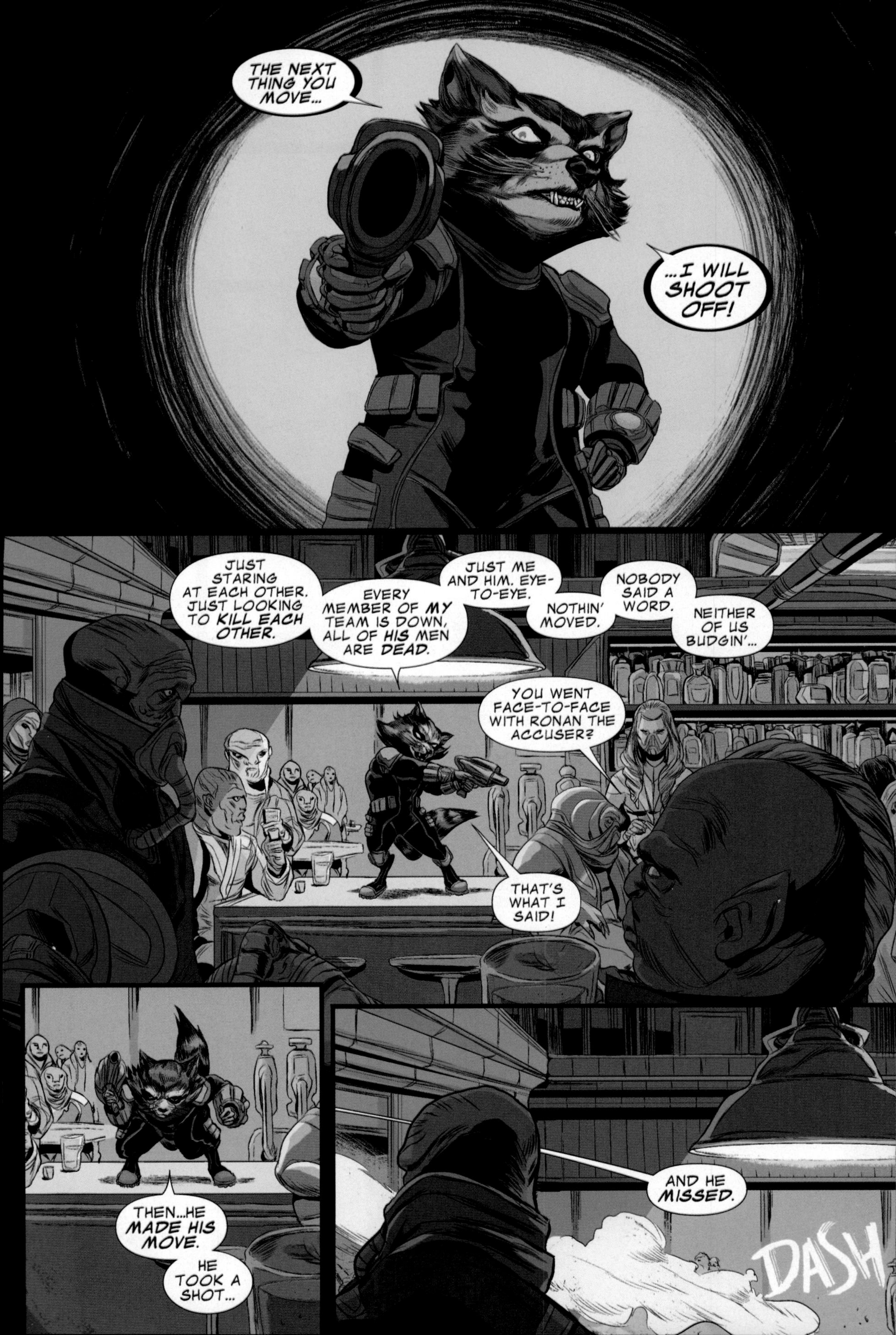
THE NEXT THING YOU MOVE...
...I WILL SHOOT OFF!
JUST STARING AT EACH OTHER. JUST LOOKING TO KILL EACH OTHER.
EVERY MEMBER OF MY TEAM IS DOWN, ALL OF HIS MEN ARE DEAD.
JUST ME AND HIM. EYE-TO-EYE.
NOTHIN' MOVED.
NOBODY SAID A WORD.
NEITHER OF US BUDGIN'...
YOU WENT FACE-TO-FACE WITH RONAN THE ACCUSER?
THAT'S WHAT I SAID!
THEN...HE MADE HIS MOVE.
HE TOOK A SHOT...
AND HE MISSED.
DASH

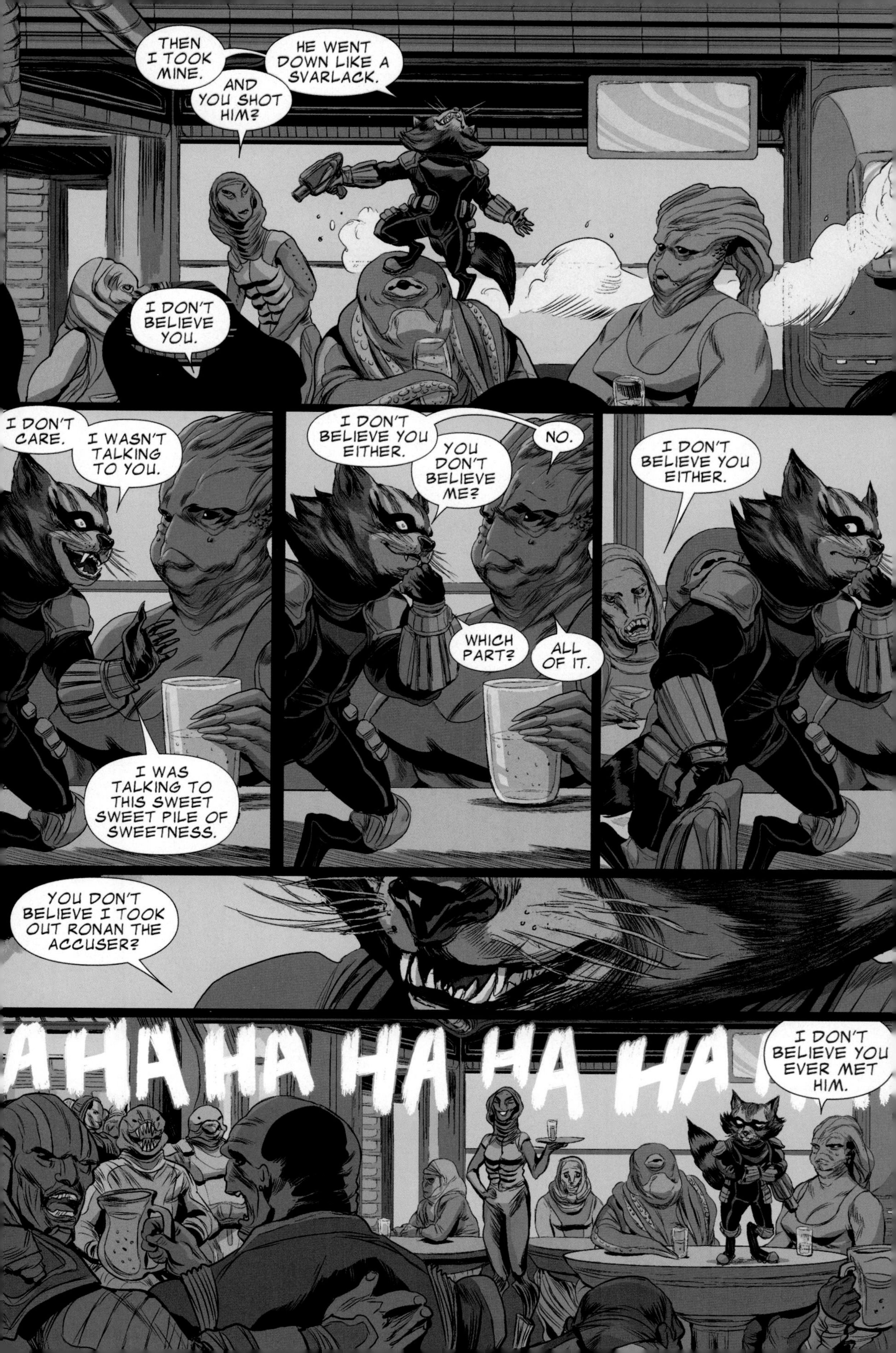

THEN I TOOK MINE.
HE WENT DOWN LIKE A SVARLACK.
AND YOU SHOT HIM?
I DON'T BELIEVE YOU.
I DON'T CARE.
I WASN'T TALKING TO YOU.
I WAS TALKING TO THIS SWEET SWEET PILE OF SWEETNESS.
I DON'T BELIEVE YOU EITHER.
NO.
YOU DON'T BELIEVE ME?
WHICH PART?
ALL OF IT.
I DON'T BELIEVE YOU EITHER.
YOU DON'T BELIEVE I TOOK OUT RONAN THE ACCUSER?
AHAHA HA HA HA HA HA
I DON'T BELIEVE YOU EVER MET HIM.

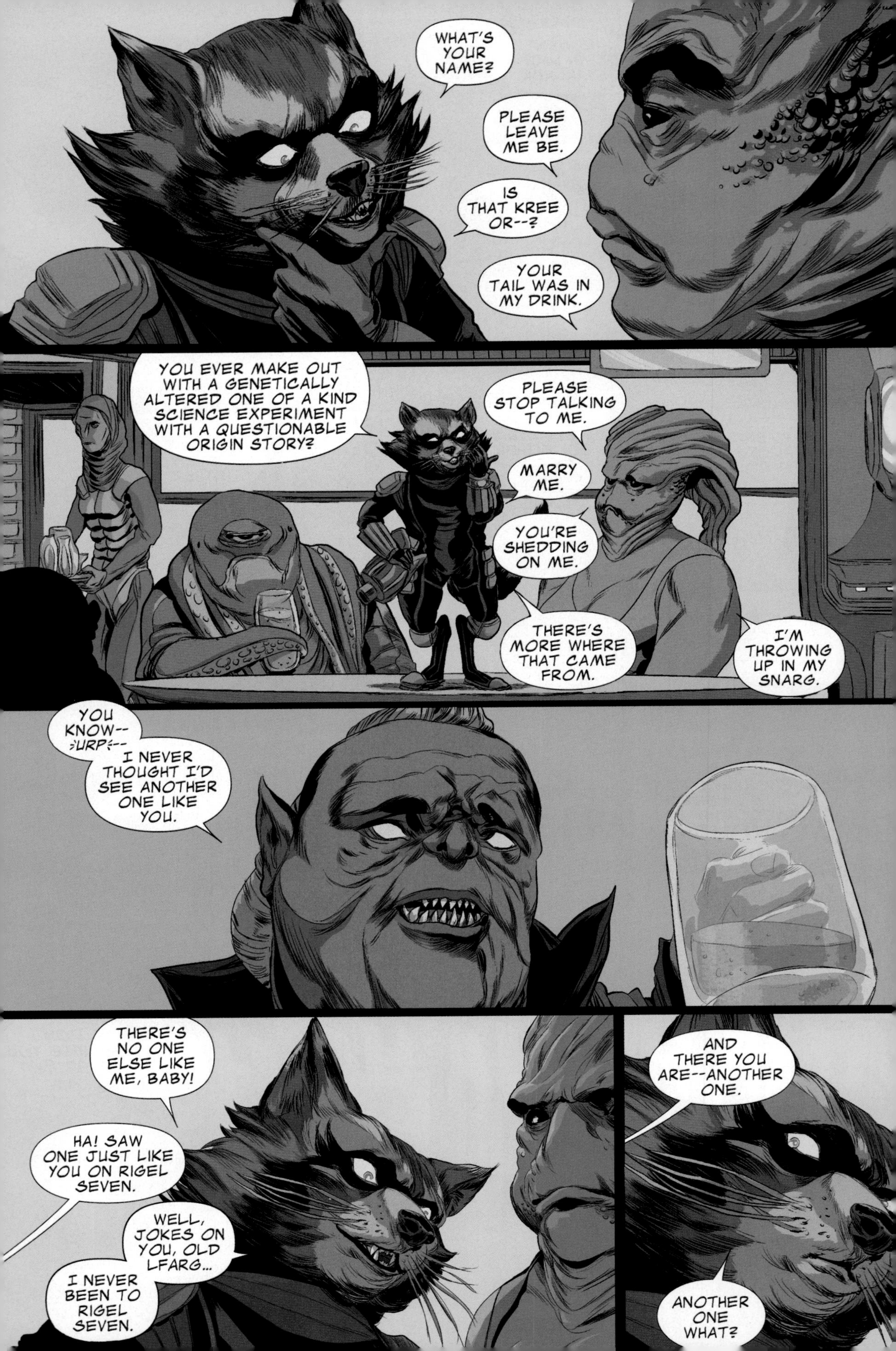
WHAT'S YOUR NAME?
PLEASE LEAVE ME BE.
IS THAT KREE OR--?
YOUR TAIL WAS IN MY DRINK.
YOU EVER MAKE OUT WITH A GENETICALLY ALTERED ONE OF A KIND SCIENCE EXPERIMENT WITH A QUESTIONABLE ORIGIN STORY?
PLEASE STOP TALKING TO ME.
MARRY ME.
YOU'RE SHEDDING ON ME.
THERE'S MORE WHERE THAT CAME FROM.
I'M THROWING UP IN MY SNARG.
YOU KNOW-- *URP*-- I NEVER THOUGHT I'D SEE ANOTHER ONE LIKE YOU.
THERE'S NO ONE ELSE LIKE ME, BABY!
HA! SAW ONE JUST LIKE YOU ON RIGEL SEVEN.
WELL, JOKES ON YOU, OLD LFARG...
I NEVER BEEN TO RIGEL SEVEN.
AND THERE YOU ARE--ANOTHER ONE.
ANOTHER ONE WHAT?

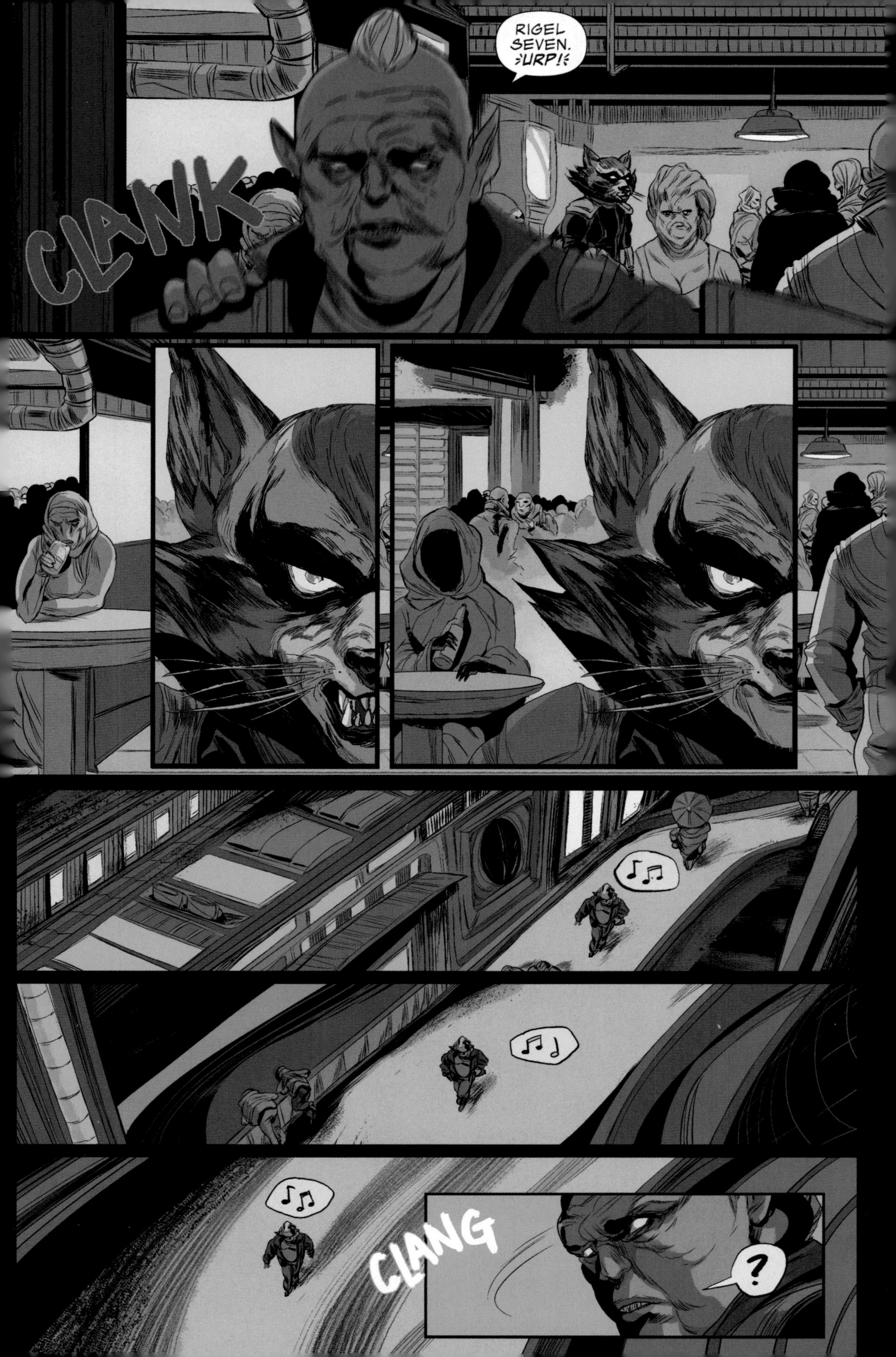
RIGEL SEVEN. URP!
CLANK
♫♫
♫♩
♪♫
CLANG
?

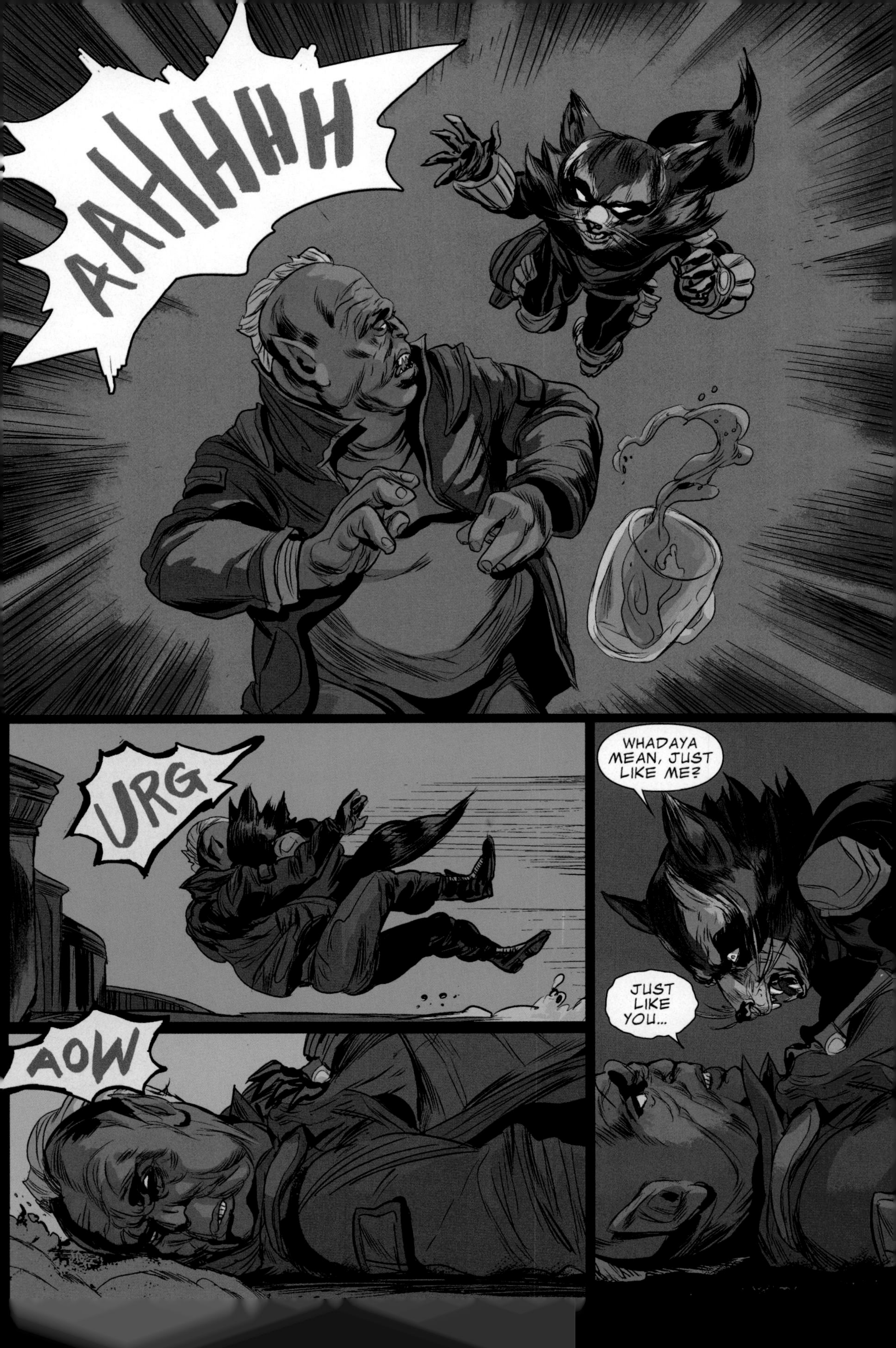
AAHHHH
URG
AOW
WHADAYA MEAN, JUST LIKE ME?
JUST LIKE YOU...

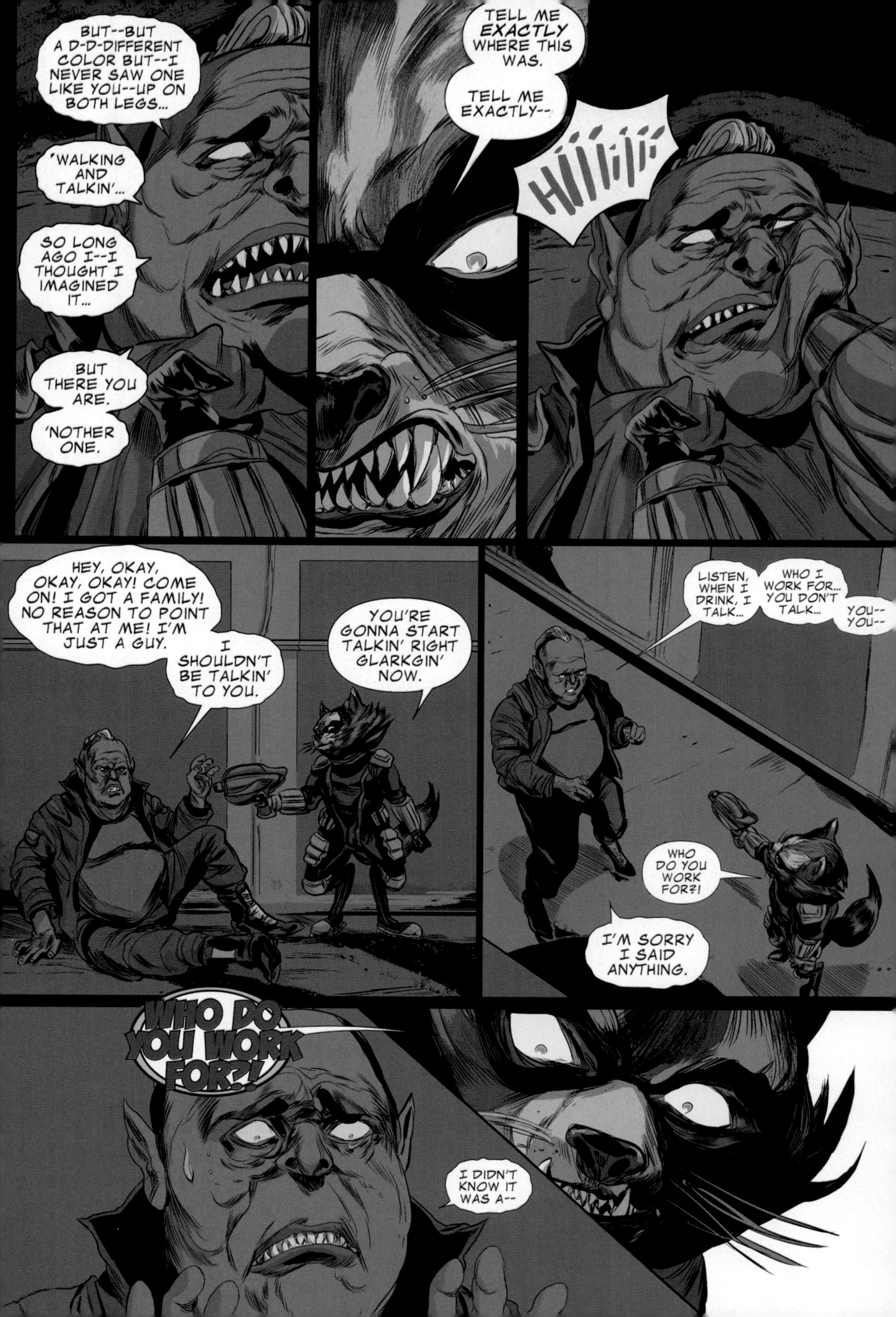
BUT--BUT A D-D-DIFFERENT COLOR BUT--I NEVER SAW ONE LIKE YOU--UP ON BOTH LEGS...
'WALKING AND TALKIN'...
SO LONG AGO I--I THOUGHT I IMAGINED IT...
BUT THERE YOU ARE.
'NOTHER ONE.
TELL ME EXACTLY WHERE THIS WAS.
TELL ME EXACTLY--
HIIIIIII
HEY, OKAY, OKAY, OKAY! COME ON! I GOT A FAMILY! NO REASON TO POINT THAT AT ME! I'M JUST A GUY.
I SHOULDN'T BE TALKIN' TO YOU.
YOU'RE GONNA START TALKIN' RIGHT GLARKGIN' NOW.
LISTEN, WHEN I DRINK, I TALK...
WHO I WORK FOR... YOU DON'T TALK...
YOU--YOU--
WHO DO YOU WORK FOR?!
I'M SORRY I SAID ANYTHING.
WHO DO YOU WORK FOR?!
I DIDN'T KNOW IT WAS A--

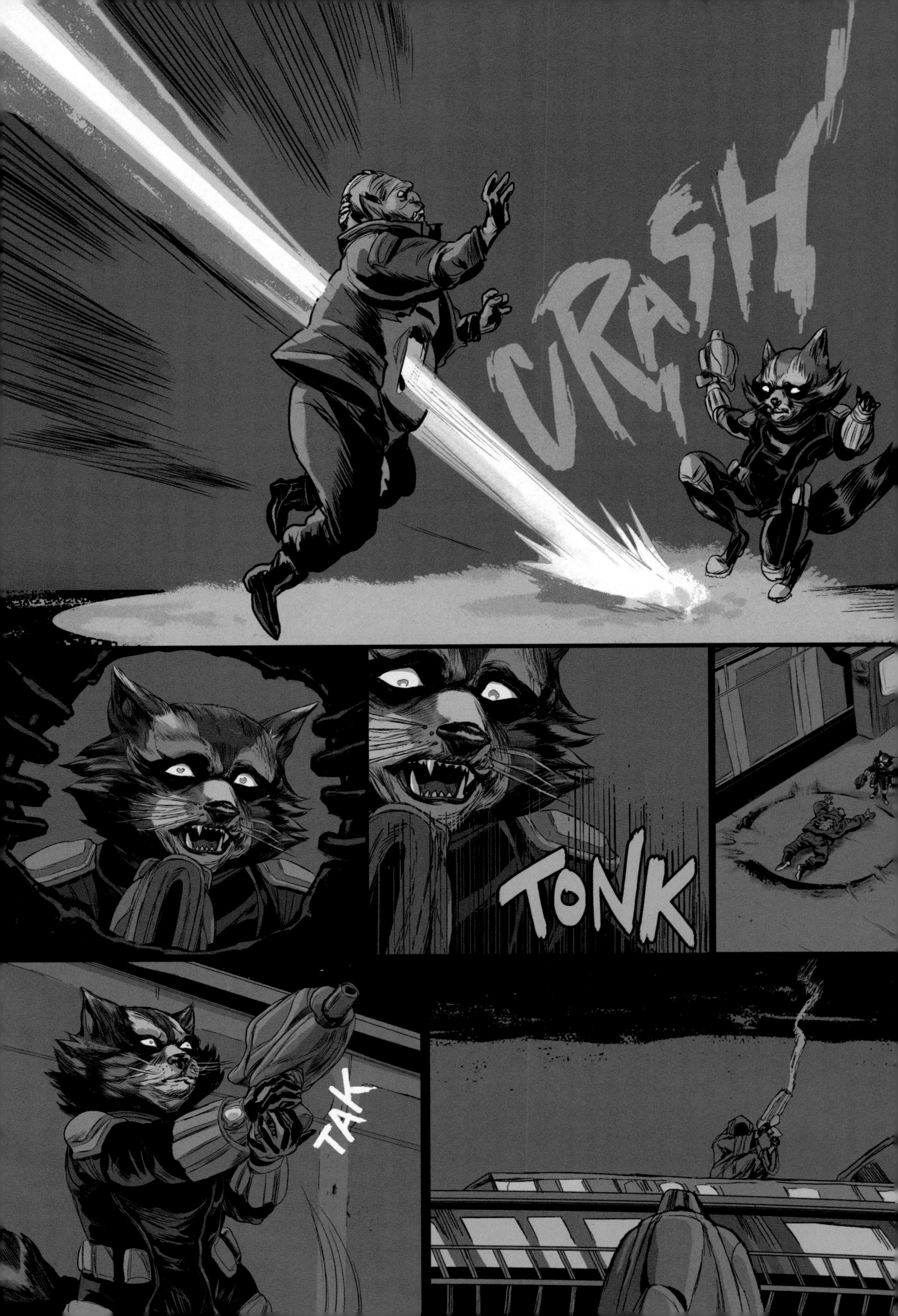
CRASH
TONK
TAK

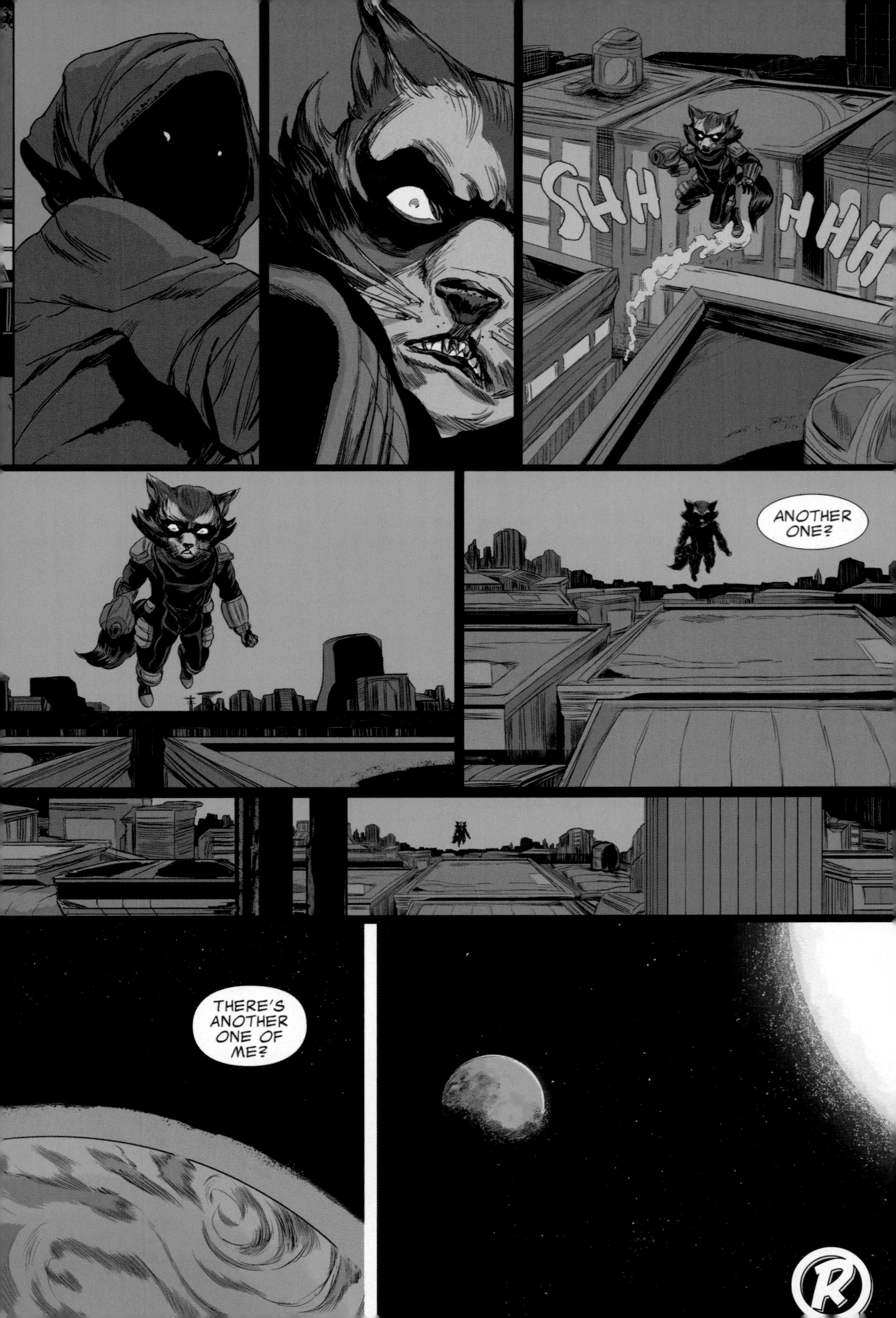
SHHHHHH
ANOTHER ONE?
THERE'S ANOTHER ONE OF ME?

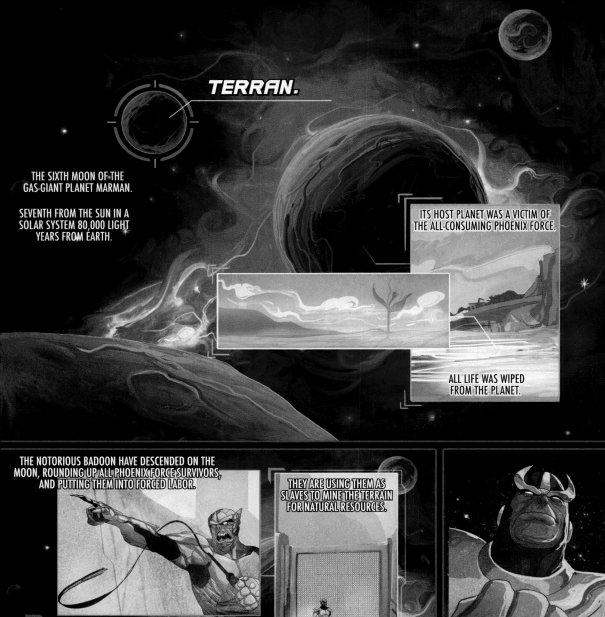

TERRAN.

THE SIXTH MOON OF THE GAS-GIANT PLANET MARMAN.

SEVENTH FROM THE SUN IN A SOLAR SYSTEM 80,000 LIGHT YEARS FROM EARTH.

ITS HOST PLANET WAS A VICTIM OF THE ALL-CONSUMING PHOENIX FORCE.

ALL LIFE WAS WIPED FROM THE PLANET.

THE NOTORIOUS BADOON HAVE DESCENDED ON THE MOON, ROUNDING UP ALL PHOENIX FORCE SURVIVORS, AND PUTTING THEM INTO FORCED LABOR.

THEY ARE USING THEM AS SLAVES TO MINE THE TERRAIN FOR NATURAL RESOURCES.

ALL FOR THE GLORY OF THE MAD TITAN **THANOS.**

BUT THANOS HAS A DAUGHTER.

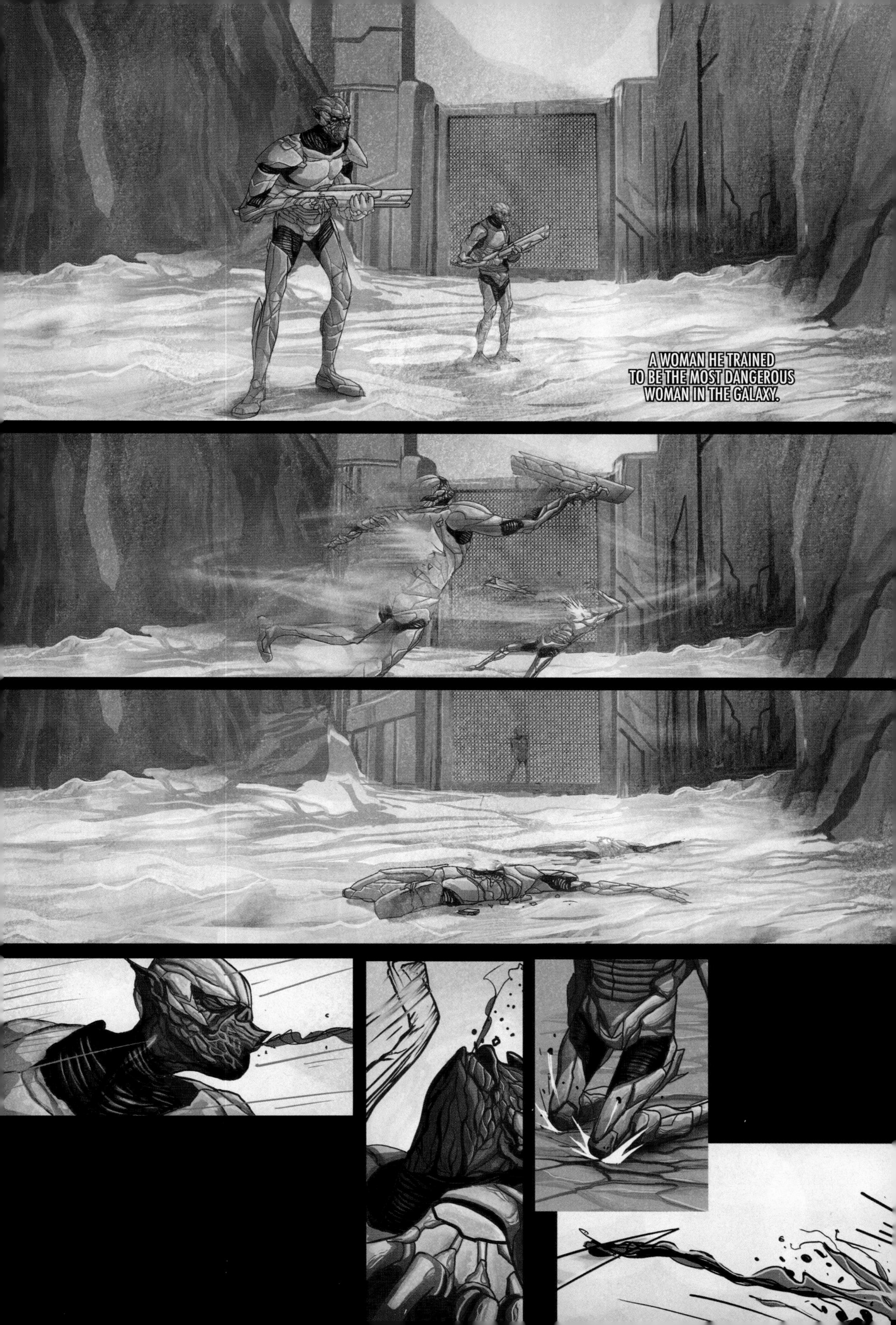
A WOMAN HE TRAINED
TO BE THE MOST DANGEROUS
WOMAN IN THE GALAXY.

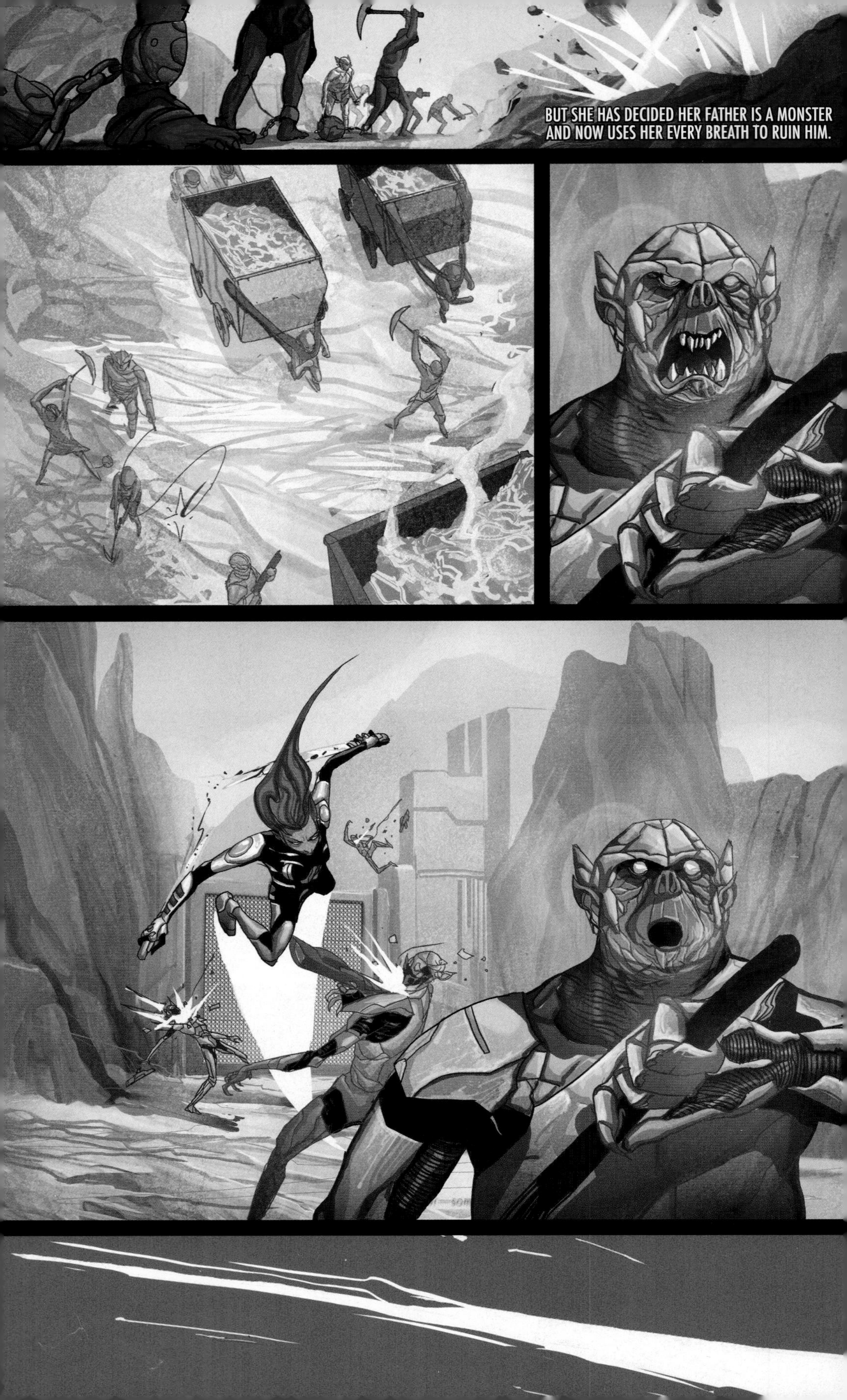
BUT SHE HAS DECIDED HER FATHER IS A MONSTER AND NOW USES HER EVERY BREATH TO RUIN HIM.

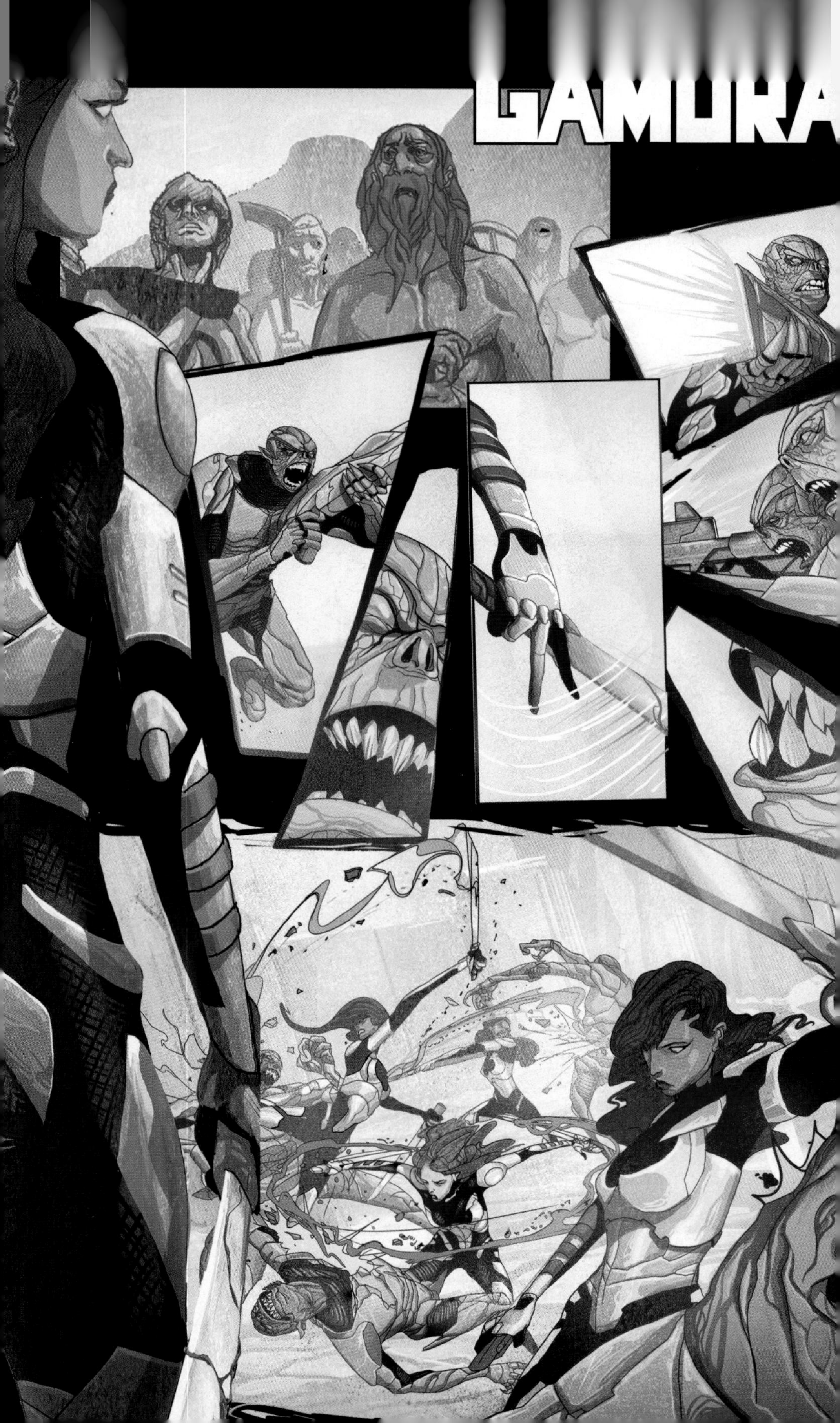
GAMORA

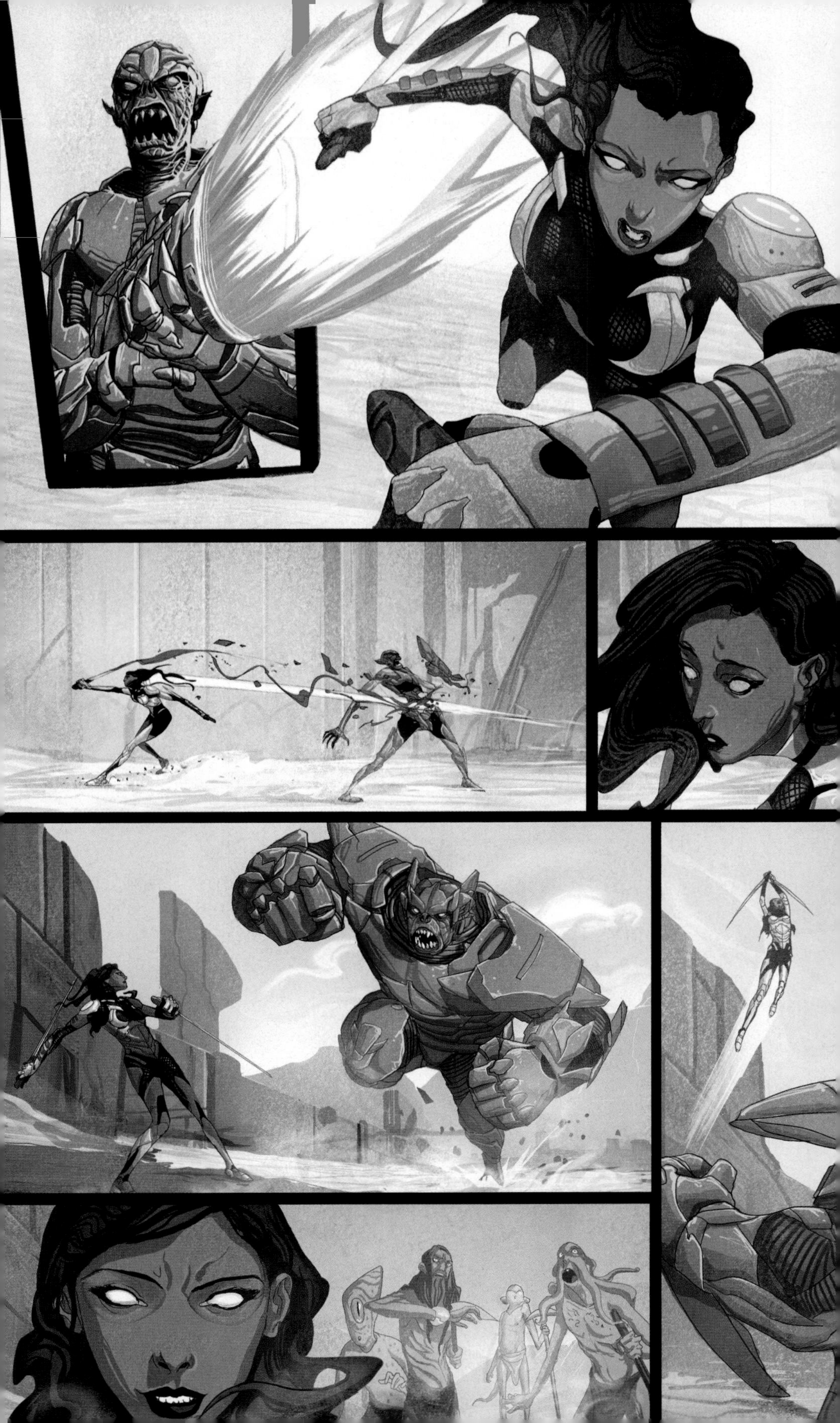

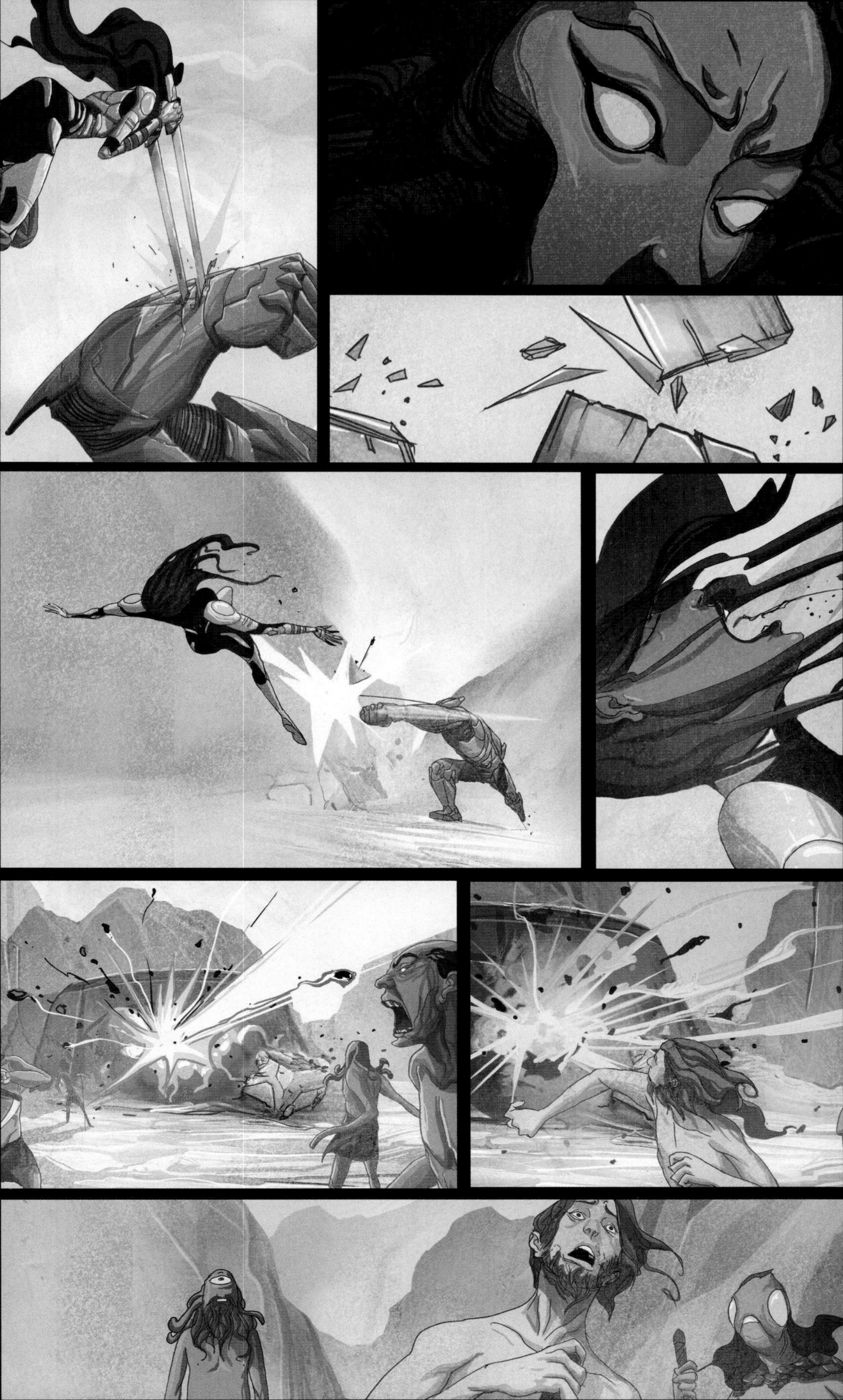

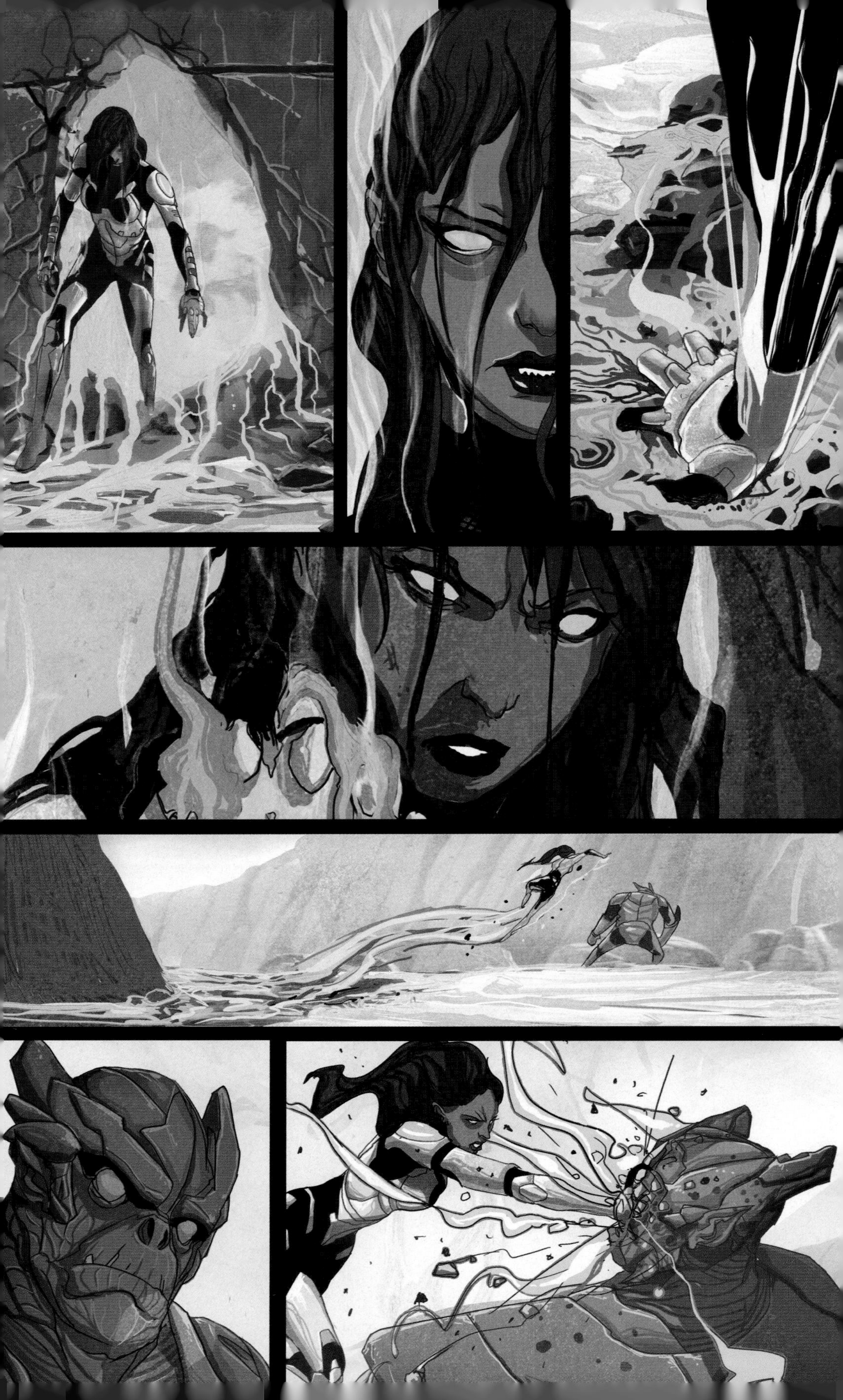

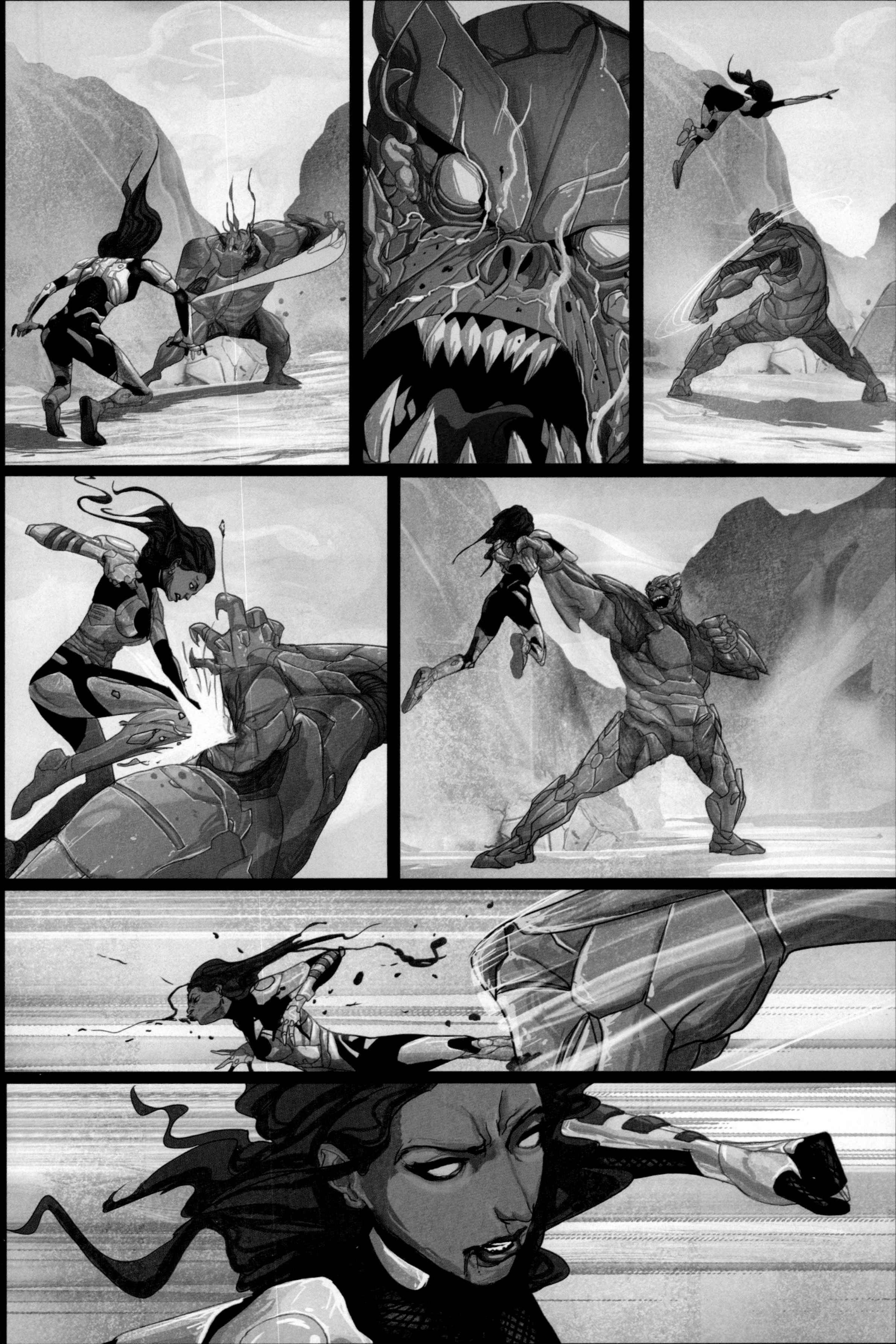

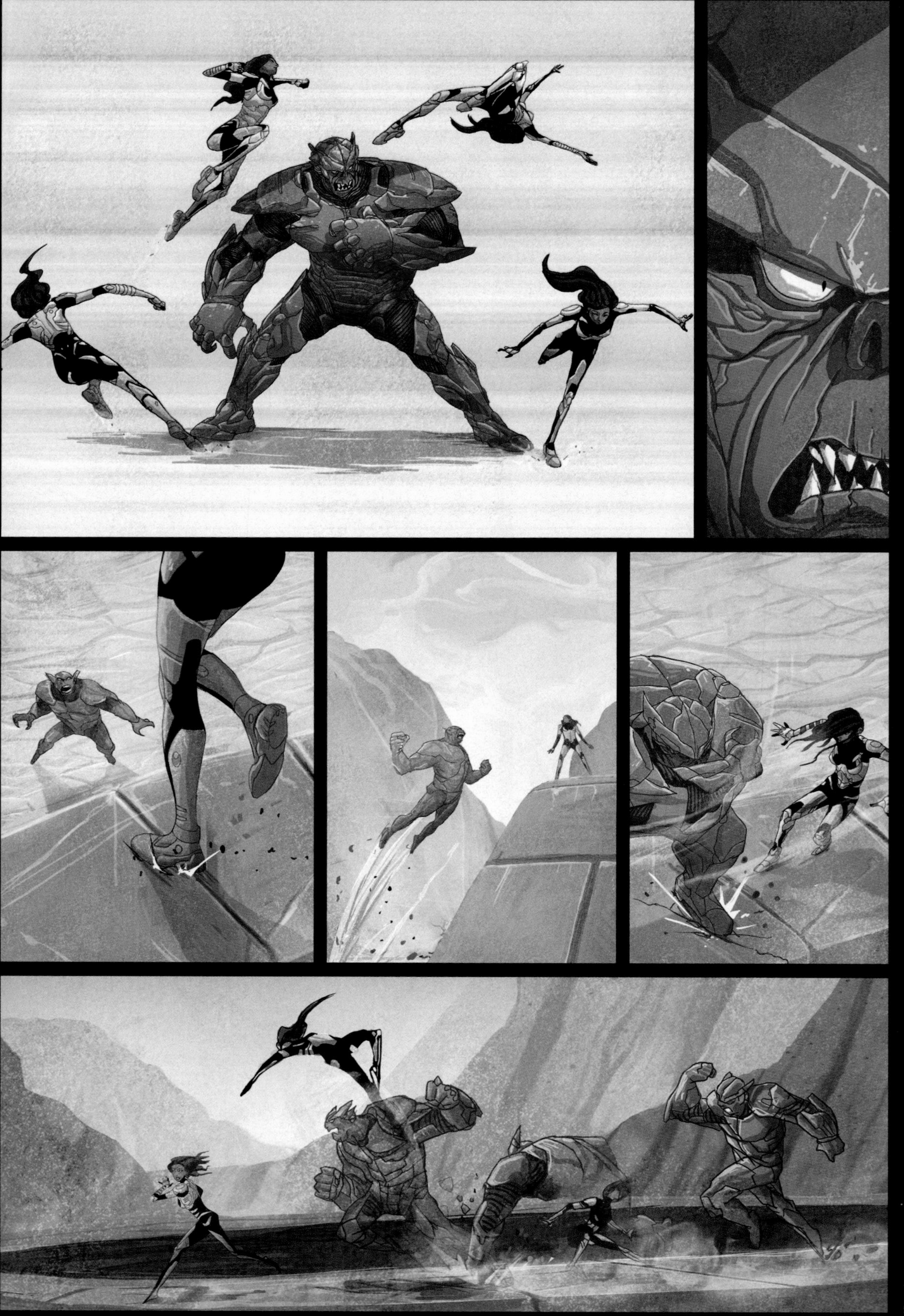

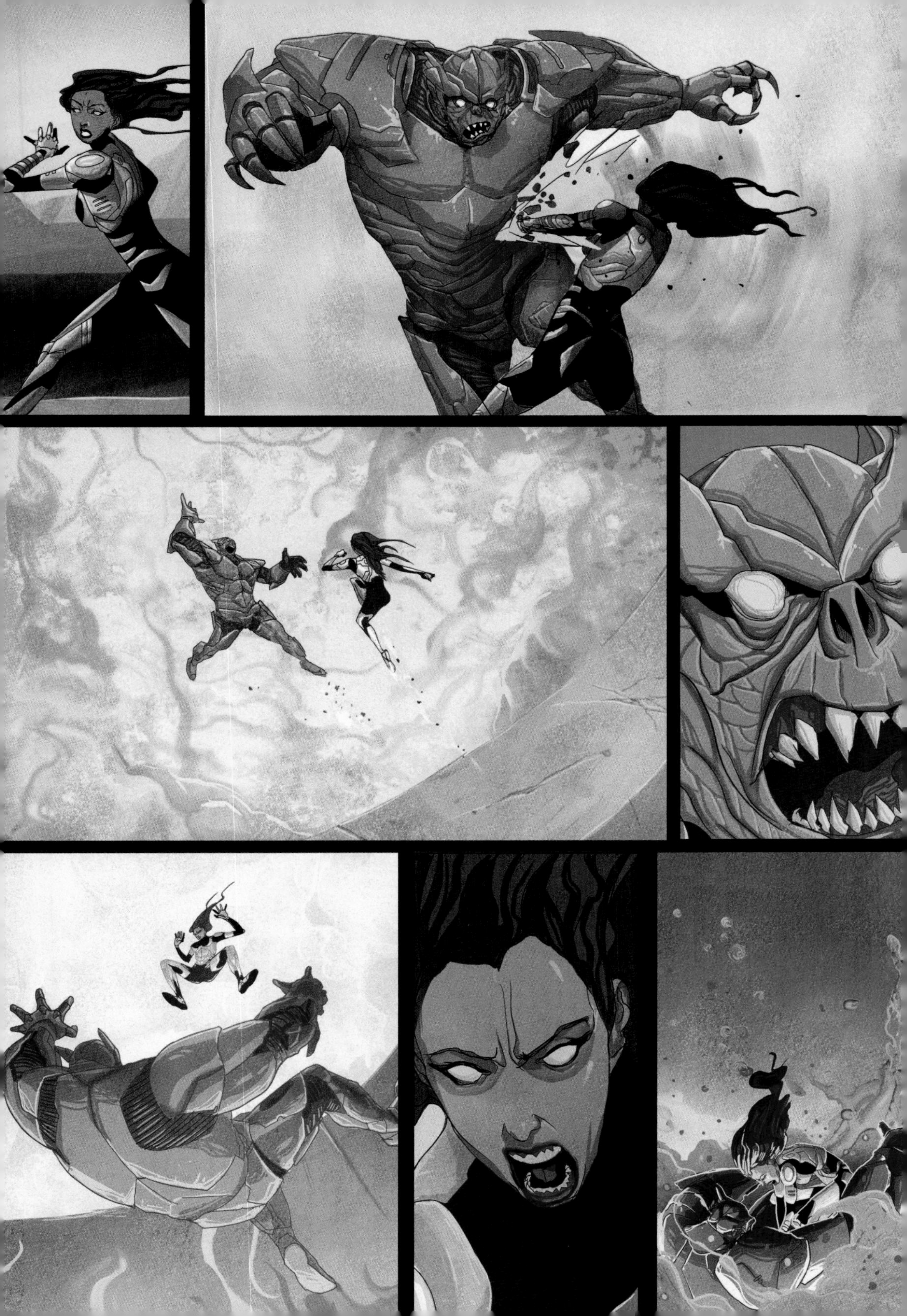

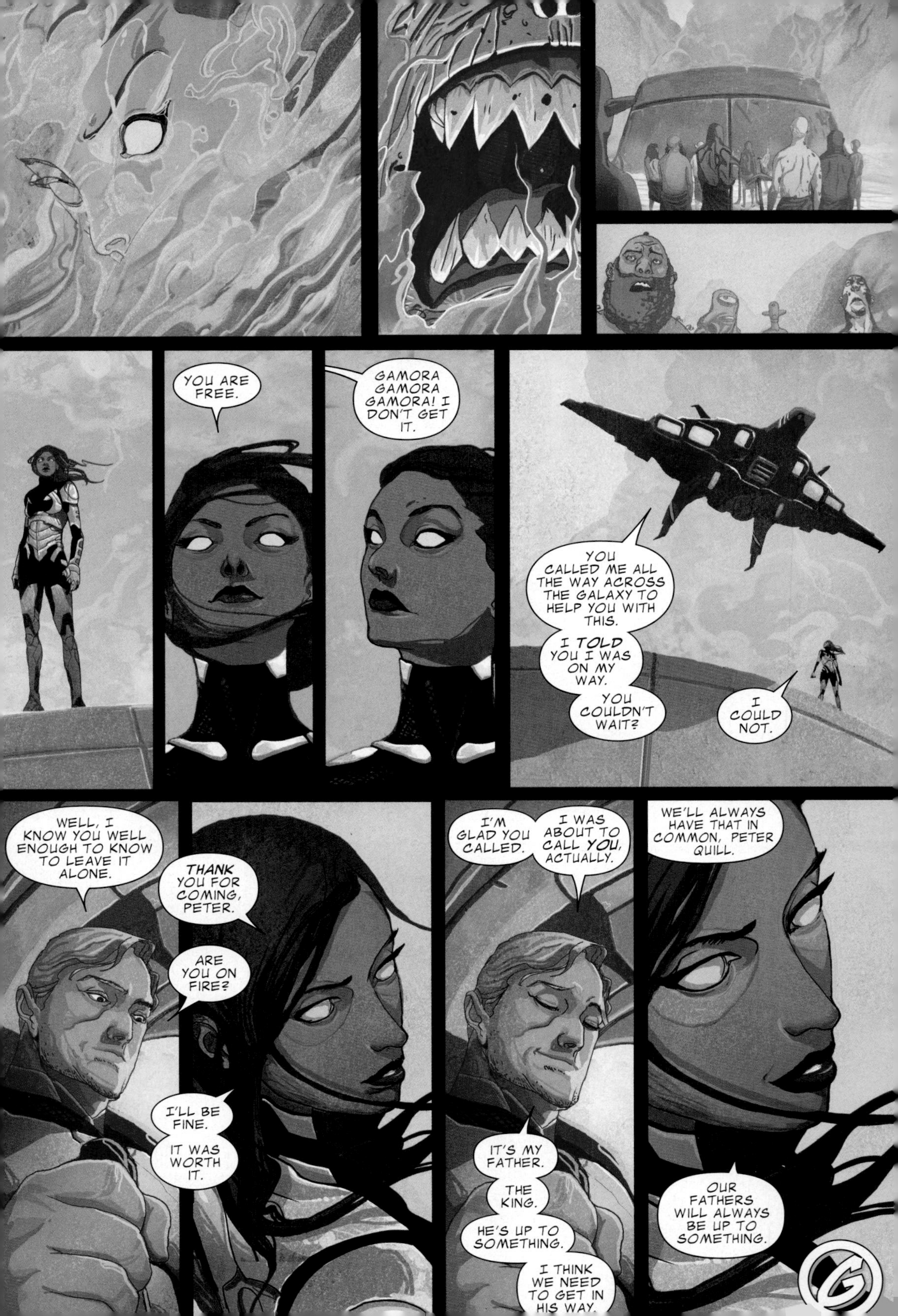
YOU ARE FREE.
GAMORA GAMORA GAMORA! I DON'T GET IT.
YOU CALLED ME ALL THE WAY ACROSS THE GALAXY TO HELP YOU WITH THIS.
I TOLD YOU I WAS ON MY WAY.
YOU COULDN'T WAIT?
I COULD NOT.
WELL, I KNOW YOU WELL ENOUGH TO KNOW TO LEAVE IT ALONE.
THANK YOU FOR COMING, PETER.
ARE YOU ON FIRE?
I'LL BE FINE.
IT WAS WORTH IT.
I'M GLAD YOU CALLED.
I WAS ABOUT TO CALL YOU, ACTUALLY.
IT'S MY FATHER.
THE KING.
HE'S UP TO SOMETHING.
I THINK WE NEED TO GET IN HIS WAY.
WE'LL ALWAYS HAVE THAT IN COMMON, PETER QUILL.
OUR FATHERS WILL ALWAYS BE UP TO SOMETHING.

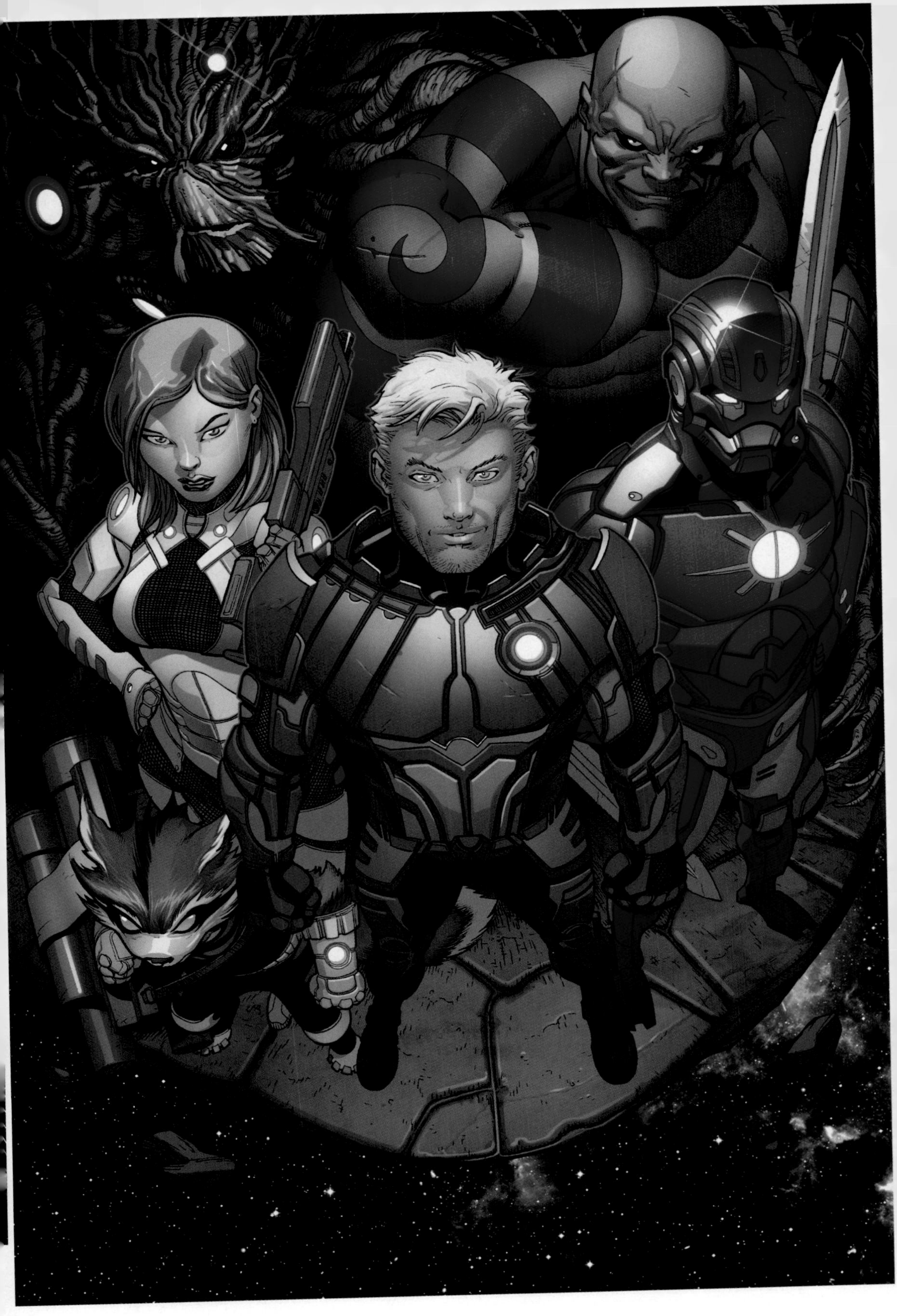

#0.1 VARIANT BY ED MCGUINNESS & MARTE GRACIA

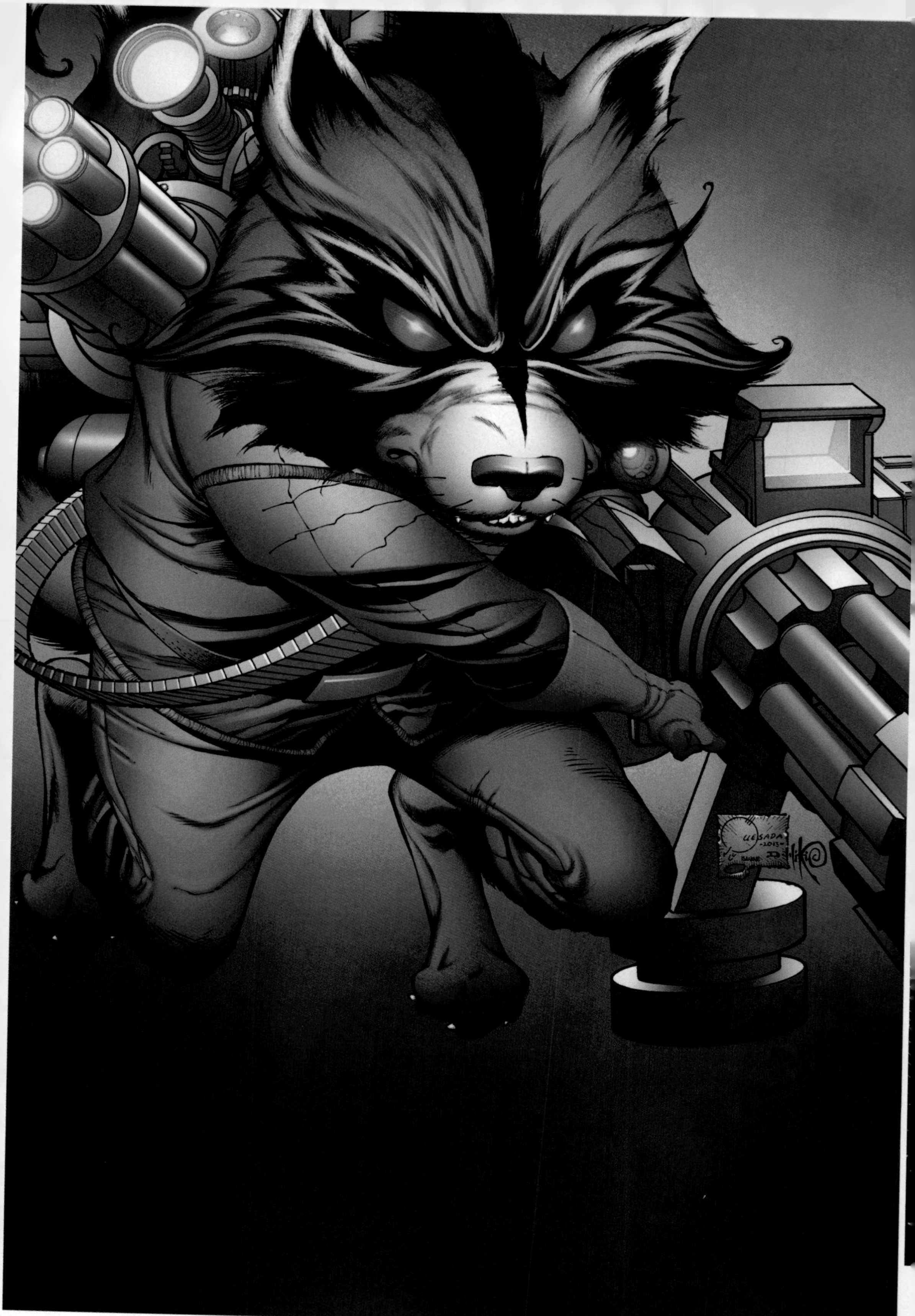

#1 VARIANT BY JOE QUESADA, DANNY MIKI & RICHARD ISANOVE

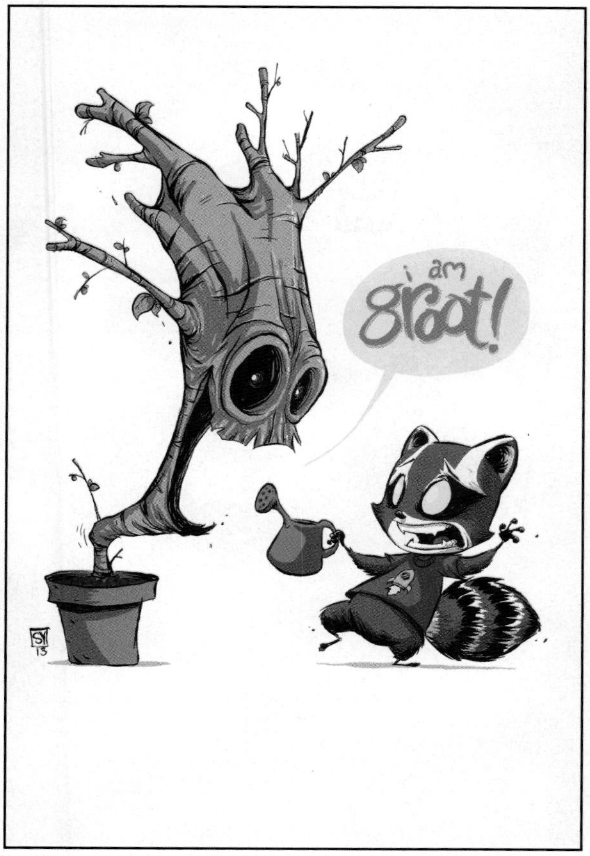
i am groot!

***#1* VARIANT** BY SKOTTIE YOUNG

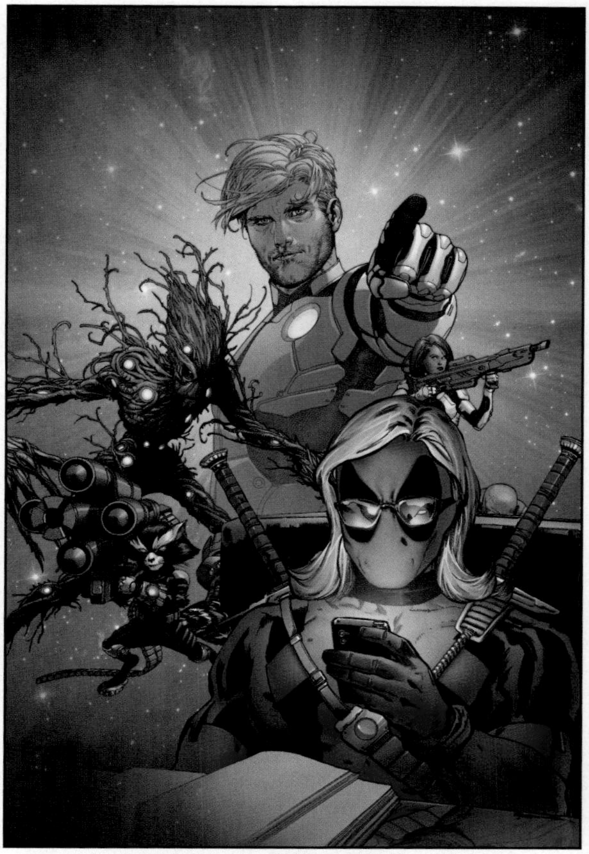

***#1* DEADPOOL VARIANT** BY PHIL JIMENEZ & FRANK D'ARMATA

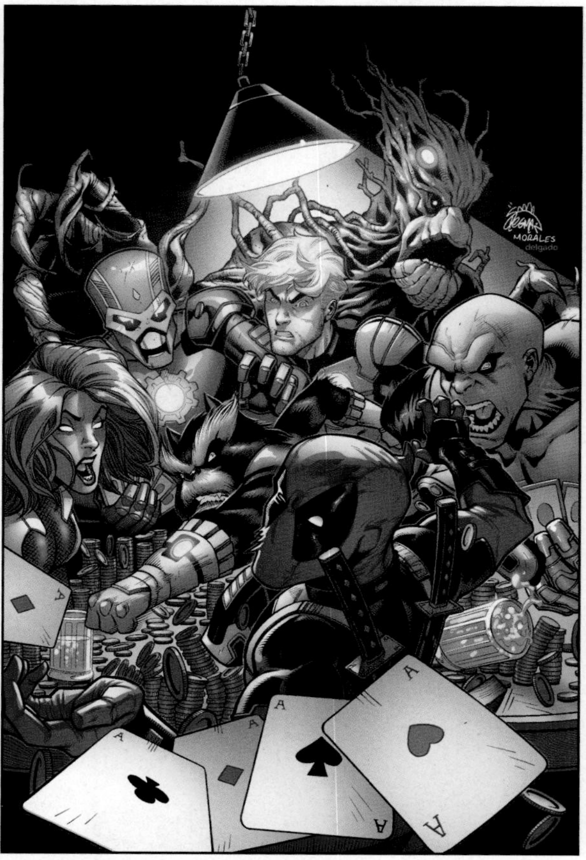

***#1* HASTINGS VARIANT** BY RYAN STEGMAN, MARK MORALES & EDGAR DELGADO

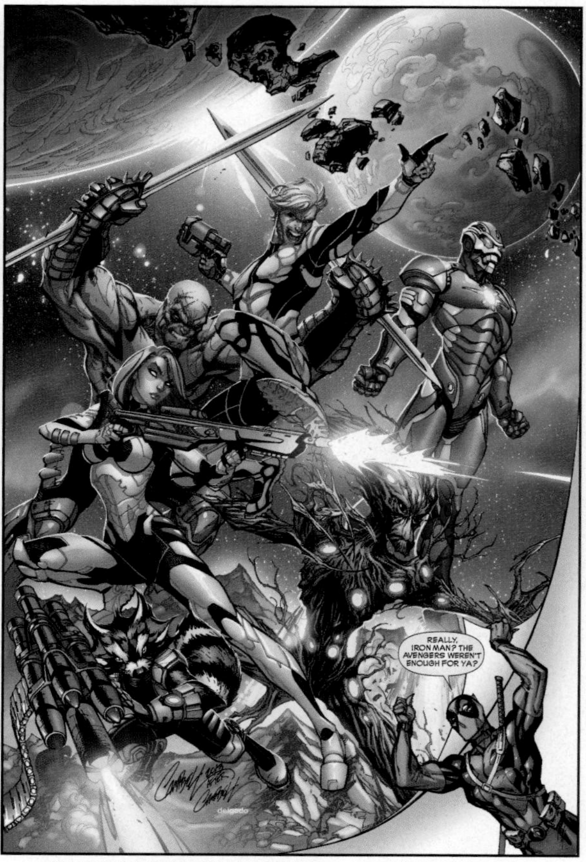
REALLY, IRON MAN? THE AVENGERS WEREN'T ENOUGH FOR YA?

***#1* MIDTOWN VARIANT** BY J. SCOTT CAMPBELL & EDGAR DELGAGO

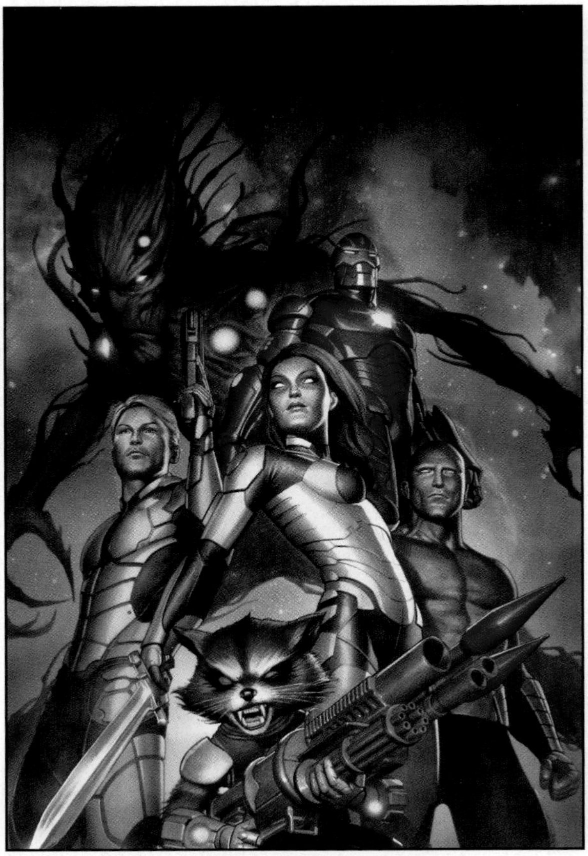

***#1* LIMITED EDITION COMIX VARIANT**
BY ADI GRANOV

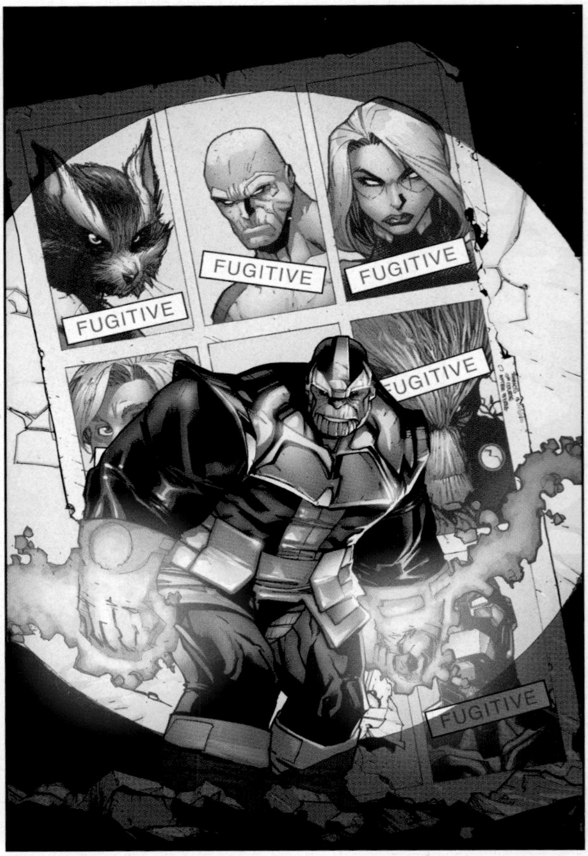
FUGITIVE
FUGITIVE
FUGITIVE
FUGITIVE
FUGITIVE

***#1* PHANTOM VARIANT** BY HUMBERTO RAMOS
& EDGAR DELGADO

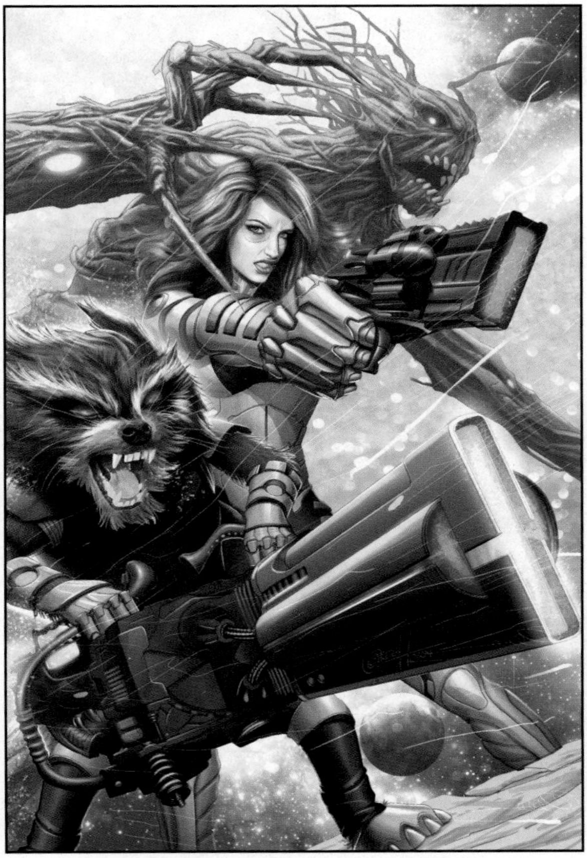

***#1* THIRD EYE COMICS VARIANT** BY GREG HORN

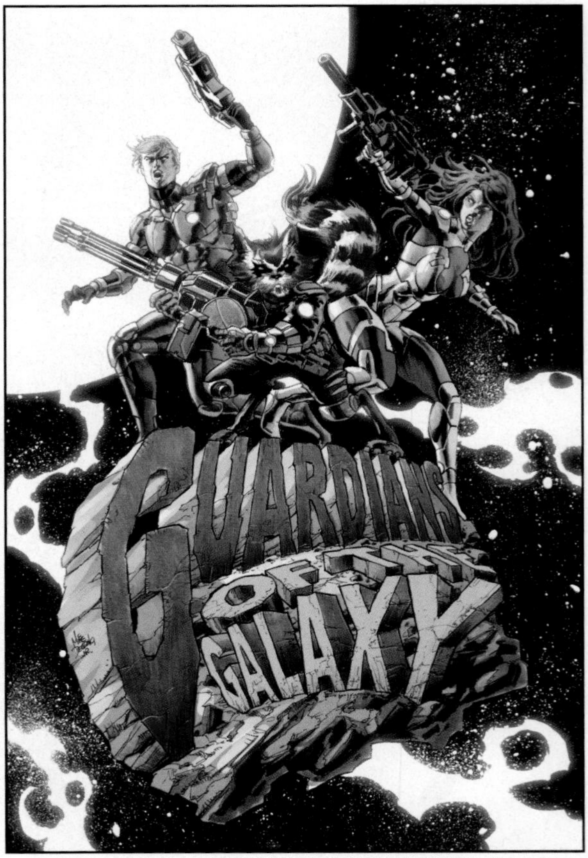
GUARDIANS
OF THE
GALAXY

***#1* MILE HIGH COMICS VARIANT** BY MIKE DEODATO
& RAIN BEREDO

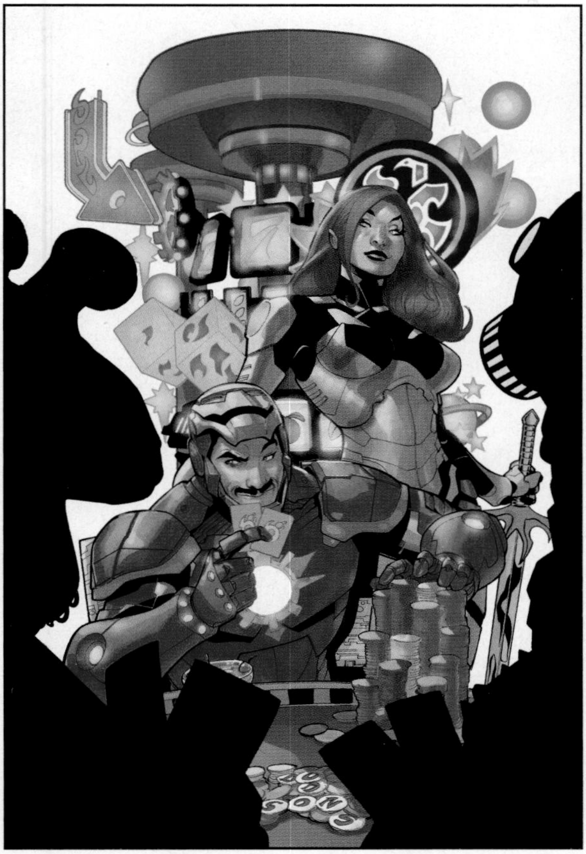

***#1* MAXIMUM COMICS VARIANT** BY TERRY DODSON & RACHEL DODSON

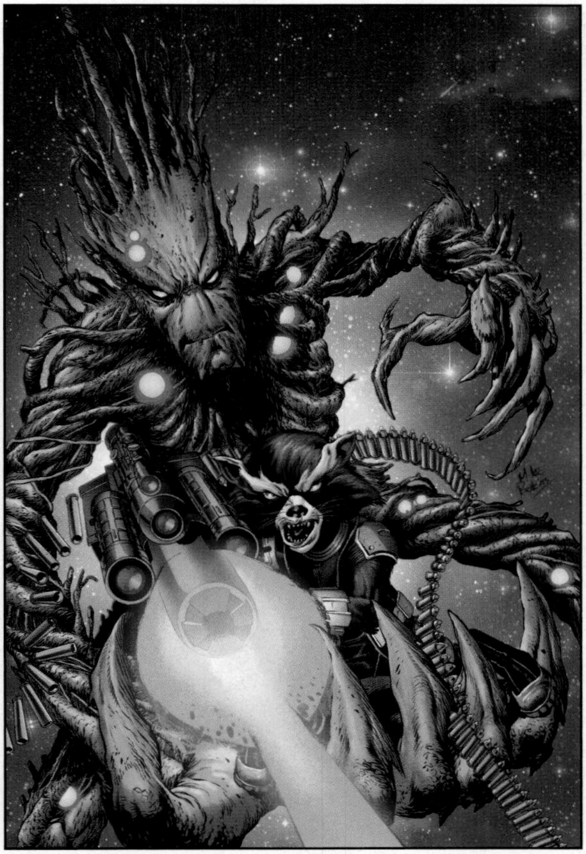

***#1* FORBIDDEN PLANET VARIANT** BY MIKE PERKINS & ANDY TROY

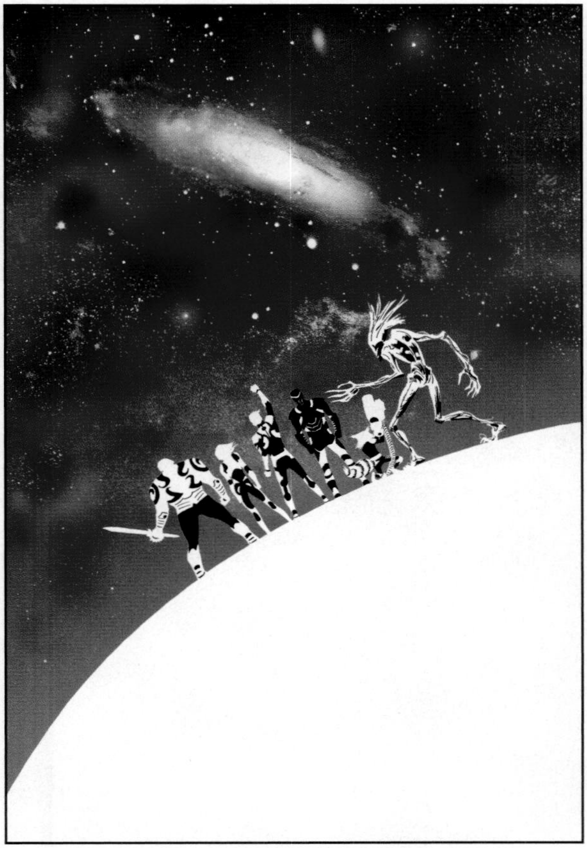

***#1* DETROIT COMICBOOK STORES VARIANT** BY MARCOS MARTIN

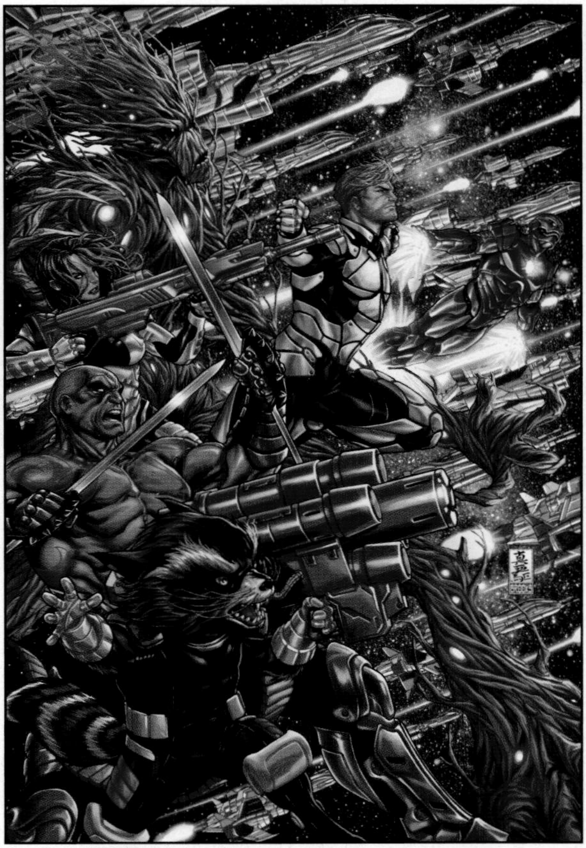

***#1* LONE STAR VARIANT** BY MARK BROOKS

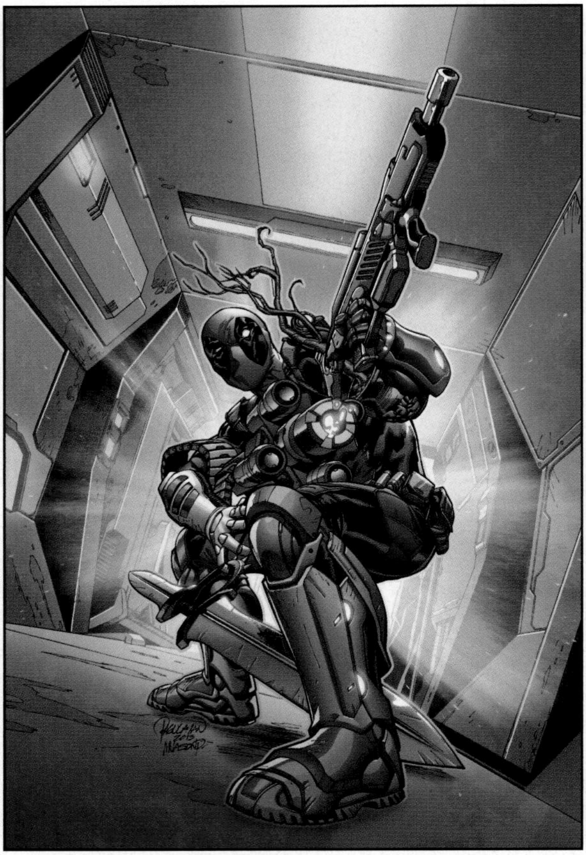

***#1* DYNAMIC FORCES VARIANT** BY CARLO PAGULAYAN, JASON PAZ & GURIHIRU

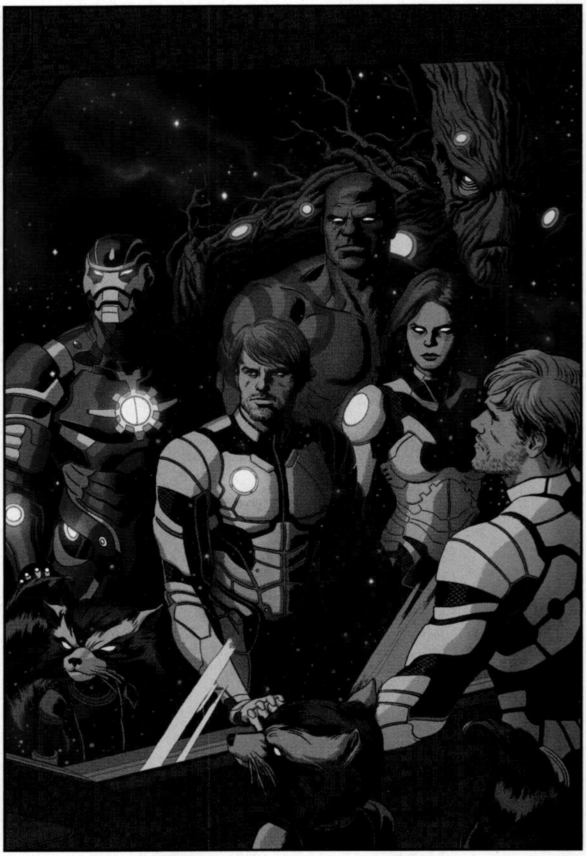

***#2* VARIANT** BY PAOLO RIVERA

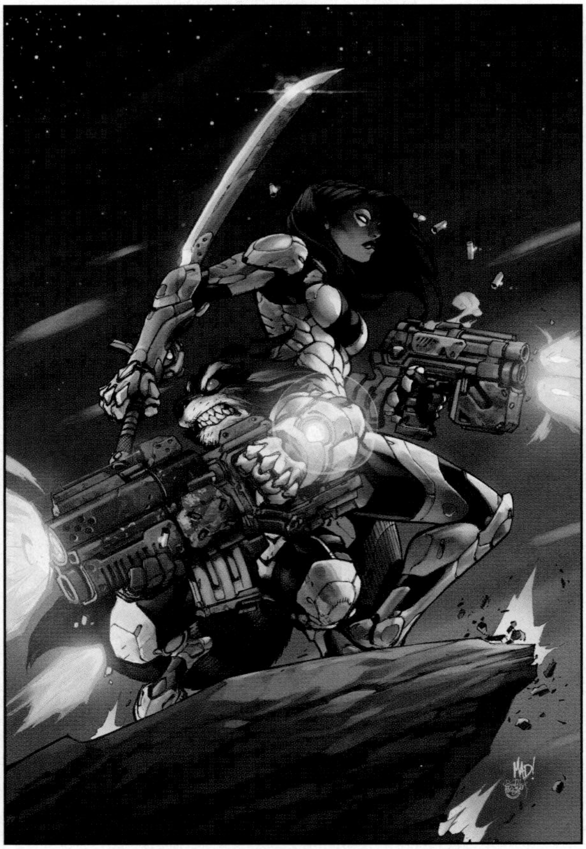

***#2* VARIANT** BY JOE MADUEIRA & PETER STEIGERWALD

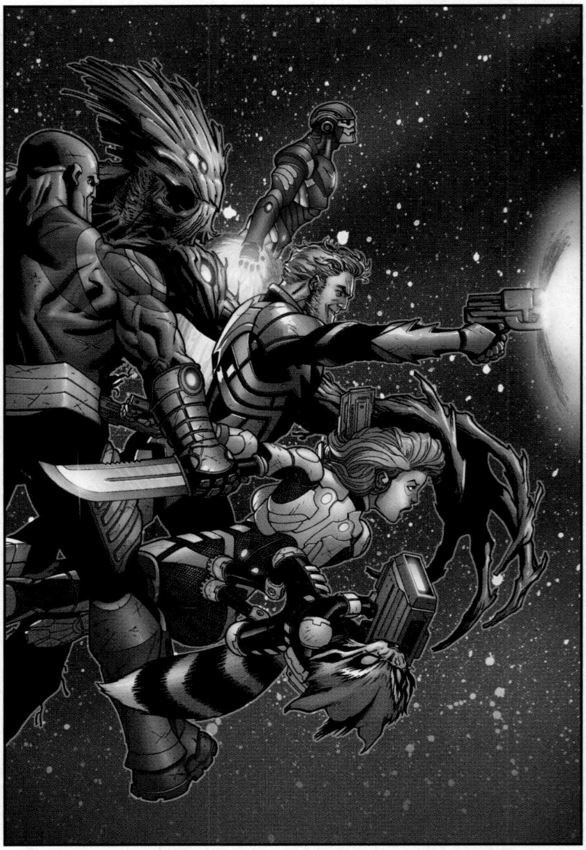

***#3* VARIANT** BY ED McGUINNESS, DEXTER VINES & EDGAR DELGADO

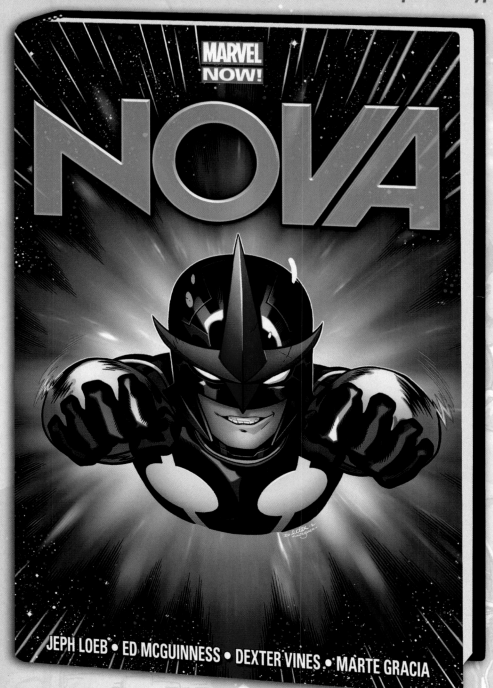

TO ACCESS THE FREE *MARVEL AUGMENTED REALITY APP* THAT ENHANCES AND CHANGES THE WAY YOU EXPERIENCE COMICS

1. Download the app for free via marvel.com/ARapp
2. Launch the app on your camera-enabled Apple iOS® or Android™ device*
3. Hold your mobile device's camera over any cover or panel with the AR graph
4. Sit back and see the future of comics in action!

*Available on most camera-enabled Apple iOS® and Android™ devices. Content subject to change and availability.

GUARDIANS OF THE GALAXY AR INDEX

MARVEL
FREE DIGITAL COPY OFFER
PEEL HERE TO REVEAL CODE

TO REDEEM YOUR CODE FOR A FREE DIGITAL COPY:

1. GO TO MARVEL.COM/REDEEM. OFFER EXPIRES ON 8/28/13.
2. FOLLOW THE ON-SCREEN INSTRUCTIONS TO REDEEM YOUR DIGITAL COPY.
3. LAUNCH THE MARVEL COMICS APP TO READ YOUR COMIC NOW!
4. YOUR DIGITAL COPY WILL BE FOUND UNDER THE *MY COMICS* TAB.
5. READ & ENJOY!

YOUR FREE DIGITAL COPY WILL BE AVAILABLE ON:

MARVEL COMICS APP FOR APPLE® iOS DEVICES

MARVEL COMICS APP FOR ANDROID™ DEVICES